WHITE UNWED MOTHER

The Adoption Mandate in Postwar Canada

VALERIE J. ANDREWS

DEMETER

White Unwed Mother:
The Adoption Mandate in Postwar Canada
Valerie J. Andrews

Copyright © 2018 Demeter Press

Demeter Press
140 Holland Street West
P. O. Box 13022
Bradford, ON L3Z 2Y5
Tel: (905) 775-9089
Email: info@demeterpress.org
Website: www.demeterpress.org

Demeter Press logo based on the sculpture "Demeter" by Maria-Luise Bodirsky
www.keramik-atelier.bodirsky.de

Printed and Bound in Canada

Front Cover: 'A Resident Looking out of Common Room Window of Victor Home' ca. 1950s, United Church Archives, VH14
Back Cover: Victor Home, Toronto, Ontario, United Church Archives.

Cover Design by Ryan Heaney Art + Design
Typesetting by Michelle Pirovich

Library and Archives Canada Cataloguing in Publication
Andrews, Valerie, 1952-, author
White unwed mother : the adoption mandate in postwar Canada /
Valerie J Andrews.
Includes bibliographical references.
ISBN 978-1-77258-172-0 (softcover)
1. Adoption--Canada--History--20th century. 2. Unmarried mothers--
Canada--History--20th century. 3. Women, White--Canada--History--
20th century. I. Title.

MIX
Paper from
responsible sources
FSC **FSC® C004071**
www.fsc.org

WHITE UNWED MOTHER

The Adoption Mandate in Postwar Canada

For my son, Christopher (1970-2008)

"Take me outside I want to feel the rain on my face,"
he said, so we went outside and sat together holding hands
and felt the light, warm Vancouver rain fall on our faces.
We talked not about our lost past, but our lost future...

I remember those days my Beloved
When we danced in the teardrops of the Goddess
And the only Angels I have ever seen
Slid down your cheeks from the windows of your soul
And the rain, the gentle rain so sweet from Heaven
Fell down over the temples of our souls
And we tasted the salt of Her ocean
Her rain washed away our pain
Pete Bernard

For Una and Jennifer, Maureen and Janet

For all the mothers...and all the children.

Contents

List of Tables
10

List of Illustrations
11

List of Abbreviations
12

Acknowledgements
15

Foreword
17

Introduction
21

Chapter One
The Construction of the Characterization and
Incarceration of the Fallen
33

Section I.
Forbidding Options: The Unmarried Mother
in Nineteenth-Century Canada
35

Section II.
The Magdalen, Rescue, Salvationist,
and Maternity Home Movement
42

Chapter Two
Recharacterizations of the Unmarried
Mother in the Twentieth Century
59

Chapter Three
The Profession of Social Work and the Influence of
Sociological Theories in Postwar Adoption Practice
83

Section I.
The Profession of Social Work
85

Section II.
The Impact of Sociological Theories on
the Adoption Mandate
96

Chapter Four
Maternity Homes in Canada
113

Chapter Five
Maternalism, the Postwar Mother Imperative,
and the Phenomenon of Mass Surrender
151

Section I.
Postwar Mother Imperative:
A Maternalistic Ideology for Whites Only Please
153

Section II.
Race and the Adoption Mandate
156

Section III.
The Phenomenon of Mass Surrender
165

Conclusion
181

Epilogue
189

Works Cited
191

Appendices

Appendix A.
Rules and Regulations of the Industrial House
of Refuge for Females (Magdalen Laundry)
221

Appendix B.
The Unmarried Mother in Mary Richmond's
Social Diagnosis, 1917
223

Appendix C.
Correspondence from Victoria Leach
to Betty Graham
231

Appendix D.
Maternity Homes in Canada: List and Images
233

List of Tables

Table 1: Daily Schedule of Maternity Home circa 1960s
131

Table 2: Number of Adoptions from Unmarried Mothers,
1942-1971 Province of Ontario
170

List of Illustrations

1. Correspondence, Sandfield MacDonald Collection 1812-1872, LAC.
30

2. *Found Drowned.* Oil on Canvas. Watts, George Frederick 1867
33

3. Ritchie, T. "In the Laundry's Steam Mangle." Photograph. 2013.
42

4. Page, Maria Danforth. Artist/Creator. YWCA WWI Poster. "Building for Health," 1914-1919.
59

5. Humewood House. Residents. Toronto, ca.1950s. Humewood House.
113

6. Armagh Maternity Home. Series of Photographs of Maternity Home Residents, PA.
132-133

7. Humewood House. Babies in Nursery. Toronto. ca. 1950s. Humewood House.
141

8. (L) McCalls Cover 1942. (R) Ladies Home Journal cover 1946 illustration Al Parker. Sally Edelstein Archives.
153

9. An ever increasing "crop" of babies born to unwed mothers in Winnipeg is creating a backlog of babies who have nowhere to go. *Winnipeg Free Press*, 1963:1.
176

List of Abbreviations

ACC	Anglican Church of Canada
ACC/GSA	Anglican Church of Canada General Synod Archives
AO	Archives of Ontario
ARCAT	Archives of the Roman Catholic Archdiocese of Toronto
ARENA	Adoption Resource Exchange of North America
ASCR	Australian Senate Committee Report
CAS	Children's Aid Society
CASW	Canadian Association of Social Workers
CCAS	Catholic Children's Aid Society
CTA	City of Toronto Archives
HSP	Historical Society of Philadelphia
LAC	Library and Archives Canada
NCW	National Council of Women
OCAS	Ontario Children's Aid Society Association
PANB	Provincial Archives of New Brunswick
PCC	Presbyterian Church in Canada
PA	Presbyterian Archives
SAA	Salvation Army Archives
SA	Salvation Army
SGS	Sisters of the Good Shepherd

SNOOLC	A Short Notice on the Origin and Objective of the Sisters of the Lady of Charity Better Known as the Sisters of the Good Shepherd
SPCMT	Social Planning Council of Metropolitan Toronto
SSCSAST	Standing Senate Committee on Social Affairs, Science, and Technology
UCMF	United Church Maternity Facilities Report
UCA	United Church Archives
UCC	United Church of Canada
VD	Venereal Disease
WHO	World Health Organization
YWCA	Young Women's Christian Association

Acknowledgements

I have received assistance and encouragement from a great many friends, colleagues, and educators, and it is my pleasure to acknowledge them. I would not have embarked on such a venture without the help of mothers of the mandate. To all those in the adoption reform movement—especially the women of Origins around the world: founder Dian Wellfare who sadly died before she could see the fruits of her work, Bryony Lake, who gave me much support and education, especially in the early days, Lily Arthur, Linda Bryant, Karen Wilson-Buterbaugh, Marion McMillan, and all the volunteers—your work continues to be an inspiration. Thank you to Sandra Jarvie for your friendship, mentorship, encouragement, and support, especially over the rough patches. Thank you to Holly and Bernard, always there, always supportive. Thank you to friend, colleague, and mother Eugenia Powell, who was there every day with a word of encouragement. I also wish to thank researchers and friends across Canada who sent me information and shared their stories. Thank you to my professors, Frances Latchford, Andrea O'Reilly, and Gertrude Mianda, who inspired, challenged, and supported me in so many ways. Finally, thank you to my siblings, Una, David, Elizabeth, and Kathleen, and to my daughters Erin and Shannon, who have shown me unwavering love and support throughout and know all too well the impact of the trauma of these events.

Foreword

The concept of reflexivity or self-reflection through an evaluation of the relationship between researcher and research by social location and lived experience is valued in feminist scholarship. Feminist Donna Haraway has suggested that the idea of objectivity be replaced with "situated knowledge," and has called for "epistemologies of location, positioning and situating, where partiality and not universality is the condition of being heard to make rational knowledge claims" (589). Models of feminist research have shifted to include the principle of location, lived experience, and standpoint.

My journey to this work has been a long one. In 1969, I became pregnant at the age of sixteen. I spent most of that summer in the basement, half hiding, half hoping, that someone would ask about my self-imposed isolation. The school year was fast approaching and pregnant girls were not allowed in school—I had to tell. I was brought to the family doctor who immediately arranged for me to be sent to the Salvation Army Home for Girls at 450 Pape Avenue in Toronto, a maternity home where I spent the next four months of my life.

While at that facility, I, along with many other young women and girls, had come to believe that I had no option except to surrender my baby for adoption. That is, until I went to my room for rest period one day and found a new roommate who informed me she was keeping her baby. I was astonished that this was even a possibility and decided I would do the same. As soon as rest period was over I went down to speak to the Brigadier about keeping my baby. I was met with a tirade of "who do you think you are" and other such comments. When I found the courage to point out that my new roommate was keeping her baby, I was told "she is twenty-seven and she is 'French Canadian'!" I did not quite know what this meant but knew it did not apply to me. I remember how I felt—so beaten down, resigned to my fate. Talk of keeping one's baby was strongly discouraged in Canada's maternity homes. I have long been plagued with guilt over this incident. By expressing my desire to keep my baby I was most probably the cause of this woman leaving the Salvation Army home within a few days. She was heavily pregnant at the time. I will never forget her.

I gave birth to my firstborn baby, a son, at the Salvation Army Grace Hospital in Toronto on 5 January 1970. I cannot begin to describe the trauma of those events, even now, after many years of counselling and advocacy work. When my son was born, I asked to see him and was told "no, that baby is for adoption." I desperately wanted to mother my precious newborn son. And even though this desire was explicitly stated by me and recorded by my social worker in her notes (which I received forty years later), without resources or support, I surrendered. This was to become the most traumatic event of my life; one from which I never recovered.

For years, I did as I had been told—"keep the secret and move on with your life." My career was ever moving upward, but my personal life was a train wreck. I subsequently gave birth to two daughters, and suffered postpartum depression after both births. Through a series of failed relationships I kept trying to reproduce the two parent family for which I had been rehabilitated. Secretly, I did motherwork. I thought about him, cried for him, prayed for him, loved him, and wondered and worried about him all the time. I looked for him in the faces of every baby, toddler, and little boy I saw at every stage of life, and wondered if that could be my son. I believed what I had been told, that I had given a gift, and that I was to go on with my life as if it never happened. I locked it away, and if asked if I wanted reunion, I would emphatically say No! —protecting myself from opening the locked vault of immense pain I held in my heart every day.

One night, when my son was twenty-nine years old, I had a dream about him. In the dream my son was riding a bike down a steep hill, and there was impending doom at the bottom. I woke up with a strong sense of urgency that he needed me desperately. The feeling was so compelling that I sat up for the rest of the night and waited until 9:00 a.m. when I called the Ontario adoption registry to obtain the forms to register. One year later, I received a letter saying that my son had registered and there was a match.

The first time we talked we found a shared interest in Mount Everest. I was in my Everest phase and he was an athlete who loved the mountains and had aspirations to climb the great peak. We talked a lot about Everest among other things during those first wonderful weeks and months. He called me most mornings before his work day started. He came for Christmases, sent me Mother's Day cards, birthday wishes, and gifts. He personified my father. He looked like him and had his distinctive commanding presence and voice. He loved his sisters. It was wonderful for all of us having him back in the family. Then, after seven years of a happy and reaffirming reunion, and only a few months after his final bike ride in the Ironman Triathlon, he called to say that his cancer had come back. He had suffered from testicular cancer as a teen, but it was back, and he was asking for our support.

The next year was an extremely difficult one. We travelled to Vancouver many times to be with him. He suffered greatly and in his last days in hospice care, he talked about his final wishes. He asked me to scatter his ashes at Tofino, his favourite place in Canada, and on the peak of a mountain. "How about Everest," I asked. "Well that would be amazing, but that would be impossible." he replied. At that moment I decided that my son's ashes would be scattered at the top of Mount Everest. Five years later, on 10 May 2013, one of the most famous Sherpas in the world, Phurba Tashi Sherpa, scattered the ashes of my son to the four winds at the top of Mount Everest. On that very same day, another baby boy entered my life... my first grandchild. Then, during the tenth anniversary year of his death, on 19 June 2018, the rest of his ashes were lovingly placed in the water at Tofino. I cannot relate what it has been like to lose him again and to lose our found future.

It had not been until reunion with my son that, very reluctantly, and with absolute terror, I began to unravel my experiences. I was compelled to question and to understand more fully the systems that had caused our separation. I became electrified as I found women all over the world talking and writing about this secret. I learned that there were many of us who had had similar experiences, and that as we connected we found that we had been told the same things by social workers, clergy and others; we suffered many of the same indignities, abuses, and ongoing trauma.

I began to gather my hospital, adoption, maternity home, and social service records. I began to research and returned to school after forty-two years to obtain my master's degree, the thesis of which is the basis for this book. I am currently an activist working to obtain acknowledgment, justice, and reparations for unmarried mothers and their children impacted by the illegal, unethical and human rights abuses inherent in postwar adoption policies and practices in Canada. I am also the executive director of Origins Canada: Supporting Those Separated by Adoption, a federal non-profit organization. My positionality is a source of knowledge, however incomplete.

Introduction

"Adoption practice works on the premise that in order to 'save' the child, you must first destroy its mother" — Wellfare, Civil 25.

While feminist research seeks to foreground subjugated knowledge and support social justice on issues that resound in the lives of women, only recently have contemporary feminists attempted to locate adoption within feminism. Dominant ideology in mainstream Canadian society and feminist scholarship typically ascribes choice to unmarried mothers who surrendered babies for adoption post-WWII, and as I argue, obscures the existence of the adoption mandate and the subsequent phenomenon of mass infant adoption (Shawyer; Solinger; Kunzel; Fessler; Chambers; Pietsch).[1]

The postwar adoption mandate could be described as a process of interrelated institutional power systems which, together with socio-cultural norms, ideals of gender heteronormativity, and emerging sociological and psychoanalytic theories, created historically unique conditions during the post-WWII decades wherein white unmarried mothers were systematically, and often violently, separated from their babies by means of adoption in Australia, New Zealand, the United Kingdom, Canada, and the United States. In Canada alone,

---

1 The term "birthmother" will not be used in this work, except as a search tool or as revealed through research since many mothers of adoption separation reject adoption industry terminology as marginalizing, demeaning, and dismissive of their lived experience as mothers. Other terms such as "fallen woman," "unmarried mother," "unwed mother," "bastard," "illegitimate," "negro," "baby-farmer," "Indian," "feeble-minded," or "mental defective" may be used in their historical context or as quoted from primary sources. The term "home," as a reference to maternity facilities, is used to reflect the historical name used during the period. However, it is acknowledged that many mothers of the mandate reject the term "home" to describe these quasi-incarceral institutions.

approximately 350,000 unmarried mothers were impacted by the mandate from 1940 to 1970.[2] The mandate was also influenced by urbanization, eugenics, social work, medical advances, and the introduction of baby formula; all within the context of two world wars. These factors came together as a kind of "perfect storm" to create an unprecedented locus in history wherein the majority of white unmarried mothers in Canada were routinely and systematically separated from their babies at birth for adoption.

This work provides evidence of the mandate in Canada, and demonstrates that mass infant adoption occurred as its result. It explores the ways in which adoption can operate or effectively function as a form of violence against women and the maternal body (Shawyer; Wellfare; Roberts). This work is original in scope. The postwar institution of adoption, its policies and practices which led to the production of contemporary adoption culture[3] are uncovered and questioned. This investigation furthers critical adoption studies, promotes feminist theory and debate about adoption in Western contexts, contributes to the feminist project of uncovering subjugated knowledges, values the lived experiences of women, supports social justice, and ultimately, leads to acknowledgement and political reform in adoption policy and practice.

Although there is still much work to be done surrounding race and the unmarried mother in Canada, the focus of this work is the white unmarried mother because it uncovers a specific Canadian history yet to be told. This focus essentially limits the scope of the research. The rationale behind a concentration on whiteness emerges through a brief exploration of contrasting institutional prescriptions for, and character-izations of, Black unmarried mothers and Indigenous women during the post-war era.

Unlike their counterparts, white middle-class unmarried mothers retained intrinsic social value by virtue of their whiteness. During the immediate postwar period when good mothers were constructed as white and married, the white unmarried mother was treated as a candidate for rehabilitation to the norms of legitimate marriage and

---

2   See Chapter Five for statistical review

3   Adoption culture is the invisible normalization of the institution of adoption, its language, policies, and practices in Western culture including the normalization of adoption as a "choice" for young healthy mothers (Andrews, *Modern*).

normative white motherhood through adoption separation; by extension, her child was effectively rendered a commodity.

Contemporary adoption discourse includes misinformation, myths, and unevenness in voices represented, along with institutional, political, and religious agendas. It is unsurprising that the perspectives of those separated by adoption have only recently emerged as a force in Canada. Those perspectives have for the most part, been methodically silenced by the secrecy and shame inherent in past adoption practice. As pointed out by Sally Haslanger and Charlotte Witt, "in fact they've been almost entirely missing!" (9). Despite contemporary tropes of openness, governments, religious groups, and social service agencies continue to restrict access to adoption-related records, which is exemplified by the fact that eight provinces and one territory have only semi-open adoption records in Canada.[4] In addition, those who benefit from, or those likely to benefit from adoption transactions have mostly remained silent with respect to human rights in adoption practice.[5]

The first law in Canada for the regulation of the transfer of children by adoption was introduced in New Brunswick in 1873, followed by Nova Scotia in 1896 (Strong-Boag, *Finding*). Other provinces followed this trend over the next fifty years. Prior to formal adoption laws children were often transferred from one family to another without documentation (LAC, *Genealogy*). In Quebec, prior to 1847, adoptions are found in notarial records and are signified by terms such as "Engagement," "Accord," "Agreement," and sometimes even "Adoption" (LAC, *Quebec*). In Ontario, the transfer of children was usually referred to as a "Guardianship," which appeared with the Guardianship Act in 1827 and "allowed a Probate or Surrogate Court Judge to appoint an individual to safeguard the child's 'property, person and education' until maturity" (AO, Guardianship 1).

Prior to WWII, adoption was not widely used as a form of child transfer since the traits of the morally fallen were thought to be hereditary. Adoption as a form of child procurement and transfer changed significantly during the twentieth century. Not only did adoption become the chief prescription to rehabilitate white unmarried mothers in postwar Canada, but the postwar adoption mandate

---

4   As of this writing, adoption records remain fully closed in Nova Scotia and Prince Edward Island.

5   This includes governments, adoption agencies, legal professionals, and adopters.

heralded the beginning of adoption culture in Western society. By the end of the twentieth century, adoption discourse shifted, as adoption practice and popular culture placed the emphasis on prospective adoptive parents, as reported in 2003 by the Special Rapporteur to the United Nations Rights of the Child, Juan Miguel Petit:

> Regrettably, in many cases, the emphasis has changed from the desire to provide a needy child with a home, to that of providing a needy parent with a child. As a result, a whole industry has grown, generating millions of dollars of revenues each year, seeking babies for adoption and charging prospective parents enormous fees to process paperwork ... the Special Rapporteur was alarmed to hear of certain practices within developed countries, including the use of fraud and coercion to persuade single mothers to give up their children. (United Nations)

This work draws upon a number of theoretical perspectives the most relevant being critical adoption studies and maternal theory. Although feminists have taken up questions of adoption since the 1990s, critical adoption studies remain a relatively under-researched area of feminist inquiry. Feminist theoretical debates surrounding critical adoption studies are emerging through history, motherhood, queer, race, transnational, and diaspora studies. Notable scholars include Karen Balcom, who explores the migration of Canadian babies for adoption across borders between 1930 and 1972, and Karen Dubinsky, who discusses the politics and tropes of adoption in the context of international adoption. Frances Latchford explores the ways in which mothers who identify as agents are silenced, whereas Shelly Park examines adoptive maternal bodies as a queer paradigm for rethinking mothering. Laura Briggs focuses on those who have lost children to adoption while examining social, cultural, and political forces influencing those transactions, and Dorothy Roberts explores modern domestic adoption in the context of race. A critical analysis of the adoption mandate will contribute to a new body of work within feminism that explores adoption through a number of perspectives.

Motherhood studies as well theory on mothers, mothering and motherhood as a distinct body of knowledge within feminist theory has emerged through theorists such as Adrienne Rich, Nancy Chodorow,

Andrea O'Reilly, and others who explore motherhood as experience, identity, institution, and ideology. These theorists are useful to draw upon when exploring the concepts of mothers and non-mothers, destruction of the maternal body, and adoption as a form of violence against women within the context of the adoption mandate.

Within the overall framework, additional theoretical perspectives and concepts are used to provide structure within various contexts. For example, relying on psychoanalytic theory is useful to uncover the underlying reasons for the drastic changes in policy for white unmarried mothers in the postwar period. In addition, standpoint epistemologies concerned with privileging vantage points as situated knowledge as they relate to the oppression of women (Harstock; Hooks; Haraway) and relates to the foregrounding of lived experiences of mothers who surrendered their babies in postwar Canada. Standpoint knowledges as expressed by Gloria Anzaldúa's concept of "borderland existence" and "identity" are useful when discussing the formation of borderland identities experienced by mothers separated from their infants by adoption.

Women's history in relation to adoption in Canada is an emerging topic. Notable scholars include feminist historian Lori Chambers, who was given extraordinary access to the case files of the Ontario Children of Unmarried Parents Act 1921-1969. In addition, Chambers concentrates on the legal history of adoption in Ontario between 1925 and 2015. Veronica Strong-Boag provides a comprehensive historical overview of adoption law and practice in English Canada from the nineteenth century to the 1990s; and Suzanne Morton illuminates the history of unmarried mothers and maternity homes in Halifax in postwar Canada. The examination of the construction of adoption in Canada is crucial to uncovering the development and implementation of the adoption mandate.

Adoption law in Canada is mostly a provincial matter and it has evolved in tandem with child welfare since the early nineteenth century. More recently provincial laws have been trending toward adoption industry economic models used in the United States. Current social justice issues for Canadian adoption activists including race, agency, pre-birth matching, consent to adoption times, sealed records, enforcement of open adoption agreements, the linking of adoption and abortion by prolife groups, and the basic human rights of persons adopted—are informed and influenced by examining past adoption law, policies, and practices.

This research uses a feminist methodological framework. It is concerned with positioning gender at the centre of inquiry to uncover interrelated power relations, ideologies, and dominant discourses as they relate to the oppression of women in social and historical contexts in order to promote social justice for women. Primary and secondary data, along with qualitative and quantitative data are examined within a feminist methodological framework which seeks to uncover androcentric bias, acknowledge difference, and reflect on the position of the researcher. Furthermore, a discourse analysis is employed to expose and analyze societal attitudes, cultural mores and media representations pertaining to illegitimacy and the unmarried mother.

This work builds cumulatively. It attempts to identify and assemble the major elements that contributed to the mandate and that came together as a perfect storm, culminating in a time in history that had never before been seen and has never since been reproduced.[6] Although this work concentrates on pre- and post-WWII events, research from the mid-nineteenth century onward provides historical context.

Chapter one concentrates on the unmarried mother in the nineteenth century to lay the foundation for the social and legal construction of unmarried mothers in a new Canada and the choices available to them. Although the postwar adoption mandate was unique in terms of prescriptions and outcomes for white unmarried mothers and their babies, various factors originating in nineteenth-century Canada led to that historical epoch. Christian Magdalenism, a redemptive punitive theory that informed and shaped policy and practice for unmarried mothers in Canada for over one hundred years is explored. Magdalenism was central to the establishment of "charitable incarceration" (Kunzel) for unmarried mothers—a practice integral to the adoption mandate.

Chapter two illustrates the major re-characterization of unmarried mothers in the twentieth century and up to the 1960s—which led to the adoption mandate—as a threat to communities, as feeble-minded, as sex delinquents, and finally, as psychologically ill.[7] Emerging

---

6   Due to the confines of this work only the major factors leading to the mandate are discussed.

7   Due to the limitations of this book characterizations of the unmarried mother after 1970 are not examined.

psychoanalytic theories pathologizing the white unmarried mother led to drastic changes in public policy in postwar Canada. In addition, pre and post-WWII research shows increasing emphasis placed on incarceration and on cures to regulate the moral and sexual behaviour of white women in Canada; all factors contributing to the mandate. Contributing subtopics such as eugenics and venereal disease are also addressed.

The profession of social work was one of the major factors influencing the adoption mandate. Chapter three tracks the progression of the "professionalism of benevolence" (Kunzel 3) and the rise of the scientific expert in the early twentieth century. It shows how social workers created a profession using scientific casework to approach social problems, particularly those pertaining to the unmarried mother. Social workers played a vital role in creating, perpetuating, and endorsing the adoption mandate in the postwar period. Several quotes from social workers expose the thinking at the time and support the fact that social work policy and practice with unmarried mothers was typical and systemic, and not isolated. In addition, this chapter establishes how sociological theories such as "tabula rasa," "clean break," and "complete break," contributed to a major shift in societal prescriptions for unmarried mothers and their newborn babies in the postwar period.[8] Furthermore, the voices of women and their experiences in Canada's hospitals document the illegal, unethical and human rights abuses pervasive in postwar adoption policy and practice. This chapter also includes a brief overview of baby formula and how its development acted as a means to separate mother and child in postwar Canada.

Chapter four concentrates on church-run maternity homes operating in Canada between from 1945 and 1970. Appendix D includes an original list of these homes and a collection of images not previously published in Canada. In addition, this chapter examines the protracted and beleaguered transfer of power from philanthropic evangelical women to social workers in connection with the so-called treatment for unmarried mothers. Maternity homes were critical in the systemic removal of babies from their unmarried mothers during the adoption mandate. This chapter takes the reader through the daily schedule of

8   Clean break theory states that children are solely a product of their environment and not their biology.

maternity home life during the 1960s, and highlights and demonstrates the coercive psychological systems functioning in these institutions to separate unmarried mothers from their newborn babies. Though not for all, many unmarried women experienced the adoption mandate in Canada through maternity homes. This chapter reveals how maternity homes were "charged sites" (Kunzel 8) in which evangelical women, social workers, clergy, and the medical community worked together to separate unmarried mothers from their newborn babies for the purposes of adoption in postwar Canada.

Chapter five highlights the social climate of post-war Canada, a period that emphasized and reinforced the construction of good women as white stay-at-home mothers, and promoted nuclear families and heteronormativity—major factors contributing to the mandate. Postwar maternalism and the mother imperative affected both married and unmarried women, and contributed to an increasing demand for white adoptable infants. This chapter also briefly explores the mandate in the context of race. Furthermore, a review of adoption statistics demonstrates the existence of the phenomenon of mass surrender in Canada. Empirical data gleaned from maternity home annual reports, provincial government reports, and other sources illustrate trends leading to the number of babies surrendered for adoption by unmarried mothers in post-WWII Canada.

The conclusion offers a brief review of the findings, an overview of the current adoption reform movement and its political activism, as well as suggestions for further feminist inquiry in the field of critical adoption studies as a specific area of study within academic feminism.

One of the shortcomings of this work is the limited amount of research I was able to uncover from the province of Quebec due to language issues and barriers to information access through Catholic institutions such as the Sisters of Miséricordia, which are private corporations with private archives that may become available later. There is still much work to do in researching Canada's Magdalen Laundries, and an in-depth study of Canada's maternity homes is an area for future examination since, due to the limitations of this work, only one chapter was devoted to those facilities.

The voices of unmarried mothers in Canada are difficult to find due to the shame and secrecy historically associated with unmarried motherhood. Most maternity home records in Canada are either destroyed or inaccessible. Social service files are becoming more available to the persons who were deemed to have received services, including unmarried mothers. The social service records I have viewed from across Canada mostly reflect notes pertaining to the adoption process, and reveal views of the unmarried mother by social workers at the time. The voices of unmarried mothers in these files are negligible. Nonetheless, I did use most of the Canadian sources available, which are limited, to allow the voices of Canadian unmarried mothers to emerge in this work wherever possible.

I am aware that since the work is laden with quotations, it may be viewed as a major shortcoming. But this was, in some instances, done by design to illustrate the pervasiveness of these attitudes in the words of the people who held them: the social workers, maternity home matrons, medical community members, and others since, even today mothers are often met with incredulity. Nevertheless, although I attempted to eliminate many of these quotations, I simply could not find words that would reproduce the power of the original—particularly those from psychiatrists, social workers, and the maternity home matrons.

It is my hope that another scholar may take this work forward in some way. In the meantime, I endeavour to document the culminating factors of the adoption mandate that not only changed the lives of myself and my son, but approximately 350,000 other women and their children in Canada.

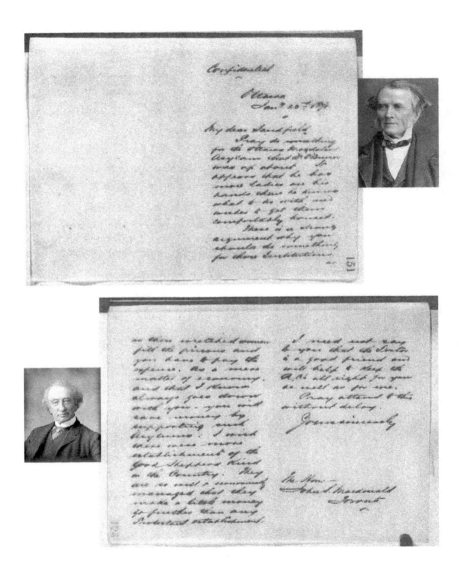

Illus. 1. LAC, Correspondence, Sandfield MacDonald Collection 1812–1872.

Confidential

Ottawa
January 20, 1871

My dear Sandfield,

Pray, do something for the Ottawa Magdalen Asylum that Dr. O'Connor
was up about. It appears that he has more ladies on his hands than he
knows what do with and wishes to get them comfortably housed.

There is a strong argument why you should do something for these
Institutions as these wretched women fill the prisons and you have to
pay the expense. As a mere matter of economy, and that I know always
goes down with you, you will save money by supporting such Asylums.
I wish there were more establishments of the Good Shepherd kind in
the Country. They are so well and community managed that they make
a little money go further than any Protestant establishment.

I need not say to you that the Doctor is a good friend and will help to
keep the RC's all right for you as well as for me.

Pray attend to this without delay.

Yours sincerely

The Hon. John A. Macdonald
Toronto

Chapter One

Constructing the Characterization and Incarceration of the Fallen

"The one fact is, that the fallen woman is socially dead. She has forfeited her womanhood, and with it her place in society. Her crime socially has been fatal, and final ... she can find no place for her repentance, though she seek it with tears."—The Ladies Repository, 1869

Illus. 2. *Found Drowned* by George Frederic Watts RA (1817-1904). 1867. Oil on Canvas. Watts Gallery, Compton.[9]

9   In Victorian art, the "fallen women" was often portrayed as literally fallen down.

Post-structural theory suggests that epistemologies are specific to social contexts and what is normalized or comes to be accepted as truth can be historically traced (Weinberg). Examining the history and evolution of the characterization and incarceration of the fallen in asylums, penitentiaries,[10] and institutions in Canada from the early nineteenth century illuminates the theories that gave rise to the distinctive un-replicated phenomenon that was the postwar adoption mandate.

This chapter concentrates on unmarried motherhood in nineteenth-century Canada to illustrate the early construction and characterizations of the fallen as marginalized identities. Section I explores influence of emerging laws pertaining to marriage, illegitimacy, and abortion in a new Canada, and the grim alternatives available to unmarried mothers within nineteenth-century society. Section II interrogates the various philanthropic movements and associated institutions to rescue the fallen such as Canada's Magdalen Laundries, which demonstrate the major influence of Magdalenism on the postwar adoption mandate. The evolution of these institutions is also examined to illustrate their role as precursors to the maternity home movement in Canada.

---

10 In Victorian Britain, a female penitentiary was not a penal institution for the punishment of crime, but a charitable enterprise entered voluntarily by members of an outcast group, such as "fallen women." "Asylum" was a place of refuge (Mumm).

Section I. Forbidding Options: The Unmarried Mother in Nineteenth Century Canada

In nineteenth-century Canada, unmarried mothers were characterized as fallen women. The term "fallen" referred to a woman who had lost her innocence and had, therefore, fallen from the grace of God.[11] Prior to and during the nineteenth century, the meaning was associated with the loss or surrender of a woman's purity and the loss of her good reputation—by seduction, rape, incest, her own free will, or the birth of an illegitimate child.[12] This term was an expression of the belief that a woman's moral and social acceptability were entwined with her obedience, chastity, and purity. Sexual experience was restricted to marriage, and women who engaged in any form of sexuality outside that institution for any reason were considered fallen. The term was associated with prostitution and unmarried mothers, both of which were regarded as the cause and effect of a woman's fall. In the work *Fallen Angels*, Gretchen Barnhill describes the fallen within ideals of womanhood in the context of nineteenth-century Victorian culture:

> The woman of the nineteenth century occupied a position of duality within Victorian culture. She was either Madonna or Magdalene, pure or ruined, familiar or foreign. Within this cultural construct, the criminal woman was defined largely by her departure from the ideal Victorian woman who was passionless, chaste, innocent, submissive and self-sacrificing. In contrast to the Victorian ideal, the woman who contravened the idealized conception of womanhood, whether by sexual misconduct or criminal act, was viewed as deviant and unnatural. (3)

The concept of the fallen woman continued during the twentieth century. Although the term is used infrequently in contemporary Western culture, the theory behind it still circulates in culture today via, for example, slut shaming women who exercise sexual agency.

11 See the Bible, Genesis 3. The concept of lost innocence denoting a "fall" has its roots in the Bible. Adam and Eve fall from a state of innocent obedience to a state of guilty disobedience.

12 See The Fallen Woman, art exhibition London UK, 25 September 2015 to 3 January 2016: "The figure of the fallen woman was popularly portrayed in art, literature and the media. Victorian moralists warned against the consequences of losing one's virtue" (Nead).

In nineteenth-century Canada, patriarchy enjoyed absolute power over the lives of women. Social roles were divided into separate spheres based on natural characteristics erroneously ascribed to men and women. Men were considered to be more intelligent and worked outside the homes in business, politics, and the marketplace, while women, considered to be weak, both mentally and physically, were relegated to the inside sphere of home and family. Characterizations of women as either good or bad—Madonna or Magdalene—were based on the norms of female roles within a patriarchal setting. Legitimate entry into motherhood relied entirely on being attached to a man through marriage—a concept that prevailed and became a major factor during the adoption mandate one hundred years later.

In British North America, the laws of illegitimacy directly affected the unmarried mother—before and after her child was born. Peter Ward suggests that these laws acted as an inducement to marry prior to birth, since a child born within marriage was treated as the legitimate offspring of a husband; the act of marriage indicated the man's acceptance of a child as his own ("Unwed" 38). In New Brunswick and Nova Scotia, legislation was enacted that held putative[13] fathers responsible for their offspring; Upper Canada adopted similar laws in 1837 (Ward, "Unwed" 41). This kind of legislation continued through the twentieth century as a scheme to protect taxpayers from the cost of illegitimacy along with adoption.

Legislation classifying the children of unmarried mothers as illegitimate continued until 1974 in Canada (Canada, *Department of Justice*). Not only did this distinction socially marginalize unmarried mothers and their children, it also allowed for legislation, regulations, and practices targeting this specific group. The laws of illegitimacy impeded the rights of a child.[14] An illegitimate child was considered "filius nullius," meaning "kin of no nobody" or "son of no man" (Chambers, *Misconceptions* 15). However, as Lori Chambers points out:

> of course the idea that a child is the child of no one and has
> no kin relations is an obvious absurdity ... the illegitimate
> child did have kin including a biological father, but the

---

13 The alleged father of the illegitimate child.

14 Those born out of wedlock and subsequently adopted continue to have their human rights impeded as they fight for the right to know their identities (Origins Canada).

designation "nullius filius" reflected the patriarchal importance of marriage and of the father as the legal head of the household. A child born to a mother who was not formally connected to a man was unlawful. (*Misconceptions* 15)

The status of being illegitimate[15] had other repercussions, including loss of inheritance rights and, usually, the support of a father. Marriage laws pertaining to children born outside marriage were enacted as part of patriarchal ideology that existed to serve men.

During the nineteenth century, the social penalties for pregnancy outside of wedlock could be severe. Having broken the code of respectable sexual deportment, unmarried mothers were generally condemned for their delinquency (Ward, "Unwed" 45). Discovery of the birth of a child outside of marriage often "resulted in disgrace, termination of employment, and severely diminished job prospects" (Backhouse 113). However, if a marriage occurred before the child's birth, penalties were often lighter: "no doubt their indiscretions earned them knowing looks, private chastisement, brief local notoriety, and some embarrassment but beyond this nothing more" (Ward, "Unwed" 45).

In Victorian Canada, as in the postwar mandate, unsupported and unmarried mothers had few options. Societal prescriptions based on religious and patriarchal values resulted in stigma, shame, and loss of family honour, which left few alternatives for those faced with illegitimate motherhood. Ward locates options for unmarried mothers as acceptance by family,[16] abortion, infanticide,[17] baby-farms, and asylums (Ward, "Unwed").

Evidence suggests that abortion and infanticide were quite common in the nineteenth century ("Unwed" 43-45). Constance Backhouse shows that infanticide was a fact of life in nineteenth-century Canada; bodies of newborn infants were routinely found in various locations in major cities (113). In Toronto, a few women were charged with the crime of infanticide, but none were given the death penalty (Strange 73). Those caught were often young and unmarried domestic servants, who had attempted to hide their pregnancy; these women were often

15 Sometimes referred to as "bastard" child.
16 This was true mostly in rural communities.
17 The murder of an infant

left with no options due to untenable economic and social realities (Backhouse 113).

Unlike those women committing infanticide, who were often from the working classes, women seeking the termination of a pregnancy were generally married and from the middle and upper classes (Backhouse 147). According to Carolyn Strange, women wishing to terminate a pregnancy often depended on women's advice networks, druggists, and midwives (*Girl* 69). Abortion in the nineteenth century often resulted in the death of both mother and child; laws[18] inflicting heavy penalties for abortion after "quickening"[19] were enacted for the person performing the abortion.[20]

Child surrender was sometimes employed by unmarried mothers, which was supported by the rise of foundling homes. Desperate mothers bundled up their babies and left them on the doorstep of a church or foundling home, where they might be taken in and cared for. It is unlikely that these mothers were uncaring abandoners; a recent exhibition at The Foundling Museum in London, United Kingdom, displayed the written petitions of mothers and the various keepsakes left with their children so they could identify and reconnect with them at a later time.[21] Nonetheless, these mothers continued to be portrayed as unnatural women. The characterization of unmarried mothers as cold, uncaring, abandoners remained prevalent during the adoption mandate and beyond. Unmarried mothers were characterized as shameless women who discarded their babies with little or no maternal sentiment. An article published in the *Winnipeg Free Press* in 1966 illustrates this sentiment: "One Children's Aid Society official said he has seen unwed mothers discard their babies 'as if they were used Kleenex'" (Dalby).

Another form of child surrender was the informal transfer of a child to strangers or relatives to raise them. Adoption was uncommon, and

18 As Ward shows, "New Brunswick made abortion a felony punishable by death in 1810, although it provided for lesser penalties if the child was not quick. At mid-century this distinction was abandoned and the penalty lowered to a maximum of 14 years in prison. In 1841 the first law in the Canadas imposed penalties of up to life in prison for convicted abortionists." ("Unwed" 42).

19 Medical term to describe the time at which the fetus can be felt by the mother, usually the second trimester.

20 Access to legal, medically safe abortions continue to be a barrier to reproductive choice for unmarried mothers.

21 See The Foundling Museum: The Fallen Women Exhibition, 25 September 2015 to 3 January 2016. Also see Permanent Collection of Artefacts at the museum which show the care and desperation of the mothers.

rarely referred to as adoption; it did not take the form in the nineteenth century that it later would. The most common forms of caring for children surrendered to stranger unknown families were indentures, or apprenticeships to farm labour for boys and to domestic service for girls. In these kinds of informal arrangements, mothers and children retained filial attachments, and mothers who entered into these transactions usually had access to their child (Strong-Boag, *Finding* 11).

In urban centres, though not a legal transaction as yet, changes in fee structure by those providing childcare from monthly or weekly payments to one time lump sum one inferred some kind of adoption or, at least, the permanent transfer of a child. Benjamin Waugh describes an adoption scam in the 1890 publication *Baby Farming:*

> She advertised, Wanted a child to adopt by a respectable married couple; premium required; apply, etc... two living babies were made over to her, one from Havre, one from Edgbaston. In neither case did the mother of the child see the advertisers' house. These brief advertisements brought her one ten pounds and one twenty pounds from persons who knew nothing of her, and not know her name and address. The children were never to be seen again. (7)

Baby-farming was an additional option used by unmarried mothers in nineteenth-century Canada. This type of informal fosterage of children rose as an industry alongside industrialism and urbanism. Much Victorian philanthropy was in response to the practice of baby-farming, which was operated by procurers of mostly illegitimate infants and children who would ostensibly take the children into a form of foster care upon receipt of a fee. Strange refers to baby-farming as a form of "passive infanticide" (*Girl* 75). Since most babies died in their care, baby-farmers were often referred to as "angel-makers."[22] Weekly payments were often not enough to ensure the survival of the children, who were weakened by malnutrition and frequent neglect. Even with a well-intentioned caregiver, children usually died.

---

22 H. Horstmann (1866) refers to baby-farmers in Germany: "In England they call these people 'baby-farmers'—here they have the more poetical expression of 'angel-makers.' The children suffer in both countries but in Germany there is some slight consolation expressed in the term, which proclaims, at least, that the little innocents, if prematurely shoved out of this world and all its troubles, are furnished with wings for a better one." (368)

Mothers who sent their children to baby-farms were reviled. In his work *Baby Farming*, Waugh refers to the "infamous creatures, mere she-things, who look out for foul and dishonourable people to consign their children to" (7). Notwithstanding Waugh's characterizations, it would seem that these mothers' actions suggest a kind of desperation difficult to conceive in contemporary Canada. Waugh describes the shocking conditions found at one baby-farm:

> It was a back room of a tumbledown labourer's cottage, scarcely fit for a coal place, about twelve feet square. Crouching and sprawling on the floor, in their own excrement, were two of them. They were tied in rickety chairs, one lay in a rotten bassinet. The stench of the room was so abominable that a grown man vomited on opening the door. Though three were nearly two years old, none of them could walk, only one could stand up even by the aid of a chair. In bitter March, there was no fire. Two children had a band of flannel round the loins; one had a small shawl; the rest only thin filthy, cotton frocks. All were yellow, fevered, skin and bone. None of them cried, they were too weak. One had bronchitis, one curvature of the spine, and the rest, rickets; all from their treatment. There was not a scrap of children's food in the house ... .and a man and his wife sat watching them die of filth and famine, so making their living. (7)

Although Waugh's accounts were made in England, baby-farming in Canada was essentially the same. Children of unmarried mothers were either procured for "adoption" or were sent to baby-farms where they were neglected to the point of death, a form of passive infanticide (Ward, "Unwed" 53). According to Strange, baby-farmers were mostly immune from prosecution "because the untimely death of infants, who, were after all, bastards, was seen as nothing more than unfortunate" (75). By the late nineteenth century, baby-farming had decreased and was mostly replaced with infant and orphan homes. Lack of societal support for unmarried mothers, including childcare and financial assistance, remained a problem for unmarried mothers throughout the twentieth century.

Another option for the unmarried mother was to leave the community for a larger urban centre to hide her shame, although Ward suggests that unmarried mothers often had family and community support, particularly in rural areas. Leniency might have been shown if a woman could prove she had been a victim of seduction and betrayal: "a pitiable figure, more sinned against than sinning" (Strange 54). According to Ward, unmarried mothers were not as ostracized as novels, legends, and general consensus suggest, and evidence supports the idea that some unmarried mothers "commonly enjoyed the support of their families and, probably, the toleration of their neighbours as well" (Ward, "Unwed" 46). Despite this, leaving home for a large urban area was for some, often the first step in leaving their shame behind when families were less than sympathetic or too poor to assist (Strange 74). Some women crossed the border to a nearby American city to hide her shameful circumstances (Ward, "Unwed" 49). Sending daughters far afield or to institutions to escape scandal and uphold the family honour was a strategy used by families of unmarried mothers until at least the 1980s.

In urban centres with few employment prospects, unmarried mothers and their children were at the mercy of social reformers and rescuers of every sort as well as the baby-farmers. As Ward suggests, "the unmarried mother found it difficult to get help from someone who wished neither to exploit nor to improve her" ("Unwed" 56). Ward's comments are profound since there are still those today who seek to improve and/or exploit unmarried mothers.

There is still much to uncover pertaining to unmarried mothers in the nineteenth century. As articulated by scholars Patricia Rooke and R.L. Schnell, due to lack of documentation surrounding illegitimacy, it is still not possible to know the fates of the pregnant, deserted, or unmarried women who were without resources or shelter and who felt forced to surrender and abandon their babies, or even, to commit infanticide (115).

Section II. The Magdalen, Rescue, Salvationist, and Maternity Home Movement

Illus. 3. In the Laundry's Steam Mangle. Home of the Friendless, Wellington St., Ottawa, circa 1917 (Ritchie).

By the mid to late nineteenth century, the rescue movement—a movement motivated by a paternalistic and philanthropic concern for illegitimacy, prostitution, baby-farming, and the moral and physical contagion they represented—created societal strategies for the moral regulation of women. Those strategies included the development of institutions to house and, ultimately, reform the moral character of the fallen. This philanthropy was directed solely at women,[23] including prostitutes, criminals, and unmarried mothers considered fallen from grace. Institutions for the fallen were already well established in Canada by 1871, as the letter from Sir John A. Macdonald to Premier Sandfield suggests. Charitable institutions based on British philanthropic

---

23 There was no corresponding class of men whose status and behaviour were targeted in this way, primarily because women seemed naturally to appear as paternalism's objects based on the sex-specific roles of nineteenth-century Victorian Britain. This raises issue of the "double standard" and the social construction of a "dangerous" female sexuality (Mahood).

models[24] included women's refuges, infant homes, poor-houses, and orphanages.[25] Some of these institutions offered refuge to unmarried mothers and their children as well as referrals to domestic service or wet-nurse situations to assist mothers in obtaining employment (Ward, "Unwed" 51). These homes were usually founded by Christian women benevolent societies, and the admittance of inmates was often determined based on the prejudices and preferences of the ladies admitting committees. Catholic Magdalen Asylums also provided refuge, though not maternity care, and they were strongly supported by the government, as MacDonald's letter to Sandfield implies. Although many institutions were founded to house the fallen, even those homes not specifically designed for that purpose housed unmarried mothers and their children from time to time.[26]

The concept of the deserving and undeserving poor also migrated from England[27] and the unmarried mother, due to her fallen state, remained the least deserving of any type of support. In *Discarding the Asylum: From Child Rescue to the Welfare State in English Canada*, Patricia Rooke and Rodolph Schnell provide us with a glimpse into some of these institutions and the fate of unmarried mothers and their babies who resided there during the nineteenth century. Protestant orphan homes mostly established in the mid to late nineteenth century had

---

24   Some institutions included: Kingston House of Industry, Toronto House of Industry, Toronto Almshouse, Hamilton House of Refuge, Halifax Poor Asylum (1759), Prince Edward Island Poor Home (1869), Montreal Orphan Asylum (1822), Hamilton Ladies Benevolent Society and Orphan Asylum (1851), Saint John Protestant Orphan Asylum (1854), St. John's Church of England Widows' and Orphan Asylum (1855), Toronto Girl's Home and Public Nursery (1856), Kingston's Orphan Home and Widow's Friend Society (1857), Halifax Protestant Orphan's Home (1857), Saint Paul's Almshouse of Industry for Girls, Halifax (1867), Montreal Protestant Infant's Home(1870), Victoria Protestant Orphan's Home (1873), Women's Refuge and Children's Home and Home for Orphans, Aged and Friendless, London (1874-76), Halifax Infants' Home (1875) Protestant Children's Home, Winnipeg (1885), Methodist Orphanage, St. John's (1888), Maternity Home, Victoria (1893), Alexandra Orphanage, Vancouver (1894), Kingston Infants' Home and Home for Friendless Women (1894), Protestant Orphans' Home, Prince Edward Island (1907), Wood's Christian Home (1915) (Rooke and Schnell)

25   Infant mortality rates in these institutions were extremely high. As reported by Backhouse, La Creche D'Youville, managed in Montreal by the Grey Nuns, looked after over fifteen thousand infants between 1801 and 1870, and between 80 and 90 percent died in institutional care (Backhouse 137).

26   Although the Kingston House of Industry "forbade the admission of unchaste women and their bastards ... between 1850 and 1857, twenty-eight unmarried mothers and their children took refuge there for periods ranging from two days to ten months" (Ward, "Unwed" 52)

27   Though, the English Poor Laws did not survive the migration and were not included in Upper Canada's Civil Law in 1792.

strict admittance requirements. Although the Winnipeg and Hamilton homes did receive illegitimate children, the Ottawa facility did not. Women were required to provide proof of marriage to the ladies admitting committee (115). Specialized homes and foundling hospitals were created for the illegitimate, which, as explained by Rooke and Schnell, caused a great stir, as it was thought these institutions "encouraged women to escape the punishments their fallen condition deserves" (115). Despite their Victorian ideals, it was often socially conscious Christian women who organized lying-in hospitals, female rescue homes, and foundling homes for women on the margins of society. Some offered after-care for the unmarried mother and her infant as well as job placement bureaus where the unmarried mother could receive training for domestic service. As an example, the Women's Refuge and Children's Home in London, Ontario, required a twelve-month stay in which a mother might be trained for a better situation or, at the very least, she might be religiously improved (117).

Some homes allowed mothers to board their children while they worked, and others required mothers to wet-nurse not only their children but the children of others. Baby formula had not yet been developed, so the use of unmarried mothers as wet-nurses was common practice throughout institutions in Canada. For example, at the Toronto Infant's Home they used a system of "mother nurses." Mothers were required to remain four months and to nurse one other baby besides their own. In the first year, a woman was expected to suckle four infants in return for room, board, and training in domestic service (118). For this service, the home received a government grant in addition to a city grant. In 1875, the Halifax Infants Home charged a $3.00 fee to those wet-nurses who wanted to keep their own infants with them (119). Despite the use of wet-nurses, infant mortality remained at approximately 30 percent in these institutions (119).

Some women judged too "low" or "fallen" usually because of multiple illegitimate pregnancies were not admitted into these homes. Despite the disapproval of those who insisted that institutions taking care of "natural"[28] children were in fact "putting a premium on vice," the Act for the Protection of Infant Children was passed in 1887 followed by the Maternity Boarding Act twenty-seven years later"

28 This refers to a child born out of wedlock, and the term "natural" mother or father is an extension of this term.

(Rooke and Schnell 121). Unmarried mothers were often required to enter these homes before birth and to agree to stay if they wanted their infants admitted. The committee of the Winnipeg Female Refuge Home was concerned about the mothers who had disdain about these rules, as they understood such disdain as an attempt to avoid the consequences or the responsibilities of their sins (123). The Friendly Home in Montreal had similar rules—"insisting that a girl attend her child during nursing and not 'add to one's sin by casting the baby off'" (qtd. in Rooke and Schnell 123). Catholic institutions were less judgmental surrounding admission, but were often criticized for encouraging promiscuity and abandonment. The higher number of infants accepted by Catholic-run institutions meant that they were more susceptible to higher numbers of infant mortality and, thus, greater criticism (123). Many unmarried mothers were forced into poor houses to deliver their babies, and the records of these institutions show a large number of "bastards" as inmates. Mothers were criticized for the "ease with which they could hide their shame at provincial expense" (Rooke and Schnell 129).

Race is mostly invisible in Rooke and Schnell's work; they do note, however, that the Halifax Infant's Home declined the admittance of children of colour who were then relegated to poor houses until the founding of the Halifax Home for Coloured Children in the twentieth century. As will be discussed, different prescriptions for unmarried mothers would continue to be employed for white women, women of colour, and Indigenous women in Canada during the postwar adoption mandate.

Magdalenism: Canada's Magdalen Laundries

To illustrate the interconnectedness and reproduction of nineteenth-century attitudes, ideals, characterizations, institutions, and practices pertaining to white unmarried mothers during the postwar adoption mandate, this section explores Christian Magdalenism—a punitive theory of redemptive penance to restore the fallen through voluntary and involuntary incarceration. With the recent revelations about and restitution to Magdalen Laundry survivors in Ireland, it seems appropriate to briefly examine Canada's Magdalen Laundries[29]—which

29   An in-depth study of the Magdalen Asylums (Laundries) in Canada is still not available.

today are largely forgotten—to uncover the use of Magdalenism in the institutionalization of the fallen in Canada. To overlook the role of Magdalenism, Canada's Magdalen Asylums, and similar institutions as forerunners to the maternity home movement in Canada, would leave out important information that illustrates not only the philosophies, theories, and principles informing the detention of women deemed morally defective, but also the forms of admittance and regulation of the daily lives of the women in these facilities, which changed little over a hundred and fifty year period. To study Canada's maternity homes during the adoption mandate without first looking at its Magdalen Asylums would neglect the historical context within which these homes evolved. With this in mind, this section explores the Magdalen movement to reform the fallen, and looks at how this movement of redemptive and punitive penance and incarceration was embraced by governments, social reformers, the citizenry of Victorian Canada, and future generations.

Named for Mary Magdalene[30]—a prostitute in the Bible who anointed the feet of Jesus as an act of faith, was forgiven her sins, and was reformed (Luke 7, 36-50)—the purpose of Magdalen Asylums was the transformation and reclamation of fallen women. Following the path of Mary Magdalene, the prior sins of the fallen, once discontinued, and appropriately suffered for, would be expunged. This would set the woman on the path to respectability and a return to the grace of God. Magdalen Asylums[31] not only confined women voluntarily[32] but also became an informal arm of Canada's criminal justice system, which, though non-statutory, allowed for Justices to incarcerate women for sexual misdemeanours, sometimes for years (Mahood).

Magdalenism was not a new idea. The Metz Convent in France 1005, is possibly the first house of this kind. The Magdalens in Germany were in existence by the thirteenth century as "attested by the Bulls of Gregory IX and Innocent IV (1243-54) which granted them important privileges" (McGahan 1). Other notable communities of Magdalens were established in Naples in 1324, Rome, established by Leo X in

---

30 Although Magdalene is spelled with an "e," most institutions were spelled "Magdalen" and penitents were known as "Magdalens."

31 They are often referred to as Magdalen Laundries due to the unpaid laundry work done by inmates.

32 Although women often entered voluntarily, they were required in most cases to agree to be detained for one year as "voluntary prisoners," although some women were detained for life (J. Smith).

1520, and Seville in 1550 (McGahan). In Marseilles, France, Magdalens were established around 1272 by Bertram, who was known as a "saintly man who associated with himself in his work of rescuing fallen women along with other zealous men" (McGahan 1). By 1696, there were several institutions in France, in Paris, Rouen and Bordeaux, although it appears that all were abolished during the French Revolution (Tait). It was not until 1821, with a resurgence of Magdalenism fuelled by the social reform movement, that another institution, the Bon-Pasteur (Good Shepherd), was established for receiving penitent prostitutes in Paris (Tait).

These institutions were often named or referred to as penitentiaries or asylums. Magdalen Asylums, and later maternity homes, were female bastions where women governed and controlled other women. These institutions were managed by women, usually unmarried Protestant matrons or Anglican and Catholic nuns. Although men were often on the board of directors, they rarely entered the internal sanctuary of a Magdalen Asylum. Most establishments had rules and regulations for the admittance of men.

Some institutions stated their purpose as giving aid to women released from jail, whereas others, such as the Lock Asylums,[33] which were locked facilities where women with venereal disease[34] were isolated and treated, although no lock hospitals such as these were established in Canada (Mahood). Most sought to reclaim the fallen, which could include perpetrators of petty crimes, alcoholics, and the feeble-minded (Mumm). Due to financial constraints by the end of the nineteenth century, many institutions allowed admittance to women for multiple reasons (Mumm). In the book *Magdalenism* written in 1842, William Tait offers an overview of the purpose of Magdalen Asylums:

> Magdalen Asylums are institutions established for the purpose of receiving such unfortunate females as appear to have experienced a conviction of the sinfulness of their conduct, and are willing to avail themselves of the advantages

---

33 The first Lock Hospital in Scotland was located on the site of the medieval leper house in Southwark. It has been suggested by Walkowitz (1974) that prostitutes became the social lepers of the industrial revolution as syphilis replaced leprosy as the symbol of social contagion and disease (Mahood). Also see Backhouse for more on the Contagious Diseases Act in Canada. In Canada no lock hospitals were ever certified even though the Contagious Diseases Act was in effect (235).

34 Often referred to as "VD", now referred to as sexually transmitted infections or STIs.

which they hold out to them. The object which these asylums have principally in view, are to afford a temporary refuge till a more permanent one be obtained – to give them a religious and other necessary instructions, such as reading, sewing, washing, glazing curtain ... to endeavour to effect a reconciliation with their friends, and restore the females to their status in society—or to produce for them such situations as they are qualified to undertake, after their residence for a certain period in the institution. (325)[35]

The theories and practices associated with Magdalenism and its associated asylums spread quickly during the nineteenth century. According to Frances Finnegan, a leading authority on Magdalen Asylums, a Magdalen charity was established in London, England, in 1758 (8). By 1898, there were more than three hundred Magdalen institutions in England. Early patrons were often royalty and aristocrats. The Patroness of the London institution in 1803 was Her Majesty Queen Charlotte, and governors included the Earl of Hertford, Charles, Earl of Romney, Hugh, Duke of Northumberland, and Thomas, Earl of Wilton, among others.[36] Rules for admission were strict, and the concept of admission requirements would transfer both ideologically and literally to twentieth-century maternity homes.

In Scotland, the Edinburgh Magdalen Asylum opened in 1797, followed by Glasgow in 1815, and Aberdeen in 1842; many more were scattered throughout the country in smaller centres (Mahood). In Ireland, a Magdalen Asylum for Protestant girls was founded in Leeson Street, Dublin, in 1767 by Lady Arabella Denny, an Irish philanthropist. Two homes operated in Cork: one was Catholic Magdalen Asylum established in 1809, and the other was a Protestant refuge founded in 1810. Another opened in Dublin in 1813 for "fallen females of every religious persuasion" (Finnegan 9). The history of the Good Shepherd Sisters—an order that ran many of these institutions, is synonymous with the worldwide spread of Magdalen Asylums. According to Finnegan, "the Good Shepherd Sisters committed to the reform of

---

35 As we shall see later in this work, the purpose of Magdalen Asylums is almost identical to the stated aims and objectives of maternity homes in Canada.

36 See *A List of Governors of the Magdalen Hospital*, 25 January 1803.

fallen women would dominate the Female Penitentiary Movement in Ireland for almost a century and a half" (10). In Australia, Good Shepherd houses opened in Oakleigh, Albert Park, Melbourne, Bendigo, Hobart, Perth, Sydney, Brisbane, and Adelaide between 1863 and 1946. In addition, houses were opened in New Zealand—in Christchurch, Auckland, and Wellington.

The Magdalen movement migrated to North America when the first institution of its kind was founded in 1800 by prominent clergymen with strong affiliations with either the Episcopal or Presbyterian Church (HSP) who formed the Magdalen Society of Philadelphia, in order to rescue and reform wayward women and prostitutes (HSP). By the 1900s, the Philadelphia home concentrated on "wayward or homeless girls rather than prostitutes," which was the trend for many of these institutions by the end of the nineteenth century (HSP 3). Other Magdalen institutions were formed in Boston in 1816, in New York in 1832 (McDowall), and in Chicago (Smith) and San Francisco in 1857.

Since religious rehabilitation was one of the central aims of Magdalen Asylums, the institutions founded in Canada were either Catholic or Protestant. The first Catholic Magdalen Asylum in Canada was founded in Montreal in the late 1820s (Ward, "Mysteries" 15). Its successor, which was subsidized by the colonial government[37] and the Catholic Church, admitted over three hundred women between 1829 and 1836 (Ward, "Mysteries" 15). It is unclear but probable that this was the Magdalen Asylum of Maria Monk,[38] who was a nun that attested she was sexually abused by a priest in a Montreal convent, that this was widespread within the institution, and that there was a method to dispose of infants created by such activities. Madame McDonnell, the matron of the Montreal Magdalen Asylum, swore before a Justice of the Peace in Montreal in 1836 that she had managed a Magdalen Asylum in Montreal for the past six years thereby attesting to the existence of that institution since at least 1830."[39]

---

37 In 1836, the colonial government was divided into Upper and Lower Canada. Montreal was in Lower Canada.

38 See The Awful Disclosures of Maria Monk. Maria Monk was widely discredited. According to the Affidavit of Madame McDonnell, Maria Monk spent time at, and left pregnant from the Montreal Magdalen Asylum.

39 See Affidavit of Madame D.C. McDonnell, Matron of the Montreal Magdalen Asylum, Ste. Genevieve Street, sworn in the Province of Lower Canada, District of Montreal.

Upon the invitation of the Bishop of Montreal in 1844, The Sisters of the Good Shepherd arrived in Montreal to found a Catholic Magdalen Asylum. The Canada Directory for 1857 to 1858 shows two Magdalen Asylums in Montreal: a Protestant Magdalen Asylum on St. Catherine Street, with Miss Veitch listed as matron, and a Roman Catholic Magdalen Asylum at Sherbrooke St., with Sister St. Gabriel listed as the superior. The Soeurs du bon Pasteur also established St. Magdalen's Refuge in 1850 in Quebec City, which was directed by Marie-Josphte Fitzback (Mrs. Roy), and received women released from jail. Although the Quebec establishment does not appear to be listed in the Canada Directory for 1857-58, it does appear in the 1865 Statutes for the Province of Canada. According to a history compiled by the Sisters of the Good Shepherd, this home remained in existence in different forms until 1975 (SGS).

In Toronto, middle-class women organized a Magdalen home to provide shelter to women as an alternative to jail: "Mrs. Elizabeth Dunlop ... joined with fifteen other prominent Toronto women to incorporate the Toronto Magdalene Asylum" (qtd. in Backhouse 234). This institution was founded in Toronto in 1852 and was known as the Industrial House of Refuge or Magdalene[40] Asylum. The first annual report states:

> The First Annual Meeting of the Friends and Subscribers to the Toronto Magdalene Asylum was held on Monday afternoon, the 20th of March 1854, in the Hall of the Mechanics' Institute. There was a large attendance of ladies and a number of the most influential gentlemen in the City were also present. (First Annual Meeting of the Toronto Magdalen Asylum, 1854 1)

The *Twenty-Second Annual Report of the Toronto Magdalene Asylum* from 1877 states that the institution was founded and "carried on for about seven years in a small two-storey house in Richmond Street. Afterwards it was removed to the old building on Yonge Street, Yorkville, which was recently sold to assist in building the present

---

40 Toronto Magdalene Asylum did use the "e" in the word "Magdalene."

commodious premises."(1)[41] In the same report, the matron of the establishment gives an overview of the asylum:

> We never reject any, however low or degraded, who ask admittance, and are willing to stay the prescribed time and submit to the rules. They have comfortable workrooms and dormitories, have plain but nourishing food supplied to them, and are kept busily employed on remunerative work such as washing, sewing &c., as well as the household duties, and are encouraged to fit themselves for the places of service to which they will be sent at the end of their term. (*Twenty-Second Annual Report of the Toronto Magdalene Asylum* 1877, 1)

These early reports that provide insight on the internal pastimes and schedules of the inmates of Magdalen Asylums in Canada are vital to examine, since the daily schedules and pastimes for women in Canada's maternity homes over one hundred years later were almost identical (see Appendix A).

Unmarried mothers were exploited for their labour in Canada's Magdalen Asylums.[42] In 1876, property was acquired at West Lodge Avenue north of Queen St. West by Archbishop John Joseph Lynch of the Roman Catholic Archdiocese of Toronto, which he then sold to the Congregation of Our Lady of Good Charity of the Good Shepherd for one dollar to establish a Catholic Magdalen Asylum in Toronto[43] (Laycock and Myrvold 37). The order supported the charity by running a laundry. An undated letter from Sister Mary of the Good Shepherd to His Grace Reverend Lynch requests steam laundry machinery in the amount of $600 along with alterations to be made for its installation, which indicates there was a large laundry enterprise at the Toronto Magdalen Asylum (ARCAT). In addition, a list titled "Sisters Names

41 From this report, it appears there may have been two separate addresses for the Magdalen Asylum in the Yorkville area as it is mentioned that the building at Yonge Street, Yorkville was sold. Most likely, the "commodious premises" referred to in the 1877 report is the Magdalen Asylum situated on McMurrich St. in St. Paul's Ward, formerly the Village of Yorkville. Also see History of Toronto and County of York, 1885 (Mulvany 290, 326)

42 The use of unmarried mothers for unpaid and unregulated work within such institutions, which were financially subsidized by governments and churches, continued for over one hundred years in Canada.

43 See Watercolour circa 1800 at Toronto Reference Library, Baldwin JRR528.

and Charges" suggests that many Sisters were actively involved in overseeing the laundry work[44] with Sister Magdalen St. Ignatius being identified as the laundry accountant (ARCAT). The work done by unpaid penitents in the commercial laundry was a source of "considerable revenue," according to the Annual Report of the Inspector of Asylums in his September 1886 report:

> I visited the Good Shepherd Refuge Toronto on the 10th March when there were in residence forty-five adult women and three girls. The premises were in excellent order and perfectly clean. I found that the structural addition to the building had been completed, and that the laundry operations, which form a source of considerable revenue to the Institution, largely extended. (72)

On 3 April 1866, the Sisters of the Good Shepherd opened the City of Ottawa's first Magdalen Asylum (Pearl-McDowell). In 1882, a book titled *A Short Notice on the Origin and Object of the Sisters of Lady of Charity Better Known as Sisters of the Good Shepherd*[45] (SNOOLC) was published by the Asylum with the use of its printing press. This book assists in understanding how women were organized by class within a Magdalen Asylum. The first class was the "Preservation Class" made up of young girls "who had not given open scandal but whose position had been such as to expose them to great danger" (SNOOLC 10). In other words, these were the girls and women who were deemed to be likely to go astray. They were kept separate from the penitents, the next class within the Magdalen Asylum. The Penitents were women who had forsaken the path of virtue. These were the fallen women, many whom entered the house of their own free will or had been sent there by family or local justices. The third class included those women who formed the

---

44 This document reveals many names and charges related to the laundry: Sister M. of St. Clare as mistress of linen room, Sister Mary De Pazzi as mistress of tacking room, Sister M. of St. Jerome as mistress of ironing room, Sister M. of St. Veronica as charge of laundry machines, and Sister M. of St. Dositheus as second over laundry machines, among several others. Sister M. of St. Martha and Sister M. of St. Philomena are listed as employed in the packing room with a notation in the document that Sister of St. Philomena was "not well, 16 years old" (1-2).

45 This book was written by a friend of the institution. See National Library of Canada.

class of the "Perserverence or Magdalens", a neo-religious order.[46] After a probationary period of one year, these women were given a new religious name and permitted to wear semi-religious garb: "they are all clothed in black, and wear a crucifix on the breast; and a rosary at their side" (SNOOLC 10). For prostitutes and unmarried mothers the option to become a Magdalen required them to maintain vows. However, reformation had its limitations. Due to their prior sins, Magdalens could not take full religious vows and be equal to the Sisters that aided them:

> These good creatures lead lives of extraordinary penance and prayer, yet for obvious reasons, no matter how pious a penitent may become, no matter what talent, rank or fortune she may have possessed, she can never be received as a member of the Community of the Sisters of the Good Shepherd. On this point the rule knows no exception. (SNOOLC 11)

The book printed by the institution provides insight into the work being done by the penitents; it reports that most of the inmates worked in the laundry, drying and ironing rooms, or in the garden. Some were taught plain and fancy sewing, whereas others made gloves or artificial flowers. The asylum also had a printing press, upon which books relating to the community, such as the one identified here, were printed (SNOOLC 23). These women were voluntary prisoners; they remained off the public purse while under the private auspices of the Sisters of the Good Shepherd, as indicated by Sir John A. Macdonald in his letter to Sandfield. Although inspected annually by the Inspector of Prisons and Asylums, the inspector's comments were mostly restricted to cleanliness, number of and disposition of inmates, the state of bookkeeping, and general orderliness of the institution.[47]

---

46   Ontario. Inspector of Prisons and Public Charities report of 1887: "I made an inspection of the Good Shepherd Magdalen Asylum, Ottawa on the 7th September, and on that day there were in residence, 100 females in four different classes into which the population of the charity is divided. I found the inmates thoroughly employed in laundry work, sewing etc. and the Asylum was in good order. The books were properly kept" (76).

47   See as an example the Eighteenth Annual Report of the Inspector of Prisons and Public Charities upon the Houses of Refuge and Orphan and Magdalen Asylums 1887. The report for the Good Shepherd Refuge for Fallen Women Toronto shows movement of inmates, religious denomination, nationalities, and place admitted from, average stay, etc. The inspector in his commentary states that "I found the Charity in its usual condition of order and cleanliness, and the inmates busily employed. The books were in good order and neatly kept" (75).

Seven years after the opening of the Ottawa institution, an Act to Incorporate the Hamilton Female Home was assented to on 29 March 1873. This home was a Protestant facility with similar aims and objectives; it was listed as a Magdalen Asylum in the Sessional Papers of 1887, which include the reports of inspections.[48] In this report, it is noted that the matron informed the inspector that she was very anxious to extend the building so that an infirmary for infants might be established. The inspector reported that "the outside laundry work has had to be given up, so the time of the adult inmates was fully occupied in the care of infants" which attests to the prior existence of a commercial laundry similar to other Magdalen establishments (Ontario. Sessional Papers 73).

In 1885, the Women's Christian Association of London was incorporated and an Order in Council was ratified in 1880 to establish the Women's Refuge and Infant's Home, which was recorded in the 1887 Sessional Papers as a Magdalen Asylum. This institution was inspected on 7 May 1887. At that time, seven women and thirteen children were reported to be in residence, and the report stated that the building had brightened up considerably since the last inspection and that it was in good order. In Ottawa, a Home for the Friendless[49] was founded in 1887, which was financed by the running of a laundry. The women in this Ottawa home received "reasonable wages and became skilled Laundresses" (Ritchie 2). Similar to other homes of its kind established near the turn of the century, this home took in women with various problems, including mothers who were unmarried.

The work of the Good Shepherd Sisters continued in New Brunswick and Nova Scotia. In 1891, the Good Shepherd Sisters incorporated the Good Shepherd Reformatory and Industrial Refuge in the city of Halifax which operated as a Magdalen Asylum. The convent of the Good Shepherd in New Brunswick was originally a federal reformatory at 133 Waterloo Street in Saint John. This institution was established as a federal prison around 1870 by King Edward VII, and the Sisters of the Good Shepherd were paid by the federal, provincial, and municipal

---

48   The inspector visited this institution on 24 June 1887 and reported nine adults and fifteen children in residence (73).

49   The image at the beginning of this chapter shows the Home for the Friendless, Ottawa. In 2013, a plaque commemorating the burials in three plots was erected at the Beechwood Cemetery in Ottawa for those who died in this home, the Protestant Orphans Home, and the Protestant Home for the Aged.

governments to run the Magdalen Asylum. Female inmates were treated as forced labourers in the commercial laundry. A publication about this institution published by the Sisters of the Good Shephard titled *Fifty Golden Years 1893-1943* states that "the Monastery is a home where young girls learn to repair the past, to be upright souls and good Christians, and thus to become useful members of society" (Slave Labour, Sheldon 11:50). These ideals continued into the following century and, in fact, became the premise on which the adoption mandate rested.

Detaining and using women for unpaid labour was not without its detractors. In a 1919 *The Toronto Daily Star*, an article appeared with the headline "Issues Writ Against Good Shepherd Home" in which it was reported that a woman named Louisa Telling had sued the institution for $20,000 for being detained against her will and forced to work in the laundries of the institution for no wages. The article states:

> It will be remembered that, during the inquest into the death of Alice Halloran, who died January 29th from injuries received while escaping from the Refuge of the Good Shepherd, Mrs. Louisa Telling swore that she was taken to the institution on West Lodge Avenue under the pretext that she was going downtown, and was kept in the refuge for one year and eleven months without any legal warrant of commitment and against her will. (28 February 1919, 2)

In 1927, this institution was again in the news with the headline "Good Shepherd Home—Inmates Not Paid for Work in Laundry," in which the home is criticized for its policy of paying no wages to those working in the laundry: "Ostensibly a charity it is a money-making laundry business where prison labour is employed in competition with capital invested in legitimate laundry businesses ... there is no wage or recompense given to those who work in the laundry" (Toronto Telegram, 16 September 1927,1,3).

Although some women did speak out about the horrors they experienced in these institutions, their claims were usually dismissed.

Georgina Williams is a survivor of the Saint John Magdalen Asylum.[50] Georgina was conceived through rape, and her mother a twelve-year-old Migmaw girl was sent to the nuns for being pregnant. Georgina alleges that she was born in this institution, sent to the laundries to work alongside her mother at the age of eight, and escaped through an unbarred window at the age of eighteen. Georgina took her case to court, and after a fifteen day trial, the Justice in the case declared that she was of unsound mind and none of the events had ever happened (Williams). The lived experiences of unmarried mothers and others confined in Canadian institutions for the regulation of women continue to be minimized and dismissed. The denial of women's accounts continues today, as women from the postwar adoption mandate begin to share their experiences as unmarried mothers in Canada's maternity homes and hospitals. They are often met with incredulity.

The Sisters of the Good Shepherd were not the only Catholic Sisters housing the fallen. The Sisters of Charity of St. Vincent de Paul of Halifax were also involved in rescue work with unmarried mothers, along with the Grey Nuns of Montreal who were involved in many areas of social welfare.[51] The Miséricordia Sisters, founded in Montreal in 1845 as a lay charity, was constituted as a Catholic order, and given their name by Bishop Bourget three years later. As the twentieth century approached, it was the Miséricordia Sisters who would loom large in the adoption mandate in postwar Canada.

Magdalenism and its institutions survived industrialization and urbanization in Canada, albeit in a somewhat reformed fashion. The nineteenth-century characterizations of the fallen and the institutions to house them, both Catholic and Protestant, evolved through the work of the major Christian churches in Canada, the Salvation Army, and the Young Women's Christian Association (YWCA). As chapter two will show, the new century became the harbinger of an increasing emphasis on incarceration and cures to regulate the moral and sexual behaviour of unmarried mothers in Canada based on Magdelanism, and the redemptive punitive penance it embodied. In fact, Magdalenism

50 See Delcinas Tears; also see Global News 16x9 "Slave Labour: Magdalen Laundries Disgraced Irish Catholic Women" which aired on 5 February 2012, in which Georgina Williams (now Bowman) is interviewed.

51 See Grey Nuns of Montreal. The Sisters of Charity, also known as the Grey Nuns, established more than sixty institutions for seniors, orphans, and the sick.

flourished in the twentieth century more than ever before, as the notion of the good and valuable Canadian woman became further entrenched as white, pure, and devoted to motherhood; and the idea of reclaiming the fallen white daughters of the nation through redemptive penance and punishment remained a prominent theme.

Chapter Two

Recharacterizations of the Unmarried Mother in the Twentieth Century

"When gender functions as a governing and normalizing force in society, those who transgress the standards are constructed as sexual, social, and moral deviants"— Pietsch, "Un/titled" 88.

Illus. 4. Page, Maria. "Building for Health," 1914-1919. The Library Company of Philadelphia.

As the twentieth century dawned and progressed, the increasingly high value placed on the white woman in Canadian society would lead to more severe systemic punishments for the unmarried mother. Moral regulation[52] intensified. New scientific theories, fuelled by Darwinism and Galtonism, created a climate that led to eugenics, intolerance, and changing approaches to illegitimacy. Embedded theories, policies, and practices related to Magdalenism continued to be reproduced without any significant change until the 1970s and beyond.[53]

This chapter builds on previously examined nineteenth-century foundations that shaped the characterization of unmarried mothers in Canadian society. The major influences examined include the four major re-characterizations of unmarried mothers in the twentieth century up to 1970.[54] Those re-characterizations analysed are: unmarried mothers as a danger to urban spaces; as feeble-minded; as sexual delinquents; and, as mentally ill. These characterizations were largely created and endorsed by experts in the emerging fields of psychology, medicine, and social work. In addition, this chapter touches briefly on the topics of eugenics and venereal disease (VD), or sexually transmitted infections (STIs) as they related to unmarried mothers.

As this chapter elucidates, the voices of experts become increasingly prominent in the lives of unmarried mothers during the twentieth century. Even though these mothers would be recast as being primarily ill by the early 1940s, they would continue to be seen as deviant delinquents toward whom harsh treatment was justified. The societal preoccupation with what was now being called the *unwed mother* in Canadian society during the 1940s and in the immediate postwar decades, led to drastic changes in public policy.

---

52 Sangster defines moral regulation as "the processes whereby some behaviours, ideals, and values were marginalized and proscribed while others were legitimised and naturalized" ("Incarcerating" 191)

53 The theory of the fallen women to be redeemed still exists today. See *Huffington Post,* "Jeb Bush in 1995: Unwed Mothers Should Be Publicly Shamed" (Basset).

54 This is true up to 1970. Further re-characterizations of unmarried mothers would emerge after 1970 such as "breeders" or "welfare moms" which were often racialized. See Chapter Five.

Recasting the Unmarried Mother in the Twentieth Century

A Threat to the Community

During the twentieth century, changing characterizations led to changing prescriptions, as the dominant discourse surrounding unmarried motherhood evolved. Illegitimacy was reconceptualised and unmarried mothers re-characterized. As articulated by Regina Kunzel, "social workers created new scripts within which to comprehend out-of-wedlock pregnancy" (52). Previously characterized as fallen victims of seduction and abandonment in the nineteenth century, unmarried mothers in the twentieth century were recast as wilful actors and as a major cause of social ills.

Dominant narratives surrounding unmarried mothers in Victorian Canada were often hyperbolic, dramatic, and racially charged; they conveyed the sexual dangers facing unmarried women living in cities (Strange 62). Numerous stories of ruined girls—victims of seduction, betrayal, and abandonment—regularly appeared in Canada's newspapers (Strange 54). The urban environment, or outside sphere, continued to be constructed as a dangerous space for women and remained male dominated.

As Canada shifted from a rural to urban society in the late nineteenth and early twentieth century, traditional values of family no longer served the same economic function they had on farms, and a broader array of choices for independence emerged for young adults (Weinberg 21). With increasing industrialization and urbanization, as well as WWI, which allowed for a certain independence to women through their participation in war-related activities, young women were increasingly drawn to urban centres. As Diana Pederson articulates, "the concentration of employment and educational opportunities in cities attracted large number of young single women" (20). Female migration to urban areas became known as the "girl problem" (Strange 3).

The YWCA was a Protestant evangelical social reform and rescue organization and it established a Toronto chapter in 1878. The YWCA viewed part of its mission as attempting to solve the "girl problem." The work of the YWCA, its project, illustrates the prevailing view of urban spaces as being dangerous to single women. The YWCA met young women at train stations coming into the larger centres. Their boarding homes strived to ensure that these young women did not succumb to the dangers of city life. The "Y" provided shelter, acquaintances of good character, and a roster of wholesome activities for Canada's most respectable young women[55] (Strange 58), providing protection from prostitution, seduction, abandonment, loneliness, and despair.

As Evangelical Christian groups such as the YWCA and other national women's organizations developed, they asserted an influence on the development of the characterization of the good woman in Canadian society as physically fit,[56] white, married, and a mother. Pederson reflects on how Canadian women were constructed in 1918 in the YWCA publication *Outlook*:

> Her tremendous energy and up-to-date training are quite indispensable to our welfare, and that just as her splendid physique is essential to the very production of the next generation, so there is abundant play for all her vision, and scope for her most magnificent ability in consecrated motherhood and sanctified womanhood. (23)

The theory of Canadian women within the meaning of the YWCA was strictly reserved for young, white, respectable, and Protestant women. Women of colour, Indigenous women, Catholic women, as well as older, disabled, or other marginalized ones were not included (Strange). Entering the interwar period, the vision of white Canadian women as "consecrated" and "sanctified" indicates the high value placed on certain women, which intensified institutionalized ideals of good women and mothers in Canadian society as white, and mothers.

Within this context, the unmarried mother became the focus of contempt in a way that differed from the previous century. Rather than being seen as a fallen sister, in need of shelter and protection, she was instead, regarded as a threat to the community (Kunzel). She was now considered dangerous not only because of the visible nature of her sexual transgression but also because of what was considered her

55 Catholics, women of colour, and those without spotless reputations were not admitted (Strange 58).
56 They needed to be fit to bear children in order to replenish the nation after the momentous loss of life in WWI.

blatant rejection of the ideal role of the good Canadian woman within the institution of marriage. Those who gave birth to babies without a clear line of parentage were seen as rejecting the existing social hierarchy and began to be characterized as a danger to respectable Canadian life. As Tamara Myers argues, "the insatiable fallen woman became the peril of the modern city" (64).

The transformation of unmarried mothers from fallen sisters or passive victims of seduction in Victorian Canada to unnatural aggressive agents in the new twentieth century promoted the notion that unmarried mothers threatened normative families and communities. It is unsurprising that single working women and unmarried mothers were recast as dangerous in the context of the first wave of feminism— an era when women became more present in public life and more vocal about their rights. Patriarchal power systems attempted to reinforce normative roles for women in the private sphere. Severe censure met those who deviated from that role. This shift in the way unmarried mothers were viewed became one of the most significant changes to impact the lives of unmarried mothers in the twentieth century.

Unmarried Mothers as Feeble-Minded

At the turn of the century, Canada became preoccupied with what was referred to as the "feeble-minded." Indications of feeble-mindedness were decidedly gendered. Feeble-minded men were associated with crime, whereas feeble-minded women were defined in sexual terms. In the report *Upon The Care of the Feeble-Minded in Ontario, 1907*—a report commissioned by the Legislative Assembly of Ontario—feeble-minded women were described as follows:

> The feeble-minded are difficult to define, but not difficult to recognize. They are below those of normal, but small, intellect, but above actual imbeciles and idiots. They are able to act and speak fairly well though usually more or less foolishly ... they lack prudence and self-control ... they have not proper will or judgement. Hence we find them in maternity hospitals, refuges, gaols and poor houses. (4)

Beginning in the 1910s, social workers embraced feeble-mindedness as a diagnosis for unmarried mothers and debated the meaning of the catchall term. Some included subjective standards such as untruthfulness as a mark of the feeble-minded person (Kunzel 52). A circular definition of feeble-mindedness eventually emerged wherein unmarried mothers were conflated with the feeble-minded (Kunzel 52).

Feeble-mindedness and the proliferation of the feeble-minded through illegitimacy became central social concerns in Canadian society. Fears of the feeble-minded reproducing their kind were initially sparked by Anglo-Saxon Protestants who were fearful about their own low fertility rates in comparison to those in the Catholic French and migrant communities. Societal concern about the losses of the "best" young Canadians in WWI while the "worst" reproduced their kind at home intensified these concerns (McLaren 43). The 1907 report on the Feeble-Minded in Ontario illustrates this fear:

> I reluctantly call to your attention the tendency, especially of feeble-minded women to lead dissolute lives, nearly all their offspring are illegitimate ... it is impossible to calculate what even one feeble-minded woman may cost the public, when her vast possibilities for evil as a producer of paupers and criminals, through an endless line of descendants, are considered. If the state can seclude such a woman and thus at one stroke cut off the possibility of a never-ending and ever-widening record of evil and expense, should it not do so at once? Can it afford not to do it? (19)

New social forces unleashed by the purity movement[57] and its organizations—including Children's Aid Societies, National Council of Women (NCW), Women's Christian Temperance Union, YWCA, The Salvation Army, mainstream Canadian churches, and social experts in the medical and social work community—contributed to the discourse of unmarried mothers as feeble-minded.

The Canadian National Committee for Mental Hygiene was founded in 1918, and its journal, *Canadian Journal for Mental Hygiene* was first published in April 1919. The editorial board included medical doctors

---

57 The social purity movement, based on Christian morality, placed emphasis on abolishing prostitution and immorality

from across Canada; the most notable was Dr. C. K. Clarke[58] of Toronto as Medical Director. The journal lists the Duke[59] and Duchess of Devonshire along with other lords and knights of the empire as patrons in October 1920. These journal publications from the early 1920s illustrate how unmarried mothers were viewed during that period.

In the first edition of the *Canadian Journal of Mental Hygiene*, in 1919, an article by Dr. Gordon S. Mundie of Montreal examines the out-patient psychiatric clinic at Royal Victoria Hospital in Montreal. The article indicates that unmarried mothers were routinely sent to the psychiatric clinic:

> The Women's Directory of Montreal looks after the problem of the unmarried mother. Their policy is to refer each case to the psychiatric clinic, but owing to stress of work and insufficient social workers, only 44 had been examined when this report was undertaken. Out of the 44 women, 25, or 56.1 per cent, were mentally deficient. (297)

A survey of Nova Scotia institutions that appeared in the April 1921 issue of the same journal notes with respect to the Monastery of the Good Shepherd that "As had been noticed in so many places where unmarried mothers are kept under observation, no less than 40 out of the 47 examined were found to be defective" (25). In the same report under the heading "Mental Defect and Illegitimacy," the Salvation Army Maternity Home and Hospital in Nova Scotia is examined and includes the categories of "dull normal" and "primitive" to describe unmarried mothers:

The Superintendent believed that at least half of the unmarried mothers cared for were of a dull type mentally and stated that less than 50% make good after they leave the hospital. Thirteen patients were seen, and while a detailed study of each case was not made, it was felt that sufficient observation was made to warrant the following classifications:

---

58 As Dean of the Faculty of Medicine at the University of Toronto, C.K. Clarke was instrumental in the creation of the Department of Psychiatry. . in Toronto, then known as the Clarke Institute of Psych. An early proponent of eugenics, The Clarke Institute of Psychiatry in Toronto was named in his honour; it was renamed Centre for Addiction and Mental Health (CAMH) in 1998 when it was absorbed into a consortium of mental health clinics.

59 Victor Christian William Cavendish, 9th Duke of Devonshire, was Governor-General of Canada from 1916-1921.

Feeble-minded...11
Dull Normal...1
Primitive...1 (30)

In this case, a Salvation Army matron was trusted as an expert in evaluating the mental health of the women under her care, and it appears that all thirteen unmarried mothers evaluated by her were seen as having some kind of mental defect. Also, some of the classifications devised by C.K. Clarke were used, including "high grade moron," or "dull class/dull normal," the latter being interpreted by Dr. Clarke as follows: "the most difficult form of all the defectives to manage, and possibly the greatest menace to the community, as they are so often attractive in appearance, and plausible, to the ordinary observer" (12). In the same issue of the *Canadian Journal of Mental Hygiene* in 1921, the Nova Scotia Presbyterian Rescue Home was surveyed. It had "fourteen beds [and] seven girls were in residence—all unmarried mothers." Furthermore, "Two who were examined proved to be low grade morons ... [and] a large proportion of the girls admitted are mentally defective" (31). A Saskatchewan survey conducted by the Canadian National Committee for Mental Hygiene published in the June 1920 issue of the *Canadian Journal of Mental Hygiene* found similar results in maternity homes (314). C.K. Clarke's study of 767 cases of unmarried mothers conducted at Toronto General Hospital from 1914 to 1920—and published in the 1921 issue of the journal—found the following:

> The 767 mothers added no less than 917 children to the population, and it goes without saying that many of this number will be defectives ... mental defect and illegitimacy go hand in hand no matter what may be said to the contrary, and the fact that 68% of those examined were abnormal should convince the most critical of the truth of the contention. (18)

By the 1920s, the notion that feeble-mindedness and illegitimacy were interconnected was entrenched not only in medicine, social work, and psychiatry, but also in broader society.

The Role of Eugenics: Controlling the Proliferation of the Feeble-Minded

The term eugenics was first coined by Sir Francis Galton in 1883 and referred to "the investigation under which men of a high type are produced" (L. Ward 738). Galton's vision of eugenics included positive and negative eugenics wherein he hypothesized that "increasing the frequency of a 'desirable gene' or decreasing the frequency of an 'undesirable gene' could be achieved" (qtd. in McLaren 15). From the assumption that undesirable traits were genetic, the idea of sterilizing people with those traits became a Canadian fascination. In fact, Acts were passed in Alberta and British Columbia in 1928[60] and 1933[61] respectively to allow for the sterilization of so-called defectives (McLaren 99-101). The Alberta Act named "mental defectives"[62] unfit to reproduce children—and also included new immigrants; alcoholics; epileptics; unmarried mothers; those with venereal disease; women seeking abortions;[63] and Indigenous women.[64]

In *The Age of Light Soap and Water*, Mariana Valverde illustrates that in the figure of Dr. Margaret Patterson, ideologies of moral purity and their perfection through science was combined. One of Ontario's first medical graduates, Patterson served on many boards and committees: the National Council of Women of Canada (NCWC), the Committee on Equal Moral Standards, the Canadian Purity Education Association, and the Moral and Social Reform Council of Canada (later renamed the Social Service Council of Canada). Patterson lectured across Canada for the YWCA and NCWC advocating for harsher punishments for prostitutes and for a "moral hospital" to which those who were "morally sick" might be sent for indeterminate sentences and punishments,

60 The Sexual Sterilization Act in Alberta was passed on 7 March 1928. The British Columbia Sexual Sterilization Bill was passed on 7 April 1933, (McLaren 100, 103).

61 This is the same year that the Nazis began their racial hygiene campaigns in Germany (Schissel and Mahood).

62 See Province of Alberta, Sexual Sterilization Act, Statutes of the Province of Alberta. The first amendment was passed on 14 April 1937, and the second amendment was passed on 19 March 1942 which broadened the scope of those who could be sterilized as mental defectives, those with psychosis and epilepsy.

63 Some women seeking abortions were forced to agree to sterilization as "part of a package deal" (McLaren 170).

64 See *The Sterilization of Leilani Muir* (1996) directed by G. Whiting. Leilani Muir is an Indigenous woman who was sterilized in Alberta because she was considered a "mental defective." Leilani Muir eventually sued the Alberta Government and won her case.

including sterilization. As an expert of the time, Dr. Patterson appealed to both religion and science to justify her stance on morality.

Helen MacMurchy[65] was another influential Canadian woman who defended the elimination of "mental defectives" through sterilization. Among other high ranking appointments, MacMurchy was the Inspector of the Feeble-Minded in Ontario from 1906 to 1916. MacMurchy firmly believed that feeble-mindedness was the cause of venereal disease, illegitimacy, and infant mortality. She referred to unmarried mothers as "illegitimate mothers" and deemed them to be feeble-minded simply by virtue of the fact that they had borne a child outside of wedlock (Valverde 108). MacMurchy's reports on the feeble-minded carried weight with medical and political leaders. While she argued that the "subnormal" deserved "justice and a fair chance," she also concluded that they could not be treated as normal because they were the "waste products of humanity" (qtd. in McLaren 39). MacMurchy contended that segregation in institutions would ultimately pay for itself, as even greater expenses would be incurred if the feeble-minded were allowed to roam free in society where they would reproduce. In 1908, MacMurchy asserted that 80 percent of feeble-mindedness could be eliminated within a generation through segregation and sterilization (McLaren 42).

The unmarried mother, through her diagnosis and categorization as feeble-minded, was not only seen as a major cause of societal ills, but within the context of eugenics, as a subject to be regulated, incarcerated, and sterilized to eliminate the reproduction of her kind. Cast as feeble-minded, the unmarried mother was no longer a fallen one or even a danger to normative families and respectable society; she was now a biological other—one to be subjected to differentiated social and medical treatment.

---

65 MacMurchy earned her medical degree at University of Toronto in 1901. She was the first woman in the Department of Obstetrics and Gynaecology at Toronto General Hospital, and was the first woman to be accepted by the John Hopkins University Medical School for postgraduate study (McLaren 30-35).

Venereal Disease

Along with Canada's societal preoccupation with feeble-mindedness, the problem of "venereal disease" or (VD), (referred to today as sexually transmitted infections, or STIs), became a major concern in the early twentieth century. I will turn briefly to this topic in the context of the increasing tide of moral regulation and harsh treatment of women which emerged later in the interwar period. As with illegitimacy and feeble-mindedness, sexually transmitted infections became a metaphor for larger societal concerns. It became a flashpoint for the regulation of immorality, sex, and vice. During WWI, societal apprehension over these types of infections intensified, as high rates were reported within the ranks of Canadian soldiers whose imminent return from the war (Mawani 148). Doctors and other experts believed that sexual immorality was the root cause of venereal disease and thus, it was viewed as a social problem. Medically endorsed government sponsorship of "anti-VD" programs sprung up around the country fuelled by the usual organizations—such as the YMCA, YWCA, and NCW—which created a hybrid "medico-moral regulatory regime" (Mawani 149). A Nova Scotia pamphlet from 1917 concludes that "all extra-marital sex was abnormal and unsafe, and virtually guaranteed exposure to VD" (qtd. in Mawani 155).

An article titled "Mental Deficiency in Relation to Venereal Disease" by London physician A.F. Tredgold was published in the July 1919 issue of *The Canadian Journal of Mental Hygiene*. In this report, Dr. Tredgold relates that the defects and moral tendencies of the feeble-minded would most likely result in their "readily contracting and spreading venereal disease, should the opportunity occur" (188). Thus, the feeble-minded morally defective girl wilfully and unashamedly contracted and spread the disease and was, thereby, an agent of immorality and social degradation, unlike the "normal" girl who contracted it as an exception (192).

Defending Canada from the ravages of STIs meant forcing soldiers to undergo treatment, but it also meant subjecting women, particularly those who were disadvantaged, to various forms of moral regulation (Strange and Loo 93). In 1918, the Ontario Royal Commission on Venereal Disease and Feeble-Mindedness recommended that free treatment clinics be established along with the imposition of fines for those who refused treatment, yet it was only women who were targeted with these regulations. Several provinces enacted such measures into law,[66] which led to the forced medical treatment and incarceration of women suffering from sexually transmitted infections or labelled feeble-minded (Strange and Loo 94). Fears over these types of infections also resurfaced during and after World War II. Educational material during the period portrayed women as either innocent victims or as "promiscuous predators" (Sangster, *Regulating* 89).

The effect was that the unmarried mother and sexually transmitted infections were inextricably linked. Not only was she a serious threat to society and families because of her biology, her immorality, and her defective mind, but also her diseased body became a locus of danger. As we shall see, unmarried mothers would continue to be routinely tested for sexually transmitted infections well into the 1960s.[67]

Unmarried Mothers as Sex Delinquents

During the interwar period, unmarried motherhood was thought to be a result of "the poisonous interaction between environmental conditions and moral degeneracy" (Solinger 17). Illegitimacy during this period began to be attributed to broken homes, poverty, poor education, domestic occupation, and even the pattern of life in certain subcultures[68] (Josie, *Caricature* 247). Moral regulation of women increased due to the rising moral panic surrounding sexually transmitted infections, sexual promiscuity, illegitimate pregnancy, and women deemed "out of sexual control" (Sangster, *Incarcerating* 190). Voluntary and involuntary incarceration continued to be a means to control the sexuality and moral behaviour of unmarried mothers during the interwar period. As in the nineteenth century, it was not only women who had already fallen but also girls and women who were viewed as "likely to go astray" who ended up in reform type institutions (Strange 132).

In the larger context of heightened public interest in delinquency and moral regulation, unmarried mothers were labelled with the new category of "sex delinquent" (Kunzel 55). The concept of delinquency had been previously associated only with boys. However, with

---

66 After the First World War, venereal disease prevention acts were implemented in all provinces except Prince Edward Island (Mawani 2006).

67 See Victor Home Admission Requirements.

68 Sub-culture in this context meant Black, Indigenous, Chinese, or any other non-white, non-European culture.

emergent theories of adolescence and fear over the deterioration of moral values, social purity reformers became interested in female delinquency (Kunzel 55). Like feeble-mindedness, delinquency was gendered. Boys were considered criminals, whereas girls were sexual deviants. The definition of female delinquency was also circular in that: "female delinquents were, almost by definition 'immoral,' and sex delinquency was perceived to be also by definition, female" (Kunzel 55). Medical and psychiatric experts played a key role in the discursive construction of female sex delinquency by inventing new labels for women, such as "delinquent," "morally degenerate," "psychopathic," "sex-crazed," "sex maniac," and "hypersexual" (Strange 127).

With the construction of the category of sex delinquent, a layer of criminality was added to the characterization of unmarried mothers. Evangelicals and other rescue workers had worked tirelessly in the nineteenth century to keep criminals and unmarried mothers separated, lest delinquents should contaminate and influence the fallen. However, in the twentieth century those distinctions blurred. The boundaries collapsed between unmarried mothers, criminals, and delinquents, until they were seen as synonymous (Kunzel 55). Sex delinquents were not viewed as fallen sisters. Instead, they were construed to have agency and a wilful agenda.

The characterization of sexual misbehaviour as delinquency for women led to various forms of incarceration (Chambers, *Misconceptions* 58). In Ontario, The Female Refuges Act, enacted in 1897, allowed a sentence of up to five years[69] (Sangster, *Regulating*). This Act gave police powers to arrest women in a pre-emptive fashion *before* they committed an act of delinquency. The Female Refuges Act targeted women who were considered promiscuous with illegitimate children, who were suspected of VD, or who engaged in relationships with Asian or Black men (Sangster, *Incarcerating*). Ontario[70] judges were authorized to commit to an institution any girl through a sworn statement by parents, a social worker, or the police (Backhouse 243). This broad statute allowed for young girls to be institutionalized for long periods of time, sometimes for very little reason. Vague charges such as incorrigibility, vagrancy, and immorality were laid with little foundation or explanation

---

69 This was amended in 1919 to two years less a day (Sangster, *Regulating*).

70 Similar statutes were enacted in Nova Scotia (1884) and Manitoba (1898) (Backhouse 243).

(Strange 133). By the late 1920s, in the aftermath of the social purity campaign, Ontario magistrates were giving younger women longer and indeterminate sentences to such institutions as the Mercer Reformatory for Women. Younger women and girls began to be incarcerated for morality crimes. During the interwar period, the Mercer[71] and similar institutions became a key site for the incarceration of unmarried mothers, prostitutes, wayward women, and those with VD (Sangster, *Incarcerating* 103).

The usual experts—including social workers, psychologists, and medical doctors—became increasingly involved in the correctional system (Sangster, *Incarcerating* 194). Parents also took an active role in having their daughters detained. Parents of "delinquent" daughters routinely sent them to maternity homes or brought them before the courts for defiance, disobedience, promiscuity, and illegitimate pregnancies. Sangster points out that: "in assessing the incarceration of these young women, one also has to take into account parents' active participation in the process and thus the broader question of how consent to the law was organized" (*Incarcerating* 198). On the advice of clergy, social workers, and the medical community, parents continued to play an active role in the quasi-incarceration of their daughters in Canada's maternity homes.

With the development of the category of sex delinquent in the interwar period, unmarried mothers began to be viewed as criminal elements in society. The legal system—as evangelism and philanthropy had in the past—became a site to reproduce Magdalenism and to proscribe women's sexuality and reform through patriarchal definitions and the Mary-Magdalen binary. After WWII, young pregnant women and girls were still being described in social work literature as delinquent, and those whose pregnancy was perceived to be the consequence of promiscuity could still come under the purview of the court. Unwed motherhood was recast as an "emblem of delinquency" (Sangster, *Girl Trouble* 154). Incarceration, cures, and harsh treatment for unmarried mothers became normalized in a "process that took away women's most basic liberties, encouraged their sterilization, and

---

71   In her memoir titled Incorrigible, Velma Demerson, who was sent to the Mercer Reformatory in 1939 for being pregnant with the child of a Chinese man not her husband—describes how she and other women were tortured with experimental treatments for sexually transmitted infections, including being operated on without the use of anaesthetic, held in solitary confinement, and kept from their babies in the nursery there.

discouraged them from keeping their children" (Sangster, *Incarcerating* 210).

The *Unwed* Mother: Psychoanalytic Theories

"Clearly, the girl's wish to have a baby without a husband is neither an adult or normal desire ... the child is clearly not a part of her unconscious fantasy and hence is of little real concern to her" — Young, *Wedlock* 36.

Although early twentieth-century psychiatry had diagnosed the unmarried mother as feeble-minded, the psychoanalytic theories of Freud which became popular in the interwar period, fuelled a renewed interest in the psychoanalysis of unwed motherhood. During the 1940s and in immediate postwar decades, there was a new preoccupation with what was now being called the "unwed mother," and unmarried motherhood was redefined once again.[72] This re-characterization, which led directly to the adoption mandate, constructed the unmarried mother as having a treatable mental disorder. Rickie Solinger explains:

The postwar, modern alternative claimed that illegitimacy reflected a mental not environmental or biological dis- order, and was, in general a symptom of individual, treatable neuroses... since society reserved deeply punitive responses for unwed mothers, a single girl who flew in the face of certain and severe censure and became pregnant had to be sick. She had, in fact, to be pregnant on purpose. Only a truly sick person could deny reality so radically. (Solinger 16, 88)

In 1946, Canadian social worker Svanhuit Josie suggested that although various theories had succeeded one another to identify the cause of unmarried motherhood, experts now explained the condition in psychiatric terms (*Caricature* 246). Psychoanalytic theories of illegitimate motherhood were granted credibility, promoted, and

---

72 Nonetheless, characterizations of the unmarried mother as feeble-minded, fallen, and delinquent continued into the late twentieth century. Young writes, "the tendency to regard all unmarried mothers as sex delinquents lingers, and is only slowly modified and diluted" (Young, *Wedlock* 11).

upheld by the usual experts and were an extension of the early twentieth century practice of drawing upon science to manage, regulate, and punish illegitimate mothers (Solinger 102).

Social workers played a major role in redefining the white unwed mother as mentally ill. The psychiatric, sociological, and social work literature for the period was changing from categorizing women as delinquent or organically flawed; psychoanalytic theories now described unwed mothers as "overly sexual and psychologically disturbed" (Chambers, *Misconceptions* 59). Those shifting characterizations—that is, from sex delinquent to mentally ill—are illustrated in a study by Lori Chambers, which includes a review of Ontario Children's Aid Society (CAS) social work case files. Chambers found the following:

> In total 1,404 of 1,992 (70.5%) non-cohabiting women were described as "delinquent," "immature," "neurotic," "unstable," "promiscuous," and "dishonest." Interestingly, the percentage of women described as "delinquent" declined steadily after the war, while the use of terms like "neurotic" and "unstable" increased, reflecting the changing social work paradigm of the etiology of unwed pregnancy. (*Misconceptions* 61)

Popular psychoanalytic theories explaining out-of-wedlock pregnancy in the immediate postwar decades characterized the unmarried mother as purposeful by nature; with emotional problems that stemmed from childhood. The unmarried mother was seen to be acting out various fantasies, and unconscious desires. Diagnoses of neuroses, personality disorders, and even schizophrenia were commonly conferred. In general, unmarried mothers were thought to be suffering from an underlying emotional problem (Daniels).

The role of the mothers and fathers of the unmarried mother within psychoanalytic theory was often invoked as a reason for out-of-wedlock pregnancy. Mother theories abounded. Most of these revolved around the idea that the unmarried mother became pregnant to present her mother with the baby, either out of revenge or love. In the book *Psychology of Women* published in 1945, Helene Deutsch, a prominent figure who wrote extensively about women and motherhood, weighed in on out-of-wedlock pregnancy: "a hateful protest against the mother often contains revenge tendencies and that promiscuity, prostitution, or illegitimate motherhood often fulfills both a fantasy and a need for self-punishment" (349). One mother theory suggested by Young in 1954 was that an unmarried mother dominated by her own mother, consciously became pregnant because she had an overwhelming drive to give the baby to the mother (*Wedlock* 58). Young describes this process: "she gives the baby to the mother; the child is no concern of hers because she does not belong to her ... in a sense having this baby concerns primarily the relationship between the girl and her mother, is a gift of love as well as an instrument of revenge" (*Wedlock* 58). In 1955 Dr. Ner Littner argued that the unmarried mother was acting out on an early childhood fantasy surrounding her own mother, that is, of having the baby for the mother and by the mother. These types of mother theories continued well into the 1960s. Psychiatrists Marcel Heiman and Esther Levitt state the following in 1960:

> We are not dealing with a mother-daughter relationship that is threatened, but rather with a relationship between mother and daughter which is already very severely disturbed. We believe that in actuality, the unmarried mother has experienced the loss of her mother, either physically or emotionally, and as Young has said, is "seeking for her mother who has deserted her at birth". (167)

In 1965 Dr. Michael Khlentzos of the Neuropsychiatric Institute in California wrote: "she is searching for a nurturance from a mother figure symbolized in the sexual act as a forbidden kind of erotized nurturing provided by the alleged father" (780).

Fathers were not exempt from the burgeoning psychoanalytic discourse surrounding unmarried motherhood. Although it was argued that unmarried mothers whose fathers dominated the home were fewer in numbers than those coming from mother-dominated homes, Young argues that overly strict, unsympathetic, even abusive fathers were responsible for their daughter's pregnancy (*Wedlock* 60), whereas Dr. James Cattell asserted that fathers in these homes were usually passive and ineffectual (98). Solinger suggests that a combination of mother and father traits were often used as reasons for out-of-wedlock pregnancy. The most frequent appeared to be "a weak father and a hypochondriacal and controlling mother, or a strong but neglectful father and a frustrated mother" (91).

Other theories advanced by experts included illegitimate maternity as a result of exaggerated adolescent psychological conflicts, including a masochistic gratification resulting from penis envy or fantasies of rape, incest, or prostitution. In 1943 Florence Clouthier imagined that unwed pregnancies resulted from masochistic gratification and rape fantasies: "some girls act out the fantasy of rape by placing themselves in situations in which they will provoke assault and if this results in pregnancy they obtain masochistic gratification" (543). Helene Deutsch reproduces these psychoanalytic themes in 1945:

> Any excessive charge of puberal conflicts can operate as such as motive [to become pregnant out of wedlock]. The motive may be that of flight from incest fantasies ... it may arise from an unfavourable identification (e.g. with a pregnant mother, sister, friend, etc.), from vengefulness toward family, from a tendency to self-punishment ... the numerous cases I have encountered have always involved a weakness of the ego that made it unable to resist the strong psychic dangers otherwise than by transference of them to the outside world. (qtd. in Deutsch, 335, 340)

A McGill University social work thesis by Dorothy Begg titled *Psychiatric Problems of Unmarried Mothers* written in 1951, echoes these Freudian themes:

> She regards her mother, who like herself is castrated, as being also inferior and blames her for having equipped her so poorly her passive masochistic development is strengthened by identification with her mother, her wish to be loved by her father as her mother is, and to have a baby by him ... maternity brings with it supreme masochistic gratification, as well as fulfillment of the long-felt wish for a child. (15)

In 1960, Heiman and Levitt asserted that the out of wedlock pregnancy and resulting baby were symbols of unsatisfactory completion of the oral stage:

Regressively, with the help of the genital apparatus, most probably on the basis of oral fantasies, a woman re-creates for herself an object. Since these objects fundamentally are a substitute for mother and since the woman has undergone a regression in order to create out of herself this object, it becomes clear that in those instances the mother is not the mother and the baby is not a baby. The very reverse is the case because the person who has regressively created the baby is the child herself, while the baby that has been created is a replacement for the mother; thus the mother is the baby, and the baby is the mother. (172)

Psychiatric diagnoses were routinely conferred on unmarried mothers in the pre- and postwar decades and cited by the medical profession as the cause of out-of-wedlock pregnancy. One study of fifty-four unmarried mothers residing in a maternity home in 1954 conducted by Dr. James P. Cattell states that: "the following distribution of diagnoses were found: character disorder, 30; neurotic reaction, 7 (anxiety, depressive, and conversion); schizophrenia, 17; pseudo-neurotic, 7; other types, 10" (339). It is interesting to note that Dr. Cattell finds that out of the fifty-four unmarried mothers studied, thirty-two percent appear to suffer from schizophrenia when it is unlikely that even one person in such a small group residing in a maternity home would merit this diagnosis.[73] Although some in the medical community found a connection between depression and out-of-wedlock pregnancy, most of these diagnoses were based on studies of mothers in residence in maternity homes or following surrender. However, in 1960 one study found that depression was, indeed, the cause of out-of-wedlock pregnancy; it existed prenatally, and was one of the prime forces motivating the pregnancy (Heiman and Levitt).

Some in the medical community went so far as to consider the physical pregnancies and deliveries of unmarried mothers to be different from those of married mothers. Unmarried mothers were purported to become pregnant more quickly; rarely experience miscarriage or nausea and delivered their babies with fewer than

---

73 Approximately 1 percent of Canadians suffer from this debilitating condition (Public Health Agency of Canada).

average complications or difficulty—and the ratio of fetal deaths was lower than that in married women. Even unmarried mothers having their first child in their thirties or forties were considered to have had no special difficulty; and regained their strength much faster than married women (Young 34). These erroneous claims furthered the notion of a biological difference between unmarried mothers and married mothers.

The unmarried mother had to be seen as different from other mothers to facilitate the normalization of the violent separation of a young healthy mother and her newborn infant. It served the mandate well to characterize the unmarried mother as different, even physically so, from other mothers. In a speech titled "The Intermediary System Is Not a Solution" given by Margaret McDonald-Lawrence at the first national conference of American Adoption Congress in Washington DC on 4 May 1979, she states the following:

> It is the child welfare establishment that has provided the picture of "birthmothers" as indifferent—as mothers who abandon their children with a wish to remain forever hidden from them. They know this is seldom true, but it helps to facilitate their work for the public to believe this.... The "birthmother" must be different, an aberration; for if it were true that she had the same degree of love for her child as all other mothers, the good of adoption would be overwhelmed by the tragedy of it ... neither society nor the mother who holds the child in her arms wants to confront the agony of the mother from whose arms that same child was taken. (1)

As illustrated, psychoanalytic theories relating to the unmarried mother flourished during the 1940s and 1950s. This mostly stemmed from the idea that a young woman had to be "ill" to dismiss the intense social stigma related to a pregnancy outside of marriage. The idea of a woman exercising sexual agency was still outside of the normative role for the so-called good Canadian woman. The fact that a girl or woman may have simply become pregnant in an era when birth control, safe legal abortion, or sexual education was unavailable was not considered as a reason for her out-of-wedlock pregnancy.

Unmarried Mothers as "Girls" and "Non-mothers"

The construction of the unmarried mother as a girl and a non-mother was integral to the success of the adoption mandate. As the teen years emerged as a separate and quantifiable stage of life in the early 1940s, not only was the unmarried mother characterized as feeble-minded, maladjusted, diseased, and neurotic, but she was also as seen as too young and immature to mother her child.[74] Unmarried mothers were often referred to as "girls" irrespective of age.[75] The tendency to generalize teenage experiences and concepts of teenage-hood contributed to the notion of unmarried mothers as being too young to be mothers. These young mothers were not simply contradicting the moral codes of society, but were also flouting childhood (Wall 65).

The psychiatric explanation for unmarried motherhood served the depiction of unmarried mothers as "childlike." The unmarried mother was constructed as not being responsible for her pregnancy; instead, she was overtaken by something larger than herself—a pathology (Solinger 88). Unmarried mothers were cast as children having children or child mothers; they were characterized as unable, not ready, and unfit to mother their children. Yet this was an era when 76.7 percent of women in Canada married between the ages of fifteen and twenty-four[76] (Canada. Statistics Canada, *Year Book*). Married women were often teen mothers, although their marital status exempted them from being an object of the state gaze, research, and psychoanalytic theories. It was the "unmarried mother' that became and continues to be, an object of intense inquiry" (Andrews, "#Flip" 3). Cast as girls, the unmarried mother could be subjected to authority and processes that severely limited her right to autonomy and self-definition, thereby transforming her into a child (Solinger 88).

An example of the characterization of unmarried mothers as girls is the CBC television program *Take 30*, which aired in 1964 and featured a segment titled "Talking Teen Pregnancy." An interview was conducted with Little Betty, an unmarried mother residing in a Calgary

74 This continues in adoption practice today. Young mothers continue to be characterized as "too young," "not ready," or "incapable" of mothering.

75 In Canada's maternity homes, unmarried mothers in their thirties continued to be referred to as "girls."

76 See Statistics Canada, Canada Year Book, 1967, Brides and bridegrooms, by Age and Marital status, 1964.

maternity home. Little Betty appears with her back to the camera; she wears a veil to ensure her identity is shielded from the audience. Although she is about to become a mother, the commentators refer to her as "Little Betty" throughout the program[77] (Talking Teen Pregnancy). A 1969 Vancouver study titled "Reaction of Unmarried Girls to Pregnancy" looked at 316 unmarried pregnant women, and although the study notes that almost 50 percent of the women were between the ages of twenty-one and thirty-six, the study refers to them as "girls" throughout (Claman et al.).

Maternity homes also referred to inmates as girls, even those in their thirties. Anne Petrie recalls how unmarried mothers were cast as girls in Canada's maternity homes: "even the oldest of us became girls in the homes. Not only were we called girls, we were not allowed to be anything else but girls. Although we were all having babies, the most obvious marker of womanhood, because we were not pregnant in the sanctioned manner we could not enter that secret sisterhood. We were girls, and we would stay girls" (11).

Characterizing unmarried mothers as girls regardless of age subjected them to institutional authority and, as "girls", their obedience to authority was expected. The categorization of unmarried mothers as girls irrespective of age, contributed to the notion that they were unfit to mother, that they had no right of choice, and that punishment for their social indiscretion was deserved. Further, as "girls", their rights over their own bodies, including their babies, remained ambiguous.

As suggested by Petrie, unmarried mothers were denied the right of passage into womanhood and motherhood afforded to married mothers. As both mother and non-mother, the unmarried mother did not fit into any category. No social rituals were passed for either the birth of or the loss of her child. The birth, which was treated as a secret non-event, placed the unmarried mother in conflict with reality. Her motherhood was outwardly invisible, but she remembered, as did her body. As one mother relates, "I was a mother who wasn't allowed to be a mother, but my body knew I was a mother" (qtd. in Alward). Although mothers of the mandate would continue to be categorized as girls, they would never be girls again.

---

77 Although unmarried mothers were characterized as "too young," they were not considered too young to sign termination of parental rights at the age of thirteen in Canada without legal advice.

As the various characterizations of unmarried mothers evolved during the twentieth century, the characterization of the unmarried mother as ill and in need of rehabilitation became entrenched in dominant discourse for practitioners. The psychiatric perspective was not simply a theoretical or conjectural construct: service providers including social workers and maternity home matrons structured their programs and services based on theories advanced by the psychiatric community in prominent medical journals. Solinger writes that "There is no public evidence that colleagues objected to their formulations or found them out of concert with mainstream psychiatric theory and practice" (88). In fact, these now seemingly ridiculous notions advanced by the medical community and other experts with respect to the unmarried mother were accepted as legitimate causes of unwed pregnancy.

There were few critics of the characterizations and diagnoses being advanced for unmarried mothers in postwar Canada. However, in the article "An Assessment of Research Knowledge Concerning the Unmarried Mother," written in 1966, Jane Kronick states that "very little of the writing is based on knowledge derived from research" (232). Kronick outlines deficiencies in the writings and publications pertaining to unmarried mothers, including hegemonic narratives, inconsistent sampling methods, research bias, lack of thesis or research question, and poor research methods (247). Another researcher Clark E. Vincent, in an attempt to more accurately portray unmarried mothers and to raise questions for future research, conducted a study in 1961 that proved sampling bias in previous studies that had only studied mothers associated with social institutions. In other writings, Vincent dispels the notion of a hegemonic mother group by attempting to study them intersectionally. Canadian social worker Svanhuit Josie suggested as early as 1955 that if an unmarried mother were to marry even the day before delivery that no questions would arise about her psychological inner conflicts or impaired abilities to raise her offspring, which suggests marital status was the central pivot of these theories and nothing more (*Caricature*). In the article "Are We Still Stereotyping the Unmarried Mother," written in 1960, social worker Rose Bernstein suggests that some unmarried mothers may have had pre-existing problems, but that others may simply be experiencing problems due to the current crisis of out-of-wedlock pregnancy. Bernstein also asserts that social workers need to think in terms of hypotheses rather than "closed systems of explanation for which we are impelled to find substantiating evidence" (117).

Kronick, Vincent, Josie, and Bernstein may have been voices of reason in the wilderness, but ones that were mostly unheeded in a prolific sea of literature that cast the postwar unwed mother as mentally ill. Many studies occurred across disciplines—social work, medicine, psychology, psychiatry, sociology—and appeared in journals such as *Canadian Family Physician, Canada Medical Association Journal, Canadian Nurse, American Journal of Psychiatry, American Journal of Orthopsychiatry,* and *The Social Worker,* to name a few. Canadian theses and scholarly works subscribed to, reproduced, and circulated psychoanalytic theories of illegitimate motherhood. Although less material was published in Canada than in the United States, nonetheless, Canadian professionals and experts subscribed to and acted on these theories which suggested unmarried mothers were ill, needed rehabilitation, and were ultimately unfit.

It was not only the theory of Magdelanism and its quasi-incarceral institutions, or the changing characterizations of unmarried mothers during the twentieth century that contributed to and impacted changes in policy surrounding the unmarried mother. As the next chapter will elucidate, the profession of social work and emerging sociological theories also become crucial elements in the unique "perfect storm" of factors that led to the postwar adoption mandate.

Chapter Three

The Profession of Social Work and the Influence of Sociological Theories in Postwar Adoption Practice

"In removing unmarried mothers from the evangelical narrative and placing them within the scientific scripts of feeble-mindedness and sex delinquency, social workers had gone a considerable distance toward achieving recognition in the field of illegitimacy ... the task of inventing their own, modern, professional identities led social workers to contribute to new sexual discourses that stigmatized working-class women's sexuality as pathological and criminal"—Kunzel 64

The profession of social work had a major impact on the adoption mandate. Section I of this chapter will track the progression of the scientific "professionalism of benevolence" (Kunzel 3) in the early twentieth century. It will set forth how social workers created a profession for themselves using scientific casework to approach social problems, particularly those pertaining to the unmarried mother.

Section II explores briefly various theories—the sociological and psychoanalytical theories of the clean slate[78] (tabula rasa), attachment,

---

78 The concept of the Latin *tabula rasa* or "unsubscribed slate" can be traced back to Aristotle. However, the modern use of the concept is attributed to John Locke (1690), as a result of his *An Essay Concerning Human Understanding*. A resurgence of the concept in postwar Canada, was due to the Freuds who assert that children were solely a product of their environment.

and imprinting, which were advanced by scholars Sigmund and Anna Freud, John Bowlby, Harry Harlow, and Konrad Lorenz. These emerging ideas informed and influenced changes in postwar adoption practice leading to the "clean break,"[79] which will be revealed as a form of violence against women and the maternal body. In addition, the idea of the complete break or the practice of sealing of adoption records in Canada is briefly reviewed.

This chapter will also show how unmarried mothers in postwar Canada were subject to draconian practices by social workers and within Canada's hospitals some of which have been constituted as illegal, unethical, and human rights abuses by adoption activists. Through the use of secondary sources, the voices of mothers are heard, and the violence, disempowerment, and unethical practices they experienced become visible. In conclusion, I will turn briefly to the topic of baby formula which, due to advances in both baby formula and food preservation became a contributing element to the mandate.

79　This is the practice of removing babies from unmarried mothers immediately following delivery.

Section I: The Profession of Social Work

In the 1910s, the newly created profession of social work claimed illegitimacy as one of its areas of expertise. This development became one of the major contributing factors to the adoption mandate in Canada. Until the end of WWI, child welfare, social work, rescue work, and moral reformation schemes remained mostly outside of the state; they were instead organized and managed by an extensive network of philanthropic groups and individuals that the Canadian governments acknowledged as experts in these fields (Valverde 52). However, with the rise and acceptance of Darwinism and the social purity movement, more emphasis was placed on science to solve social problems. In *The Search for Order 1877-1920*, Robert Wiebe asserts that a fundamental shift took place between 1877 and 1920 wherein the new urban middle class embraced science as a way to create order in unruly and expanding urban environments. These new reformers were instrumental in "extolling the virtues of bureaucracy, efficiency, rationality, and scientific management all of which would help bring order to the chaos of a developing urban-industrial society" (Irving 11). The view of many in the emerging field of social work at that time was that unless a scientific basis for social work was firmly established, it would not thrive as a profession (Irving 14).

After a meeting of the Social Workers Club and the Social Science Study Club in 1913, a resolution in support of formalizing social work training was presented to the Board of Governors of the University of Toronto[80]; the first school of social work in Canada was established a year later. McGill University followed in 1918, and courses were introduced at the University of British Columbia in 1928. On 20 March 1926, approximately sixty social workers from Winnipeg, Montreal, Ottawa, Halifax, and Toronto met in Montreal formed the Canadian Association of Social Workers (CASW), with 197 charter members from across Canada. The Canadian Conference of Social Work met for the first time between 24 April and 27 April 1928; 710 social workers were in attendance. The Association journal, *The Social Worker*, was published for the first time in October 1932 (Jennissen and Lundy).

The Great Depression and two world wars were vital in expanding

---

80 The University of Toronto calendar for 1915-16 listed a course titled "Statistics and Social Research – methods of analysis; collection and interpretation of data" (Irving 14).

the social work profession (Hick). It was not until 1941 that the Maritime School of Social Work in Halifax opened its doors with six students (M. Smith). In 1943, the Laval School of Social Work opened in Quebec City followed by the School of Social Work at the University of Manitoba (77). Canadian social workers continued to rely mostly on American social work conferences and associations for professional growth, and Canadian education and research were influenced greatly by developments south of the border until after the Cold War (Irving 10).

The professionalization of social welfare would reshape the approaches and attitudes to illegitimacy and the unmarried mother (Kunzel 37). The early twentieth century was an initial period of growth for social work, as early practitioners working with unmarried mothers sought not only to distance themselves from nineteenth-century philanthropy but also to create a new scientific profession. The new social workers did not consider the unmarried mother as their "unfortunate sister" and had no philanthropic ideals about saving them. While extolling the virtues of the scientific method, social work leaders found the values of nineteenth-century reformers to be unprofessional, outdated, and overly sentimental (Kunzel 44). Although evangelical and other Christian women continued to claim authority over unmarried mothers, their proficiency was questioned by those in the emerging social science community. Beginning in the late 1910s, social work practitioners began to claim illegitimacy as part of their expanding domain (Kunzel 50). Social workers constructed themselves as experts, enlisting and developing scientific methods, such as "differential casework" (Friedlander 71).[81]

The use of differential casework as a method resulted in the introduction of the case file, which included a detailed record of interactions between the social worker and client, including interviews, and was used to provide social diagnosis and treatment. Extensive and detailed instruction as to how to achieve this was outlined in *Social Diagnosis*, written by Mary Richmond in 1917. A chapter devoted to unmarried mothers includes a lengthy sample interview for social workers to use when interviewing them. Questions regarding the social

81 Differential casework is a social work practice based on the premise that under certain conditions, certain casework goals and techniques are appropriate; and under other conditions, other goals and techniques may be appropriate (Friedlander 71).

history of the unmarried mother included those about the background of the unmarried mother and father, school achievement, employment, paternity, sexual morality, community, attitude of parents, and plans for pregnancy, delivery, and care of the child (See Appendix B). As an example:

> If this is the girl's or woman's first child, does she appreciate the seriousness of her act and its consequences? Did she leave her home to hide her shame? To give the baby to strangers so that her misconduct might remain unsuspected at home? Does she love her baby? Does she want to keep it? (Richmond 414-419)

The methodology of the unmarried mother interview was to remain virtually unchanged for the next fifty years or more.[82] Social workers asserted that the objective of the case file was to collect all information that may indicate the nature of the client's difficulties in order to provide a solution (Chambers, *Misconceptions* 58). The goal was no longer to provide short-term solutions for illegitimacy but to uncover the underlying causes of out-of-wedlock pregnancy to permanently resolve the problem (Weinberg 26).

Prior to the introduction of social work, unmarried fathers had been portrayed as predators, seducers, and irresponsible cads. However, by the 1940s the social worker had shifted the responsibility for unwed pregnancy away from unmarried fathers. Social workers argued that viewing all men as seducers and betrayers was unfair and that saddling a man with the support of a child that he may not have fathered could possibly endanger his marriage prospects (Crawford 134). Social workers reversed the narrative surrounding unmarried mothers: the burden of responsibility and guilt for illegitimacy shifted away from men to women. Solinger states that "the girl or woman who 'got herself pregnant' was the locus of blame, the target of treatment programs and punishments" (Solinger 36). This narrative further stigmatized and vilified unmarried mothers. A 1949 *Maclean's* article titled "The Forgotten Fathers" asserts that although the public viewed the unmarried father as a "low scoundrel" with no sense of responsibility

---

82 Later in the century, records of the Children's Aid Society of Ontario show similar detailed interviewing methods for unmarried mothers (Chambers, *Misconceptions*).

toward either the "unfortunate woman" or "hapless infant," social workers viewed the unmarried father as a normal, personable youth who was worried about his situation (qtd. in Crawford 113). Further, unmarried mothers were not considered trustworthy in their assertions of paternity. Social workers stated that often the father remained unknown—alluding to moral laxity on the part of the woman—and that women were manipulative in naming fathers who might not have actually been the fathers. This characterization of men as victims of predatory scheming women highlights social workers' perceptions of unmarried mothers (Crawford 113). For those mothers that did attempt to name the father to obtain financial support, most provinces required that her paternity testimony be corroborated (Boyd et al. 67).

A review of the Canadian Association of Social Work journal, *The Social Worker*, from 1936 to 1970 reveals interesting developments in the field pertaining to unmarried mothers. The 1937 Manitoba report on unmarried mothers released in *The Social Worker* identifies possible causes of unmarried motherhood: lack of moral training, idleness, misuse of leisure time, lack of wholesome recreation, moving pictures, immoderate use of alcohol and drugs, increased opportunity due to more social freedom, and financial difficulties (7). The report also identifies a need for comprehensive services for unmarried mothers to be provided by one organization instead of a patchwork of services by various social service agencies. The Manitoba report recommends that only agencies with the highest level of training and skill should be charged with the responsibility of casework with unmarried mothers; it suggests that either Children's Aid Societies or other family agencies are well placed to do so. In this report, we are offered a rare glimpse of how the adoption mandate came to be administered by Children's Aid Societies and social agencies with the powers of adoption in Canada:

> Although a somewhat irregular one, the Unmarried Mother and her child constitute a family unit, and might be handled by a family agency ... there is an advantage in that a Children's Aid Society has the machinery for court action ... in addition the Children's Aid Society has powers of adoption which a Family Agency has not ... since the Children's Aid Society movement has extended throughout the Province of Manitoba, and Family Agencies are largely

restricted to urban centres, the Children's Aid Societies would appear to be the logical media for the provision of service on a provincial wide basis. (7)

By 1943, *The Social Worker* was directing women to contact their local Children's Aid Society if they were single and pregnant. During the war years, *The Social Worker* concentrated on topics mostly pertaining to the war effort, such as safety, emergency plans, overseas efforts, child health, and women war workers. However, in the February 1948 issue, an article appears titled "Case Work and Adoption" by Mary Speers, the supervisor of the Adoption Department at the Children's Aid Society of Toronto, and she writes the following:

> Good adoption practices began with good case work done with the unmarried mother who is usually a sick girl. Her pregnancy is a symptom, not the cause of her condition. Her illness might be of a neurotic, psychotic or pre-psychotic origin, springing from maladjustments in her own home, deprivations and frustrations which interfered with her psycho-social development ... the healthy girl protected herself. (18)

In this article, Speers reproduces the major postwar psychoanalytic theories of unmarried motherhood, and social work methods, that is, for the sick unmarried mother, the child is not real, or the child is used unconsciously as a weapon to punish her parents—and through good casework, the unmarried mother can reach a more mature adjustment toward life (Speers 18).

Betty Isserman, the Chief Medical Social Worker at St. Anne's Hospital in Montreal, wrote an article titled "The Casework Relationship in work with Unmarried Mothers," which appeared in the October 1948 issue of *The Social Worker*. Isserman shows that for social workers, the preferred solution to unmarried motherhood was adoption:

> The social worker does not persuade [sic] the unmarried mother either way. Today we say that unmarried mothers need real assistance in making a decision to give up or keep their children, and this help is offered by a social agency

through the casework relationship ... we believe in adoption as a good solution in many situations. We might say adoption is best in all cases where the mother chooses a more normal life for her child. (12)

More articles pertaining to unmarried mothers appeared in *The Social Worker* during the 1950s along with an increasing number of advertisements for social workers to work in Children's Aid Societies. By 1953, there were approximately six pages of advertisements. It is interesting to note that although adoptions from unmarried mothers in Canada reached their highest level in Canada during the 1960s, *The Social Worker* was unusually silent on the subject; only one article pertaining to unmarried motherhood was published during the entire decade. However at the same time, the number of pages advertising for employment for social workers at Children's Aid Societies increased to twenty-five pages by 1963.

By the 1950s, social workers were entrenched in adoption work with unmarried mothers in Canada and increasingly used adoption as the casework treatment. Social workers were more likely to favour adoption since the prevailing view was that being unmarried equated to being "unfit" (Kunzel 129). Relinquishment of the child was considered to be the solution to the problem of "unmarried motherhood". Casework was used to assist mothers in arriving at a "realistic plan"—a trade euphemism for relinquishment found in many social work journals, books, and practicums. This term was widely used in social work practice as the following examples exemplify:

The more healthy unmarried mother, on the other hand, usually has faced her situation *realistically*, has a plan in mind, usually adoption. (my emphasis, Speers 19)

She may find herself ill-prepared to make *realistic plans*. (my emphasis, The Canadian Welfare Council, *Services* 3)

Each of the girls spends on average at least one hour a week in a formal counselling or therapeutic relationship, with opportunity to assess her past and to make *realistic plans* for the future. (my emphasis, qtd. in Drew 126)

> Counselling services to unmarried mothers were extended with the wish to contact all unmarried mothers prior to confinement and to assist the unwed mother to face her dilemma *realistically* and by doing so to bring about her re-establishment into society on a sound basis; also to protect the interest of the child and afford it maximum security. (my emphasis, Ontario. Dept. of Public Welfare, 1958-1959, 32)

> Social workers and others serving unmarried mothers have arrived, as a result of experience, at the conviction that adoption is the best plan for most illegitimate children as well as for most unmarried mothers. This does not disregard the unmarried mother's right of choice, but with more understanding of the complications of the problem, the caseworker is able to approach the situation more objectively and to help the unmarried mother arrive at a *realistic* decision. (my emphasis, qtd. in Petrie 147)

During the postwar mandate, social workers worked closely with maternity homes and hospitals to effect adoption outcomes. Social workers often visited unmarried mothers in maternity homes and hospitals prior to and after the delivery of babies. In some cases, a written agreement existed between the parties. Gwen Davenport, director of Armagh maternity home, reports that in 1961 "The relationship with Peel County CAS and Armagh is different than that of other Children's Aid Societies. There is a written agreement covering ways of working together" (Armagh, *Report of Director 1961*). Although I was unable to find evidence of written agreements with other maternity homes, this does not preclude their existence. In any case, collaboration between maternity homes and Children's Aid Societies and other social welfare agencies is well documented.

Many mothers of the mandate report coercive means used by social workers to extract consents in hospitals and afterward, including the use of falsehoods, threats, and trickery. Lori Chambers found that young women were subjected to unrelenting pressure to conform to the adoption mandate—"the high pressure, and at times unsavoury tactics that CAS workers could use are well illustrated in a case that came before the court in Toronto" (Chambers, *Misconceptions* 96). Most unmarried mothers signed consent forms with only themselves and a social worker or two present. Unmarried mothers were neither given nor offered legal advice in the majority of cases. One mother reports, "I was 17 years old, alone in a room with three social workers. I was very reluctant to sign. They said sign, it will be better for him and so on. It took a while, but I ended up signing."[83] Another mother recalls, "I cried, I begged, I screamed, I threw furniture around. They tried to put a pen in my hand and tried to make me sign. I threw the pen away. I tried so hard. Then they threatened to call the police ... and so I signed" (Goldhar). Mothers of the mandate assert that "we did not give up our babies, we gave up because of the coercion, and the pressure and the lack of support. We just surrendered" (qtd. in Alton).

Social workers told mothers that their life as a sole parent would be a bleak one. Many were told that no one would give them housing or a job, that their children would be called "bastards," or that they would fail at mothering and would end up bringing their child back when it was older and unadoptable: "CAS workers had a responsibility to ensure that mothers were aware of the financial difficulties that they would inevitably confront raising children alone, but lurid descriptions of abject poverty were used to dissuade mothers from keeping their infants" (Chambers, *Misconceptions* 96). Mothers report being told that unless they signed consent for their newborn to be adopted, the child would end up languishing in an institution. They also report being told that no one would marry them and that their future prospects would be ruined unless they surrendered. Social workers routinely warned that unmarried mothers would have many difficulties and that "'men don't want used goods', meaning that their marriage prospects would be bleak, and that society would not be accepting of the mother or the child" (Chambers, *Adoption* 161). As one mother aptly puts it, "We were put to the challenge to prove we loved them by letting them go" (qtd. in Alward).

Most mothers were told by social workers that they would forget about their baby and go on with their lives. In the film *The Forty Year Secret*, a social worker reveals the thinking of social workers at the time, "the message was get over it. You made a mistake, get on with your life. You will have other children who will replace the child that you placed up for adoption ...you won't even remember that child" (qtd. in Alton).

---

83 This was my experience in Toronto, Ontario, 1970 recounted it at Origins Canada, Adoption Experience Conference, October 2012.

One mother recalls, "I was told repeatedly of the mature woman who longed for a child and could give my baby what I couldn't. And, I was assured that giving up my child was an unselfish act of love ... I was told I would get over my loss and move on" (Walton). Another mother reports, "I was told I would forget this baby and that I would be a 'real' mother later."[84] Referring to social worker narratives, one mother states that mothers were generally told "Don't worry dear. You'll go home and forget about this and go on with your life" (qtd. in Alton). One mother recalls, "I couldn't figure out why I wasn't forgetting him because the nuns told me I would forget him and I was raised Catholic... I thought there was something wrong with me because I wasn't forgetting ... I didn't forget him, I never forgot him" (qtd. in Alward). Another reports, "I was told that I would eventually get married and forget about my baby. How does a mother forget her baby?" (Powell, Witness, SSCSAST, 2018).

These mostly young mothers, many isolated from their families and communities, had no experience to know their rights or to question those in authority over them—including maternity home matrons, social workers, nurses, doctors, and the clergy—all entities to whom they were socialized to respect and, in some cases, obey. Unaware of their rights, many young mothers believed they had to surrender; that it was a law or some other unknown rule. Still recovering from birth and the associated ill treatment, traumatized over the violent act of their babies being torn away from them at delivery, breasts bound, these young mothers were released from hospital with no aftercare or counselling whatsoever. Instead, as this mother articulates, callous treatment was all that was in store: "The social worker stood in front of me. Coldly she said, 'You will never see your baby again as long as you live. If you search for the baby, you'll destroy his life and the lives of the adoptive parents'" (Jarvie, Witness, SSCSAST, 2018).

The regulation of social work is a provincial matter. Although various voluntary associations were in existence prior to regulation, social workers remained an unregulated body in Canada during the postwar decades; therefore, the conduct of social workers during the mandate was, for the most part, not subject to any disciplinary or

---

84 This was told to me by a social worker in 1969.

regulatory body.[85] Upon examining the dates across the provinces wherein a formal regulatory body for social work was instituted, a surprising disparity is uncovered. Whereas British Columbia instituted a regulatory body for social workers in 1969,[86] Manitoba did not do so until 2014 when the Social Work Act of 2009 was passed into law. In fact, Manitoba was the last jurisdiction in Canada to regulate social workers (CBC News, "Manitoba"). In Alberta, registration of social workers became mandatory in 1995. However, it should be noted that the Alberta Department of Children's Services and social workers employed by First Nations were exempt from this registration until the Alberta Health Professions Act of 2003. Ontario passed the Social Work and Social Service Act in 1998 and instituted it on 15 August 2000; social work then became a regulated profession in the province (Ontario College). Prince Edward Island and New Brunswick established regulatory bodies in 1988 and 1989, respectively, and Saskatchewan regulated the profession in 1995.

Unregulated social workers during the mandate operated within a conflict of interest,[87] since they not only controlled the processes for access to support from putative fathers but counselled unmarried mothers, prospective adopters, and organized adoption matching; moreover, they processed adoption transactions while being, at the same time, the source of newborn babies for adoption. Judges relied on the recommendations of social workers in adoption matters, which "ensured that the CAS was largely unsupervised and indirectly awarded the agency enormous discretionary power" (Chambers, *Misconceptions*[87]).

Social worker Svanhuit Josie was one of the few critics of her profession during the mandate. In *Canadian Welfare*, Josie states the following:

---

85 For example, The New Brunswick Association of Social Workers which was formed as a voluntary body in 1965, and only became a regulated body in 1988.

86 Social Workers Act, BC, and Board of Registration for Social Workers, 1969; Social Work and Social Services Work Act, Ontario, received Royal Assent in 1998; Social Workers Act, Saskatchewan, 1 April 1995; Manitoba College of Social Workers, 1 April 2015; New Brunswick Association of Social Workers, 1988; Prince Edward Island Registration Board, 1988; Alberta Health Professions Act, 1 April 2003.

87 "They [social workers] did not recognize that simultaneous control over adoption and affiliation proceedings placed child welfare workers themselves in a position of conflict of interest" (Chambers, *Misconceptions* 91).

One of the basic principles of casework is self-deter-
mination. Yet today it seems to me that casework with the
unmarried mother has come to mean the process of
convincing her that it is impossible, if not absolutely
immoral for her to plan to keep her own child. She must
be made to face the *reality* of her situation which means to
give it up for adoption. Things are made so difficult for her
that in the end she has no choice. (my emphasis, *Caricature*
248)

However, Josie's statement was not well received, since a statement
placed directly below hers in the same issue of *Canadian Welfare* written
by the superintendent of the Unmarried Parent's Department strongly
rejected Josie's assertions.

Section II: The Impact of Sociological Theories on the Adoption Mandate

Clean Slate Theory

The concept of the Latin "*tabula rasa,*" or a clean slate, can be traced back to Aristotle (Duschinsky 511). The clean slate theory was reintroduced in modern times by John Locke in the seventeenth century. Locke asserted that the human mind is a blank slate and that all forms of thought processing and development in the human mind is experiential. During the 1940s there was a resurgence of this concept in part due to the work of Sigmund and Anna Freud related to the developmental psychology of children, which raised the importance of environment as a factor in normal child development (Mayes and Cohen).

Earlier in the twentieth century, the popularity of eugenics[88] had contributed to the idea that children to be adopted were tainted with the moral, mental, and physical impediments of their parents. In addition, genetic concerns resulted in delays in adoption finalizations so that adopting parents could be "assured of the genetic quality of their adopted children" (ASCR 20). Until the mid-to late 1950s, adoption practice had considered not only the intelligence of the unmarried mother but also the baby to be adopted. Newborn infants to be adopted in Canada were routinely given "psychometric" examinations (Speers 19). As concluded by Lillian Romkey in her 1951 master's thesis at the University of Toronto titled *The Disposition of Children of Unmarried Mothers with Limited Intelligence*, "young infants placed for adoption are selected on the basis of known and hereditary factors. Children cannot be placed for early adoption if there is knowledge of poor background" (15).

As eugenics fell out of favour, developmental theories such as clean slate were embraced and began to be applied in adoption practice. With the application of clean slate theory, perceived inherited intellectual impediments in an infant to be adopted were now understood to be erased. By the 1950s, adoption practice changed, as experts "argued for the early separation of [unmarried] mothers from their babies" (ASCR 22). Intelligence testing for newborns or intellectual matching, which had been prominent in adoption in the 1930s and 1940s, "diminished

---

88   See more about the connections of eugenics and adoption in Chapter Two.

notably in the case records of the 1950s and 1960s ... as the predictive value of intelligence testing was challenged by social scientists who emphasized the influence of environment" (Melosh 75). One of those challengers was British psychiatrist John Bowlby, who in 1951, asserted that the various tests used on infants to predict intelligence had little or no value (Bowlby 103).

By the late 1950s, it became common for babies of unmarried mothers to be placed in adoptive homes much earlier in life than had been the former practice. At a University of Toronto seminar about adoption practices in 1948, prominent social worker Dorothy Hutchinson from the New York School of Social Work stated that "the most progressive American agencies were now placing a number of babies under six months of age, and even from hospital" (qtd. in Speers 19). *The Thirteenth Annual Report of the Department of Public Welfare, Alberta, 1956-1957*, reports that "it is gratifying to note that most infants who are accepted as wards by this method [application to surrender], are placed for adoption at the age of a few weeks" (Alberta, Dept. of Public Welfare 1956-57 28).

Clean Break

Following WWII, concerns in the global north extended to the impact of war on children, including those displaced, orphaned, or otherwise affected. This was in addition to the 1930s studies of hospitalized infants that documented the effects of institutionalized care, limited physical contact, and changing caregivers (Melosh 75). In this climate, psychologists and social scientists began studying the mother-child dyad and the importance of the mother's presence in early development. Anna Freud argued that the child develops an attachment to the mother early in life and that "the mother child attachment was thus the cradle of the emotional self" (qtd. in Vicedo, "The Father" 272). A number of influential analysts in the United States came to the conclusion that "maternal care and love are vital necessities for a child's psychic and even physical development" (qtd. in Vicedo, "The Father" 272). These studies about mother love and the importance of mothering for child development came at a time when there was a growing concern about the rising number of women working outside the home (Vicedo, "The Social").

Springing from these and other prominent studies, the "clean break" was instituted in adoption practice. Clean break was the practice of removing babies from unmarried mothers immediately at birth so as to prevent bonding[89] and to promote attachment to a surrogate as early in life as possible.[90] Social worker Mary Iwanek writes that "clean break theory exercised a considerable influence on adoption legislation and practice" (14). The manifestation of clean break was partly based on Bowlby's attachment theory published in a World Health Organization (WHO) report in 1951, which suggests children are biologically preprogrammed to form attachments for survival very early in life. Influential studies by Bowlby promoted early infant bonding: "a child should be attached to a mother figure as early as possible as a key determinant in parenting success" (Welbourne 60). Bowlby introduced the idea that the mother of origin was of little to no importance to the child as long as the infant could be introduced to a surrogate early after birth. Bowlby also advocated for the unmarried mother to make a realistic plan sooner rather than later. In the 1951 WHO report, Bowlby writes the following: "Moreover, it is in the mother's interest to make the decision to keep or part with her [sooner] rather than late[r] ... if the mother has sought care reasonably early it should be possible for the experienced case-worker to help her reach a *realistic decision* either before the baby is born or soon after." (my emphasis, 102). Bowlby was a strong supporter of early adoption, and suggested that it was not only in the interests of the unmarried mother but also clearly in the interests of adoptive parents. Ontario adoption practice strongly echoed Bowlby's ideas. The contents of the *Adoption Policy Guide of 1966* states that "The earlier a child is placed, the more favourable are his chances of healthy emotional development and the greater the satisfaction for the adopting parents" (Ontario, Dept. of Public Welfare, 1966).

Bowlby was a proponent of the earlier work of scientist Konrad Lorenz,[91] which concentrates on "social imprinting"—the process by which some animals form attachments for survival during a critical period, early in life (Hess 72). Lorenz's method was to remove the mother from newly hatched ducklings; note how they followed him

---

89 This was attempted even though the mother had most likely already bonded with her child in utero for nine months.

90 Indigenous mothers also lost their newly born children soon after birth: "it was common practice in BC in the mid-sixties to 'scoop' from their mothers on reserves almost all newly born children" (Sinclair, *Identity* 2).

91 Lorenz was a zoologist, an ethologist, and an ornithologist.

soon after hatching, which, for Lorenz, illustrated that within the first few days of life, an imprinting with a mother figure occurs. Lorenz allied himself with child analysts who emphasized the importance of the mother-child dyad and the consequences of its disruption (Vicedo, "The Father" 265).

American psychologist Harry Harlow also contributed to sociological studies surrounding clean break adoption practice. Harlow conducted a study titled "The Nature of Love" in 1958, in which he compared infant monkeys raised by their own mothers with those introduced to surrogate mothers—in this case, a "wire mother" and a "cloth mother." The control monkeys developed affection or love for the cloth mother, but that the interval of delay in exposing the infant monkey to the surrogate "depresses the intensity of the affectional response to below that of the infant monkeys that were surrogate-mothered from birth onward" (Harlow 684). Harlow concluded that "as far as we can observe, the infant monkey's affection for the real mother is strong, but no stronger than that of the experimental monkey for the surrogate cloth mother, and the security the infant gains from the real mother is no greater than the security it gains from a cloth surrogate" (684).

Harlow's experiments, which were widely distributed and popular at the time, contributed to the justification of the brutal adoption practice of clean break in human beings by "substantiating the adoption-friendly theory that 'nurture' was a far more contributing factor in healthy psychological development than 'nature,' and that infants should be introduced to a surrogate as soon as possible after birth" (Adoption History Project 1).

Bowlby's WHO report came to be the authoritative document of the consensus within this field of research (Vicedo, "The Social" 408). The work of Bowlby and other attachment theorists created a major shift in adoption practice that survives to this day. Environmental and psychodynamic concerns became more prominent instead of the hereditary and genetic determinants, which had been the major concerns prior to the adoption of Bowlby's ideas. Mary Iwanek explains:

> The work of Bowlby influenced the use of psychodynamic theory of personality, particularly Freudian theory, in

social work practice.... Bowlby's work also provided the social work profession with an opportunity to lay claim to an area of work which they could truly call their own, thereby increasing their status as a legitimate professional body. (15)

Another important factor influencing clean break was the drive to achieve heteronormative gender roles and nuclear families in the immediate postwar decades. Adopters wanted newborns, and they were in demand. One of the driving forces influencing clean break practice was the increasing market demand for newborn infants for adoption, particularly white newborn babies. In the article, "Attachment Theory and Children's Rights," Thoburn, notes that "it was responsiveness to the needs of adopters that motivated the 'clean break' approach to adoption" (qtd. in Welbourne 66). In her work "Silenced, Denigrated and Rendered Invisible: Mothers Who Lost their Babies to Adoption in the 1960s and 1970s," Sandra Jarvie refers to the Report of the Committee on Adoption in Alberta (1965), which summarizes the results of questionnaires sent to 2,167 couples who had adopted. This questionnaire not only illustrates the demand for white newborns by adopters but also alludes to the social work practice of removing babies from their mothers directly from the hospital. The report also suggests the desirability of newborns as being one of the central reasons this practice was instituted: "most adoptive parents ... wanted a newborn to 2 months old ... virtually none wanted a child over 4 years, indicating, of course, the desirability of placing a child as soon as possible after birth. Ideally, perhaps the child should be placed by the time it leaves hospital" (qtd. in Jarvie 76).

Clean Break: Operating as a Form of Violence against Women, Infants, and the Maternal Body

The hospital experiences of Canada's "unwed mothers" are characterized by systemic disempowerment. The assumption that the babies of unmarried mothers were to be adopted was reinforced by hospital protocols. The identification of the unmarried mother upon arrival in Canadian hospitals prompted processes and procedures that were in contrast to those for married mothers. From the accounts of Canadian mothers and hospital files obtained, it appears that the identification of Canada's unmarried mothers in hospital mirror those which took place in Australia. The Australian Senate Committee found that unmarried mothers were identified by their files being flagged with BFA, or, "Baby for Adoption" and "UB-", meaning "Unmarried, Baby negative" (45). Others were prominently marked with MISS to indicate an unmarried mother. While these types of identification may have appeared in cases where mothers had explicitly stated that they did want to have their child adopted, the committee concluded that these acronyms appeared on the files of most unmarried women. Mothers arriving on a regular basis from local maternity homes were readily identified as unmarried mothers.

Figure 1. This image shows the notation "baby for adoption" on the hospital file of an unmarried mother in Canada (Torn Apart, Sheldon).

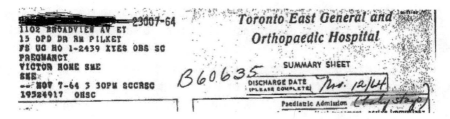

Figure 2. This image shows the hospital file of an unmarried mother in 1964 indicating clearly that she is from the Victor Home (United Church Maternity Home) and notes that the "baby stays" (Provided by mother to the writer, with permission).

Upon admission to hospital, unmarried mothers were routinely not consulted by nursing or medical staff about their wishes concerning their babies. Adoption was the assumed protocol for the majority of unmarried mothers, especially for those arriving from maternity homes. By the late 1950s and early 1960s, the arrival of an unmarried mother at a Canadian hospital activated several different hospital protocols: isolating unmarried mothers in wards separate from married mothers, removing babies directly from the delivery table prior to the completion of all stages of birth, denying the mother access to her baby, and suppressing lactation. These protocols were instituted without consent of the mother, and prior to the signing of adoption consents. This occurred most frequently in hospitals with religious affiliations to maternity homes—such as Miséricordia Hospitals and Salvation Army Hospitals—although most hospitals in Canada had similar protocols.

Social workers working closely in conjunction with hospitals were at the forefront of these policies. Policies at the Mt. Sinai Hospital in Toronto stated that all mothers contemplating adoption "be referred to the Social Service Department of the hospital" (Brock 126). The contents of the *Adoption Policy Guide of 1966* offer insight into the close relationship that existed between social workers and hospitals regarding adoptions. This guide documents the protocols of various Toronto area hospitals on direct adoptions or adoptions made directly from hospital; it instructs social workers in detail, especially for nursery protocols. As an example, "very informal hospital, no pass needed. Nurses aren't too aware of confidentiality re/baby's surname; no bottle needed, but one day's formula is given to adoptive couple" (Ontario, Dept. of Public Welfare, 1966).

Mothers in Canada report hospital treatment that was draconian in nature. Hospital staff were often unsympathetic, judgmental, and harsh. Unmarried mothers, particularly those from maternity homes, were usually dropped off at hospital and left to labour alone. One Canadian mother reports, "I was left alone in labour; they came maybe twice ... the nurses were very judgemental ... as soon as he was born I asked to see my baby and the doctor said no" (qtd. in Alward). Another mother states that "my labour was on my own in a dark room, I cried for help many times. A nurse came in and shut the door." (Humewood House, *100 Years*). In the book *Gone to An Aunt's*, Anne Petrie recalls, "I was put in a room alone on the gynecological ward, as was the practice for unwed mothers" (Petrie 182). Another mother remembers,

"I was left alone for most of my labour ... it was pure fear and abandonment and a pathetic ignorance of what was happening to my body" (qtd. in Petrie 185).

Mothers report verbal abuse by nurses: "I told the nurse I hurt, and she told me it was a good lesson for me" (qtd. in Alward). Another mother alone at 17 in the Salvation Army Grace Hospital in Toronto in 1970 reports that when she complained it hurt while being shaved roughly, the nurse responded, "it's less than you deserve."[92] Referring to hospital staff, another mother confirms that "the looks and the tone of voice that they gave you told you that you were bad and that this is your punishment" (qtd. in Alward). The general principle was to make the experience so traumatic that it would not be repeated, since repeaters were not readily tolerated.

Clean break was the routine protocol for unmarried mothers in most Canadian hospitals. In the article, "They're 'More Children Than Adults': Teens, Unmarried Pregnancy, and the Canadian Medical Profession, 1945-1961," Sharon Wall suggests the following:

> Evidence clearly shows that some women were not permitted to see their babies even once, whether as a matter of policy or due to individual circumstances. Ramona B. explained, "I wasn't allowed to go to the nursery. I wasn't allowed to go see her or hold her." Likewise, in the case of one Burnaby Home resident in 1948, with a girl deemed 'suicidal,' the superintendent recorded that, "it was tho't [sic] best that she...not see her baby at all." (62)

Mothers report having their faces covered with sheets and pillows or having their heads restrained in order to block the view of their baby in the delivery room. Delivery room mirrors were either covered or averted so that mothers would not be able to see the birth. Mothers report that they were either given no medication or medicated to the point where they could recall little about birth and delivery. One mother reports that "I was drugged for the first and kept drugged for three days. I was tied to the bedrail when I came to" (qtd. in Torn Apart, Sheldon).

92 As experienced by the author.

Mothers from the postwar adoption era are speaking out about their experiences in Canada's delivery rooms.[93] One mother in Canada reports seeing "a little mop of dark hair poking out of the blanket" (Origins Canada, *Past Adoption*) as her child was whisked away from the delivery room never to be seen again. In an article celebrating 100 years of Humewood House, one mother states, "I was not allowed to see my infant son after he was born ... when other babies were wheeled into the ward for feeding, I sat alone and watched. Eventually I became hysterical with grief" (Ferenc). Another mother who gave birth in 1964 wrote, "my head was restrained when I begged to see my baby ... I never had the chance" (Humewood House, *100 Years*). Another states that "it wasn't a surrender, it was more like having my baby torn from me...after the baby was born the ache in my body was so horrible ... I wanted to hold my child, my milk was there to feed her and I was supposed to "act like none of this happened" and go back to my "normal" life" (Origins Canada, *Sue's Story*). Another mother of the mandate corroborates this: "removing a child from a mother, under any circumstance, is an act of violence ... it is violent because it feels like its 'ripped away' physically ... you feel it physically" (qtd. in Alward). One mother reports screaming "bring me my baby! I want to hold my baby!" as her baby was speedily removed from her following birth (qtd. in Torn Apart, Sheldon). Another mother who delivered twins reports that "all I could see were little dark heads" as her babies were removed from the delivery room (qtd. in Alward). Some mothers remember being restrained on delivery tables, whereas others describe being put on different hospital floors from that of their babies to prevent contact.

A few mothers of the mandate in Canada have come forward after being told their babies died when in fact they were adopted: "my mother was told that I passed away overnight" (qtd. in Torn Apart, Sheldon). Lise Pageau, regional director at Mouvement Retrouvailles, a non-profit Quebec agency supporting those separated by adoption, states that, "In those days, it was just said the child was dead because that way the mother wouldn't look for it ... [nurses and doctors] would show the mother a very, very, sick baby and say the child would not pull through the night. Sometimes the child was already promised to a couple" (Carlson, "Your Baby Is Dead" 1).

93 The writer was prevented from seeing her baby. I was told "you can't see that baby, that baby is for adoption" at the Salvation Army Grace Hospital in Toronto, 1970.

Although it is impossible to determine the number of cases like this in Canada, it raises concerns, particularly with those unmarried mothers who were told their babies had died. Today, there are still some women in Canada that grapple with unimaginable questions. Did my baby really die or was my baby adopted? Should I be looking for my child, or is my child really dead?

Preventing lactation was routine treatment for unmarried mothers. Mothers were given lactation suppressant medications without consent in most cases, which assumed adoption. Some mothers believe that they were given the cancer causing drug Diethylstilbestrol (DES)[94] and although it was a lactation suppressant and may have been used, I was unable to find evidence to support this in Canada.[95] DES was developed in 1938 and used for "symptom relief from estrogen-deficiency states, postpartum lactation suppression, and treatment of prostate and breast cancer" (Goodman et al. 2083).

Many mothers report being bound tightly with breast binders. Singer Joni Mitchell who gave birth to her daughter in a Toronto hospital states that "one of the barbaric things they did was they bound the breasts of unwed mothers to keep the milk from coming" (qtd. in Johnson, *Joni's Secret*). Another mother recalls her experience of being back at school after her child's birth: "sitting there with bound up breasts, still recovering from a birth in every physical way, no child in your arms, and you are sitting in a math class ... with not even a minute of counselling" (qtd. in Alward). Although many unmarried mothers in Canada report the use of breast binders and hospital documents corroborate this, it is unclear whether breast binders were also used on married women who were not breastfeeding. In any case, married women were most likely given the choice to breastfeed their babies, whereas in the majority of cases, unmarried mothers were not.

Mothers who were victims of these practices have reported it as a trauma from which they have never recovered and studies corroborate

---

94 Diethylstibestrol (DES) was approved for medical use in 1941 to treat vaginitis, gonorrhea, menopausal symptoms, and to suppress lactation. Doctors confirmed the link between DES and a rare vaginal cancer, Clear Cell Adenocarcinoma (CCA) in 1971. Effects of DES exposure include structural damage in reproductive organs of DES sons and daughters, high risk pregnancies and miscarriage for DES daughters, Increased risk of CCA in DES daughters, increased risk for infertility in DES sons and daughters, and increased risk of breast cancer in DES mothers and DES daughters over forty years of age (Goodman et al.).

95 This does not preclude that DES may have been used as a lactation suppressant on unmarried mothers in Canada.

this. Mothers of the mandate are more likely to suffer mental health issues, such as disenfranchised grief, post-traumatic stress disorder, anxiety, and depression (Commonwealth of Australia, *Past Adoption Experiences*; Askren and Bloom; Blanton and Deschner; Carr; Kelly; Lake; Pengilley; Wells). In effect, these inhumane and harsh adoption practices were a form of violence against women that resulted in a lifelong psychological impact.

There is ample evidence that social workers and maternity home matrons knew at the time that mothers would be affected for the rest of their lives. However, mothers were not advised of the adverse mental health effects that they and their children would suffer; instead, they were told they would forget about their babies. A 1966 *Globe and Mail* article refers to the annual conference of the Ontario Association of Children's Aid Societies in 1966 where a social worker told the group that "unwed mothers who give up their children go through at least three years, and perhaps a lifetime of mourning" (qtd. in Kirkwood). An edition of "Your CAS," published by the Ontario Association of Children's Aid Societies in 1966, states clearly that "if she gives up the baby she may go through years of grieving for it" (13). Salvation Army Major Mildred Tackaberry, superintendent of Grace Haven in Montreal, observed in 1968 that "It's not just a case of having a baby. It's something the girl lives with the rest of her life. It's really a traumatic experience for her" ("The Problem," *The War Cry*, 30 November, 1968:10). In addition, Jerry Diamond of Jewish Family and Children's Services stated in 1966 that: "We find girls whose delayed sense of loss is so powerful that long after the birth they are trying to go back and look for what they left behind ... years later the repressed grief may arise to destroy a marriage or distort feelings about a child born in wedlock" (qtd. in Landsberg, "Failing" 29). In her article "Smooth System" in 1963 Landsberg explores future psychological impact on these mothers with a social service agency director: "Caseworkers feel the backlog of hurt and guilt may swamp the girl several years later, a sort of psychological delayed reaction, 'it may happen when the girl is married and has her first baby. We've known them to reject the baby entirely in an excess of remorse over the one they gave away'" (9). Even though social workers were aware of the severe psychological impact on mothers, they continued to advocate for adoption and clean break as prescriptions for unmarried motherhood.

Since the 1950s, attachment theory has remained a cornerstone of birthing and adoption practice. The clean break theory survives, and its expression in modern domestic adoption is no less traumatic. In current practice, adopters are often present in delivery rooms, cutting the cord, holding, and bonding with the prospective adoptive infant while the mother continues the final stages of birth[96] (Andrews, "Sales"). This practice is rooted in the adoption mandate and has been normalized in adoption culture. The study of attachment in adopted children is still a focus of research and assessment in contemporary adoption practice (Johnson and Fein; Houlihan). In addition, theories of birth bonding and attachment continue with the "skin to skin"[97] practices between mothers and their newborns today. Raylene Phillips articulates that "being skin to skin with mother protects the newborn from the well documented negative side effects of separation, supports optimal brain development, and facilitates attachment" (1). This raises implications for the impact on and outcomes for those babies literally ripped away from their mothers on delivery tables in postwar Canada—practices that continue in modern domestic adoption practice.

Today, many adoption activists argue that the taking of babies from their legal mothers in hospital delivery rooms prior to the signing of a legal consent was not only violent and unethical, but also illegal. Dian Wellfare, founder of Origins and prominent Australian adoption activist, writes:

> In having introduced de-humanising labour ward procedures of violently snatching newborns from their mothers' wombs during birth, at a time when still in labour, a mother was bound by stirrups, awaiting the expulsion of the placenta; by introducing policies forbidding eye contact between mother and child to prevent bonding (culminating in a violent trauma to the female psyche from which no mother is ever able to recover). In preventing lactation by the use of drugs or breast binding prior to a consent being taken; by sedating mothers

96 The birth process has three main stages: contractions resulting in the dilation of the cervix, delivery of baby, and the expulsion of the placenta.

97 This is the current practice of mothers and fathers holding babies bare chest to bare chest as often as possible for the first few days after birth.

postnatally with hypnotic barbiturates: by hiding babies from their own mothers therefore denying mothers free access to their own babies; by separating and transporting mothers without their babies to distant locations—all without due consultation, permission or written consent from the mother ... I contend – were all violations of the law. (*Civil* 25)[98]

Complete Break: Closed Adoption Records

Not only did the practice of the clean break become entrenched in adoption practice but so did the practice of "complete break" or the sealing of adoption records. As Chambers explains, "ties between the child and his or her natural parents were irrevocably severed and the relinquishing parent had no right to information about the child" (*Legal* 64). This paternalistic practice spread, and by the 1940s, most provinces had implemented laws to maintain secrecy in adoption records. The closed adoption system in Canada meant that original birth registrations were sealed. New, legally falsified birth certificates showing the adopters as mother and father were issued. Indeed, any identifying information pertaining to the child's original family was removed, sealed, and kept secret by provincial governments.[99] According to Dukette, this practice had many advantages:

[it] disrupts any interference by a natural parent; leaves parties free to make their own lives; cuts off any immoral or unpleasant background; provides class security; provides greater sense of entitlement or possession of the child to adopters; ensures privacy and autonomy of the family which are essential to the survival of adoption as an institution. (qtd. in Griffith 12, 4)

98 These policies were acknowledged as being illegal in Australia. The Apology for Forced Adoption given by then Prime Minister Julia Gillard on 21 March 2013 states, "you were forced to endure the coercion and brutality of practices that were unethical, dishonest, and in many cases illegal" (Commonwealth of Australia).

99 Although the current trend in adoption practice is openness, as of this writing, adoption records continue to be sealed in Prince Edward Island, and Nova Scotia, and only semi-open subject to a veto in British Columbia, Alberta, Manitoba, Saskatchewan, Ontario, Newfoundland, and New Brunswick. In Quebec only adoptees have a right to information if not vetoed, not mothers, as in other provinces.

Keith Griffith concurs that the practice of complete break played three main roles: "[a] protective role for adoptive family; [b] constructive role emphasizing formation of new relationships; and [c], a destructive role to destroy any connection with the past" (12, 6). As alluded to by Griffith, adoption records were not closed for the protection of the unmarried mother, but to protect adopters. Original families were viewed as suspect, whereas adoptive families were viewed as being in need of protection from them. This is suggested in a statement made by the British Columbia government in 1967: "every effort is made to protect the interest of the adopted child and his adopted parents" (British Columbia, *Vital Statistics* T22). Although records were closed for the protection of adoptive families, unmarried mother privacy continues to be used as a reason for keeping adoption records closed; even though many unmarried mothers from postwar Canada assert that they were not promised secrecy, nor did they ask for it. In fact, in some cases, unmarried mothers were given assurances by social workers that they would be able to contact their child at the age of majority. This was, of course, untrue and simply a tool of coercion to convince a mother to surrender her child. Notwithstanding any assurances that may have been given by individual social workers acting upon their own authority, there are no legal documents known to the writer in Canada given to any unmarried mother that guaranteed privacy. Recently, Joanne Bernard, Minister of Social Services in Nova Scotia, has stated that "I have absolutely no intention of opening up the adoption act in this province" (CBC News, "Nova Scotia"). Bernard cites unmarried mother privacy as the reason.

In Canada, at the time of writing, adoption records are semi-open[100] in eight provinces. I could not find evidence to support negative consequences to postwar unmarried mothers as a result of open adoption records, although there are still unmarried mothers from the postwar mandate that continue to keep the secret[101] mostly due to the shame and secrecy with which they were indoctrinated. Citizen engagement into open adoption records was held by the provincial

---

100 Semi-open refers to adoption records being subject to a veto by either party to prevent the other from receiving identifying information. Vetoes remain controversial, as many adoption reformers seek to remove them entirely from existing and newly drafted legislation.

101 Many unmarried mothers who lost their children to adoption during the adoption mandate era are forming support groups and sharing their accounts on social media.

government of New Brunswick in the spring of 2014.[102] Eight regional public sessions were held to determine public sentiment for the opening of adoption records. The study found that eighty-five percent of all respondents were in favour of opening the records, and in April 2018, adoption records were opened in that province. In early 2018, Prince Edward Island embarked on a similar public engagement, and as of this writing, many activists hope for a positive result in that province as well. If that happens, Nova Scotia will stand alone as the only province in Canada with completely closed adoption records.

Baby Formula as a Factor in the Separation of Mother and Child

I will turn briefly to a the development of baby formula as an important factor in the separation of mothers and babies during the adoption mandate due to the newfound ability to nourish infants safely away from their mothers. The historical evolution of infant feeding practices and norms includes breastfeeding, wet-nursing, the feeding bottle, and formula use (Stevens; Patrick et al.). As discussed in Chapter One, wet-nursing was the practice of a newly delivered mother suckling other babies along with her own and was often employed by unmarried mothers as a way to support their illegitimate child in nineteenth-century Canada. Wet-nursing quickly declined with advancement of the bottle and the availability of animal milk. Not all physicians were in favour of using artificial methods to sustain infants, since infant mortality remained high for those not fed by mother's milk, as exemplified by this physician statement in 1907:

> What [is] more suitable to its delicate digestive apparatus than its mother's milk, the food elaborated by nature for its use! Yet, breast feeding is not fashionable either among rich or poor. A mother has no option but to nourish her unborn child, but, too often, alas, the moment her own free will can be exercised she denies her infant's right to look to her as the source of its food, and condemns it to the miseries and dangers of artificial feeding. (Budin, vi)

102 See Province of New Brunswick, Public Response Paper, Opening of Sealed Adoption Records, August 2014.

Although alternative feeding methods were evolving, they still fell short of mother's milk, and infant mortality remained high in the nineteenth and early twentieth centuries. Animal milk was often used depending on the type of animal available, and cow's milk was the most prevalent. In 1865, Justus von Liebeg developed, patented, and marketed an infant food. Liebeg's formula consisted of cow's milk, wheat and malt flour, and potassium bicarbonate. This type of formula was followed by condensed milk, which was often recommended as a substitute to mother's milk in the 1930s and 1940s by pediatricians. In 1930s Canada, mothers were urged to breastfeed their babies for at least nine months to ensure a healthy, thriving baby (Miller). The evolution of baby formula and food preservation led to increased replacement of breastfeeding by formulas and a decline in infant breastfeeding worldwide between the 1930s and the 1970s—the very timeframe in which the adoption mandate took place. Indeed, "by the 1940s, breastfeeding was no longer considered the norm for infant feeding" (Nathoo and Ostry 12).

The fact that infant breastfeeding had severely declined and bottle feeding became the norm for infant feeding during the period in which the adoption mandate took place was not a cause of the mandate itself. However, since safe bottle feeding was now possible and it had become the established and recommended norm for infant feeding, the physical separation of mothers and infants at birth became possible, an outcome that served the mandate well. This history makes baby formula an important contributing factor to the mandate—particularly considering that breastfeeding had been one of the main reasons used to keep the unmarried mother and her child together postnatally in the past.

The profession of social work—which advocated and advanced the realistic plan of adoption as the casework solution for unmarried mothers—along with the sociological theories of attachment and "clean break" was a major influence in the shift in adoption policy and practice in postwar Canada. The rapidly increasing demand for newborns also impacted the shift, and ushered in current adoption culture—that is, the normalization of practices, language, and policies that concentrate on the desires and needs of prospective adoptive parents, and that focus on, and emphasize adopter narratives of infertility, miscarriage, or failed adoptions. Furthermore, despite myths of openness in contemporary adoption practice, the era of closed and secretive adoptions continues to reverberate in the lives of mothers and adoptees, as many try to find one another through social media, DNA, and other methods.

In the next chapter, I will explore the maternity home movement in Canada. This chapter will illustrate that the theory of Magdalenism was alive and well in these facilities in postwar Canada, for which the Magdalen asylums and other institutions were precursors. I will examine the coercive psychological system at work in these institutions, another major factor in the "perfect storm."

Chapter Four

Maternity Homes in Canada

"The world of maternity homes in postwar America was a gothic attic obscured from the community by the closed curtains of gentility and high spiked fences. The girls and women sent inside were dreamwalkers serving time, pregnant dreamwalkers taking the cure. Part criminal, part patient, the unwed mother arrived on the doorstep with her valise and, moving inside, found herself enclosed within an idea"— Solinger

Illus. 5. Humewood House, Toronto, circa 1950s.

By the 1890s, the rescue movement and accompanying institutions to house the fallen were changing, which gave rise to the maternity home movement in Australia, the United Kingdom, Canada, and the United States. At the turn of the century, most Magdalen institutions in the West were either closing or changing their mission.[103] The Magdalen movement which previously had as its patrons, royalty and aristocrats, gave way to the middle-class influence of the social purity movement, now driven by white Protestant social reformers in the new Dominion of Canada.

By the 1910s, maternity homes were on the rise in Canada. Maternity homes were places of quasi-incarceration, in which unmarried mothers resided during pregnancy and the postpartum period, although the use of these homes for postpartum stays decreased as the twentieth century progressed. Often referred to as "Homes for Unwed Mothers," "maternity homes", "girl's homes", or "homes for unmarried mothers," these facilities were usually located in inner city neighbourhoods or in hidden rural settings; often in Victorian-type mansions to accommodate several internees.

Maternity homes in the twentieth century continued to be rooted in Magdalenism—the theory that a woman could be redeemed to some degree for the sin of out-wedlock-pregnancy through remorse, penance, religious improvement, and training and occupation in domestic work. These elements remained the foundation upon which maternity home practice was based until at least the 1970s. This was reflected in the daily schedules. The rules, regulations, and daily routines in maternity homes in postwar Canada were virtually identical to those of the Magdalen Asylums and other institutions set up to house the fallen of one hundred years earlier (See Appendix A).

Maternity homes used coercive psychological systems to facilitate the separation of mother and baby. In the article "Not by Choice," Karen Wilson-Buterbaugh refers to the work of Margaret Thaler-Singer, psychologist and expert on psychological coercive persuasion.[104] Thaler-Singer argued that six systemic practices are required for the success of coercive psychological systems: create a sense of power-

---

103 Exceptions are noted in Chapter One

104 This was formerly known as "brainwashing," "thought control," and "thought reform." It is now referred to by experts as coercive persuasion, coercive psychological systems, or coercive influence (Lifton; Thaler-Singer).

lessness; control environment and time; keep person unaware; use rewards and punishment to inhibit behaviour reflecting former identity; use rewards and punishments to promote group's beliefs or behaviours; and use logic and authority that permit no feedback (qtd. in Wilson-Buterbaugh 1). Wilson-Buterbaugh suggested that the elements required for a coercive psychological system as identified by Thaler-Singer can be applied to the maternity home experience.

In this chapter, I attempt to illustrate the "smooth system" (Landsberg 9) that operated in the maternity homes of postwar Canada, which led to the separation of mothers and babies through adoption.[105] Building on Wilson-Buterbaugh's concept, I explore in detail the coercive psychological systems that were intrinsic to these institutions in Canada. In addition, I have compiled a list, and collection of images of maternity homes that operated in Canada during the twentieth century; both are original in scope[106] (See Appendix D). I acknowledge that although there were many unmarried mothers across Canada in the postwar years that spent their pregnancies and gave birth without public or social assistance, this chapter concentrates on those unmarried mothers who were residents in Canada's maternity homes.

Charitable Incarceration

By the 1940s, mainstream Christian churches in Canada were deeply involved in the maternity home movement— the confinement of unmarried mothers within maternity homes—including the Catholic, Salvation Army, United,[107]Anglican, Presbyterian, and Evangelical churches. The YWCA ran at least one facility. Those with the largest number of facilities in Canada were the Catholic Miséricordia Sisters and The Salvation Army.[108] In addition, many homes operated outside of the church as private enterprises—such as the Ideal Maternity Home in Nova Scotia, Molly Breen's Boarding House in Newfoundland,

---

105 Not all unmarried mothers were sent to maternity homes. Some were sequestered within the homes of their families for the duration of their pregnancy or were sent to live with relatives. Some lived independently, and others were sent to Wage Homes by social service agencies (Marshall and MacDonald 4).

106 This work attempts to identify all church-run maternity homes in postwar Canada, and although this list, to the best of this writer's knowledge, is the most comprehensive in Canada to date, there may be errors or omissions.

107 This was previously mostly Methodist, but later it merged with other churches and became The United Church of Canada.

108 Also, United Kingdom, United States, Australia, and New Zealand.

The Strathcona in Toronto, Annie Montgomery's in Toronto, or the Beulah Home in Edmonton.[109] Due to high birthrates in the immediate postwar decades, many homes were renovated to increase capacity, or new homes were built. Most facilities remained in operation until the early to mid-1970s when they closed down altogether. A few continued well into the 1980s, while others changed their mission to assist pregnant and parenting teens.[110]

Early Salvation Army facilities were known generically as "rescue homes," but as the twentieth century progressed they were often identified by "Booth," "Bethany," or "Haven" (i.e., Grace Haven or Faith Haven). The name "Booth" was for William Booth, the founder of the Salvation Army; the name was often used for Salvation Army maternity homes and hospitals. The Evangeline Home in Saint John, New Brunswick, was named after his daughter. The name "Bethany" was often used in reference to unmarried mothers. Many Salvation Army homes were called "Bethany Home for Girls," "Bethany Home," or other derivatives. To call homes for unmarried mothers "Bethany" is notable, as its roots lie in Magdalenism. Biblical scholars argue that Bethany is the location where Mary Magdalene anointed Jesus with oil and wiped his feet with her hair (John 12, 1-8). The name "Bethany" is still used widely in reference to unmarried mothers and adoption. One of the largest adoption agencies in the United States is Bethany Christian Services.

The first officially organized women's social work by the Canadian Salvation Army began in Toronto in 1886 with a rescue home for fallen girls on Albert St. and one on Esther St. in 1889 (SA, "Brief" 2). A 1965 report by the Salvation Army boasts sixteen Girl's Homes across Canada: Vancouver, Calgary, Regina, Saskatoon, Winnipeg, Fort William, Windsor, London, Toronto, Hamilton, Ottawa, Montreal,

109 It would be impossible to accurately identify every private home that took in unmarried mothers in a nonofficial capacity across Canada in the twentieth century. See Nova Scotia, Department of Child Welfare, Forty-First Annual Report of the Director for the Fiscal Year Ending 31 March 1954 which states that the Nova Scotia government granted eight licences for the operation of maternity homes. These include Mrs. Harry Burrell, Yarmouth, Mrs. K. O'Donnell, Enfield, Miss Sylvia Kinsman, Caledonia, Mrs. Amy S. Nickerson, Doctors Cove, Mrs. Evangeline Townsend, Crowell's P.O., in addition to the religious mainstream homes operating in Nova Scotia (21). Also, see Petrie, Molly Breen's Boarding House. Petrie also names a Moncton widow, and a couple in Calgary who took in unmarried mothers as examples of non-official homes (48).

110 Examples are Victor Home in Toronto (now the Massey Centre), Humewood House in Toronto, and Bethesda Home in London (recently closed).

Sydney, Halifax, Saint John, and St. John's. This report says that accommodation is available for 567 girls[111] and that for the year 1965, the
Army received 3,782 and that 3,727 "passed out satisfactory" (SA,
Army on the March 17).[112] It is unclear what "passed out satisfactory"
means in this context, but presumably it means the women stayed for
the duration of their pregnancy, gave birth, and eventually returned to
their homes.

Together with the Salvation Army, the Catholic Church operated
the largest number of maternity homes in Canada. The organization of
the Catholic Church is centred on a diocese, which is a geographic area
of parish churches presided over by a bishop. Most Catholic maternity
homes were not operated directly by the local diocese, although a few
were; they were mostly operated by nuns—such as the Sisters of
Miséricordia, Ursiline Nuns, or Sisters of Good Shepherd—who
conducted business under separate incorporations.[113] Some homes
operated with the assistance of Catholic charities.

In 1925, the United Church of Canada was formed as a union of the
Methodist Church, the Congregational Union of Canada, and seventy
percent of the Presbyterian Church of Canada. Some homes existing
prior to that date were taken over by the United Church, and one
remained with the Presbyterian Church. The United Church was
responsible both solely and jointly for five homes for unmarried
mothers, one postnatal care facility, and other institutions that may
have housed unmarried mothers from time to time (UCMF 5). The
flagship Fred Victor Mission in Toronto took in an unmarried mother
in 1900, and at that time, the mission reserved two rooms, especially
for unmarried mothers and their babies (UCMF 5). A year later, the
Victor Mission opened the Door of Hope at 295 Jarvis St. in Toronto,
which relocated to 266 Jarvis St. donated by Chester Massey in 1904.
After several more relocations the home, renamed Victor Home, moved
to 1102 Broadview Avenue in Toronto in 1947 where continues to
operates today as the Massey Centre, supporting pregnant and
parenting adolescents.

---

111 This is across Canada.

112 The remaining fifty women were most likely still in residence awaiting the birth of their child.

113 The archives of the various orders of Sisters are private and closed, and the author was unable
to obtain access.

A pamphlet issued by an Anglican committee formed in 1911 stated that there was no maternity home in Canada operated by the Church of England, which was "a great and serious reproach to us all" (ACC/GSA, *Humewood, 1912-1962* 1). After consultations with social workers, the Anglican committee was convinced that there was a real need for a home for unmarried mothers, and Humewood House[114] was formally opened in Toronto on 23 April 1912 with one girl in residence (ACC/GSA, *Humewood, 1912-1962*). Most Anglican Church homes were run by individual diocese or in collaboration with other churches. Elizabeth House in Montreal was a joint effort of the Anglican, United, and Presbyterian churches while The Church Home for Girls in British Columbia was a joint effort with the United Church. The Marion Hilliard House[115] opened in Kamloops, British Columbia, in 1965, followed by St. Monica House in Kitchener, in 1968, which was a $300,000 project of the Huron Diocese (ACC/GSA, *Trend*). Other homes were operated by Anglican or lay sisters, including Bishops Messengers of Faith in Manitoba and St. John's House in Alberta.

By 1910, the Presbyterian Church operated seven homes in urban centres across Canada. However, after church union in 1925, only the Toronto home remained (PCC, *Presbyterian Record*, 1964). The Presbyterian Home for Girls employed Miss Ratte as superintendent from 1925 until her retirement in 1930. Requirements at that time were that unmarried mothers remain in the home and look after their babies. In 1930, Miss Myrtle McKinnon succeeded Miss Ratte until the home closed in 1953, when the Board of the Presbyterian Church authorized the sale of the Yorkville property. Plans were made for a new building located outside of the city of Toronto in what was then a rural setting in Clarkson, Ontario (PCC, *The Presbyterian Record*, 1953). The new home, named Armagh, opened in 1955, and had accommodation for eight residents. After a new wing was built in 1957, capacity was increased to twenty-two. The Armagh home was supported by grants from the Board of Missions, the Province of Ontario, and the United Appeal of Metropolitan Toronto.

---

114 The flagship Humewood House in Toronto is now a residential facility for parenting teens offering transitional housing, childcare, education and training for pregnant and parenting women ages thirteen to twenty-one. Records from 1912 to present continue to be located at 40 Humewood Drive and are accessible to former residents.

115 This house was named after Dr. Marion Hilliard of Women's College Hospital.

By the late 1950s, most maternity homes were funded through the provinces, churches, local community chests, and fees paid by families. However, on 1 April 1966, the Canada Assistance Plan (CAP) was enacted. This plan provided for direct federal sharing in the costs to the provinces for maintaining persons in a wide range of residential institutions known collectively as "Homes for Special Care." Specifically identified under CAP's "Homes for Special Care" were "Homes for Unmarried Mothers" This meant that federal funding was provided to the provinces specifically to fund these homes. Under CAP, provinces were required to name the homes and to submit claims to the federal government monthly or annually in order to be reimbursed directly for cost sharing (Canada, Canada Assistance Plan, *Annual Report 1968-69*).

Similar to the Magdalen Asylums and other institutions of the nineteenth century, maternity homes were strictly female, as women simultaneously "served and regulated other women" (Morton, "Managing" 133). The generally accepted purpose of a maternity home was to offer shelter and assistance and increasingly, a place to hide for unmarried mothers from the social stigma of out-of-wedlock pregnancy. The United Church stated their purpose as the following: "To protect unwed mothers from the intense social stigma and poverty that could result from having a child outside of marriage, and ... to offer a safe retreat from the curiosity, criticism, and condemnation of neighbours and townspeople and all those with whom the girl has been associated" (UCMF 3). One Anglican Church publication suggests that residences for unmarried mothers acted not only as a refuge from a "hostile" community and overwrought family, but also as a means to keep the problem secret (ACC/GSA, *One Parent*).

Most homes kept record of resident demographics including employment status, age, religion, and average stay. A presentation made at a joint Anglican and United Church conference in 1965 describes the residents of Canada's maternity homes as follows: "Age 17 appears to remain the time most vulnerable for pregnancies to occur— and 11th grade ... most of the girls are in the normal and slightly superior intelligence range. Most come from a middle-class situation, are physically attractive and mature looking, are well-nourished and have better than average health" (ACC/GSA, *Out of Wedlock*).[116] Also in 1965, a report for

116 This description is in stark contrast to that of unmarried mothers earlier in the century who were documented as being 'substandard' in every way.

Armagh, the Presbyterian home, shows 126 of the 141 residents were between the ages of 16 and 22, with nine aged 15, and fourteen ranging in ages between 23 and 34 (Armagh, *Annual Report 1966*).

Although most of the homes claimed to offer a place with "no distinction made to race, colour, nationality, language, or creed" (UCMF 7), it was predominantly white unmarried mothers who resided in Canada's maternity homes. This is not overtly stated in maternity home demographic reports. The following statistical study, which appeared in the Annual Report of Humewood House in 1955, shows that residents were in all likelihood white, predominantly between the 16-23 age range, and primarily office workers or students.

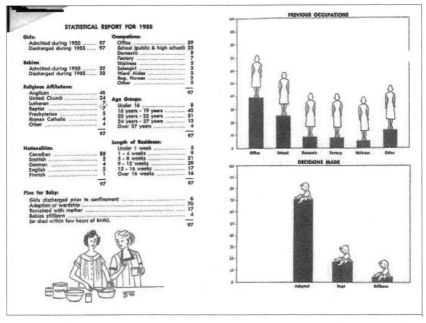

Figure 3. ACC/GSA, Humewood House, Annual Report 1955.

Women of colour were rare in Canada's maternity homes not because they were denied entry but because these homes catered to the rehabilitation of the mostly white, middle-class, unmarried mother; a covert versus overt exclusion. A study of five Toronto maternity homes in 1958 by the Social Planning Council of Metropolitan Toronto found that out of 585 residents studied, 577 were white and 8 were non-white: "including one Negro, five Indian[117] and two from the British West Indies" (SPCMT, 12). In Halifax, the Salvation Army professed to be "open to all 'races and creeds'... although the specific mention of the presence of a 'coloured girl' in 1953 in the home's minutes suggest this was an unusual occurrence" (Morton, "Nova Scotia" 336). There were some maternity homes for Black women organized by women's groups in the United States.[118] However, I was unable to uncover any maternity homes in Canada that provided services specifically to Black unmarried mothers, although there may have been private or informal ones.

Pregnant women and girls entered these homes anywhere from the fourth to ninth month of pregnancy depending on their situation and vacancy rate; the average being the sixth month of pregnancy (Dexter). Expectant mothers were referred to maternity homes by social service agencies, clergy, physicians, family, or friends.[119] Social agencies referred the majority of cases. For example, in Toronto, "the two Children's Aid Societies accounted for nine of every ten referrals" (SPCMT, 11). This number reflects that fact that most homes required mothers to register with a Children's Aid Society or other social service agency prior to admission to ensure a social worker was assigned to the case.[120] In this way, those entering maternity homes were streamed to adoption. The admission requirements for Humewood House state that "it is important that all applicants to Humewood contact, prior to admission, a Children's Aid Society" (ACC/GSA, Humewood House, *Information Sheet*). Rejections for admittance were mostly due to no vacancies or month of pregnancy—such as "too near delivery" or "too early in pregnancy"—but it is also recorded that "ten girls [out of 230 rejections] were rejected because they refused to contact the appropriate Children's Aid Society" (SPCMT, 16).

---

117 The term "Indian" used here in 1958 would have referred to Indigenous women.

118 See Solinger 66-68, Phillis Wheatley Home in Columbus, Ohio; Talbert Home, Cleveland; Kansas City, Topeka, and Little Rock also supported Black maternity homes. Also see Liebmann, G.W., Harriet Tubman House in Boston, and homes in New York, Philadelphia, Baltimore, Norfolk and Washington operated by the National Association for the Protection of Colored Women. Also see Morton, M. And Sin No More: Social Policy and Unwed Mothers in Cleveland, 1855-1990 1993.

119 After the 1970s, mothers were also referred through prolife crisis pregnancy centres (CPCs) and organizations such as Birthright or Planned Parenthood.

120 Humewood House, Victor Home, Salvation Army Homes, Armagh, and Catholic facilities all required preregistration with a Children's Aid Society. In 1963, all three Winnipeg homes required as a condition of admission a referral from the Children's Aid Society (Telpner).

Unmarried mothers continued to be targeted as a threat for spreading sexually transmitted infections and expectant mothers were routinely tested. Admission to maternity homes required a positive pregnancy test, and prior testing to screen for STIs. Anglican Humewood House required written reports of Wasserman test[121] and smear tests prior to admission (ACC/GSA, Humewood House, *Information Sheet*).

Staffing included an administrator with varying titles, such as executive director or superintendent. In Salvation Army facilities, a Brigadier or Major might preside. Additional staff included nurses, secretaries, housemothers, program workers, tutors, cooks, house-keepers, and maintenance staff. Some staff lived on the premises. With the emergence of the profession of social work early in the twentieth century, maternity home matrons, mostly women religious, and secular social workers were in conflict. Maternity home matrons continued to aspire to religiously improve or "save" the unmarried mother, while the social worker sought to use scientific methods to diagnose and treat the unmarried mother through individual casework. Underlying this struggle for power over the unmarried mother was the overriding principle of competing forces of "female moral authority" versus professional expertise (Kunzel 116). The competition for power was palpable as The United Church minutes of the Executive, Board of Evangelism and Social Services in 1966 shows: "Miss Beatrice Wilson reported that there was a paper written by a student at the School of Social Work which criticized the policies of the Home and the spirit of antagonism shown by staff to professional social workers" (UCC, *Maternity Home Assoc. of Canada* 3). As the profession of social work gained more power and legitimacy in the area of child welfare, it also became more vocal in its criticism of the traditional religious maternity home matron, who acted as a quasi-vision keeper of Magdalenism and other nineteenth-century philanthropy. Until the late 1960s, secular and religious models continued to operate in tandem, although the relationship remained tenuous at best. At the Juvenile and Family Court Judges Association Meeting in 1963, an address by Miss C. Johnson exemplifies the tension between traditional maternity home matrons and social workers. In the address, Johnson poses a series of questions about maternity home processes: "1.Why haven't maternity homes

---

121 Test for syphilis, named after bacteriologist August Paul von Wasserman.

taken the lead and increased proportionately their social services to clients? 2. Why are they [maternity homes] not staffed with the most skillful of trained persons? 3. Why is social casework not one of the most important tools of service? 4. Why do they not offer rehabilitation services to the girl on her own?" (AO, *Juvenile and Family Court Judges Assoc.* 2). Social workers criticized religious matrons as being untrained, unsophisticated, and unprofessional in their work with unmarried mothers, and religious matrons viewed social workers as intruders in a field they had dominated for over one hundred years. Until the early 1940s, Humewood House managers—including Gertrude Hill, the motherly matron of Humewood from 1912 to the early 1940s—criticized the work of social workers (Murray 269). Nonetheless, as maternity homes increasingly relied on government funding, and as the profession of social work became more legitimized, requirements for the use of theoretical knowledge and educated matrons also increased. As a result, increasing numbers of social workers were employed by or affiliated with maternity homes.

With the appointment of Miss Mary Smedley as Superintendent in 1949, Humewood House hired its first professional social worker; soon after, Humewood House hired Elizabeth McLaughlin, a graduate of McGill University Social Work (ACC/GSA, *Humewood House 1912-1962*). At Catholic Rosalie Hall in Scarborough, Mrs. Margaret Johnson was hired as the first professional social worker in the 1960s "to help them [the girls] make practical plans for the future" (Miséricordia Sisters 13), and at Presbyterian Armagh in 1955, the director, Gwen Davenport, was a social worker and a prior Children's Aid caseworker in the Unmarried Parents Department in Toronto. Davenport was succeeded in 1961 by Mrs. Herrig, also a social worker and a former Children's Aid Society caseworker (PA, *Annual Reports*). A 1965 report titled *Casework in a Maternity Home*, by social worker Mary K. O'Neil, outlines that the use of a social worker within the maternity home, in this case Catholic Sundale Manor in Chatham, would provide "needed casework ... if diagnostically she [the girl] was able, and if she was to gain from her stay at the home" (4). Sister Miriam de Lourdes—who in 1943 worked at the Home of the Guardian Angel in Halifax—held a diploma in social work and had prior experience as a teacher and educational administrator prior to joining the staff at the home. Subsequent sisters at the home would be instrumental in the field of social work and social services, although their counterparts at the Halifax Bethany Home rejected modern social work approaches (Morton, "Managing" 124, 127). On Prince Edward Island, Sister Mary Henry, executive director of the Catholic Family Services Bureau, held a master's degree from St. Patrick's School of Social Welfare in Ottawa (Turner 175). Whether religious or secular, moral rescue or casework, both schools of thought promoted their view of rehabilitation. However, as trained social workers began to dominate maternity home practice, the emphasis changed from redemption to casework treatment, which predominantly meant the *realistic plan*, the separation of mother and baby by adoption. As a result, maternity homes were no longer simply a place for women to hide.

Coercive Psychological Systems I: Create a Sense of Powerlessness

Although referred to and propagandized as "homes," along with "motherly matrons" to care for the "girls", maternity homes were integral to an interrelated institutional power system targeting the unmarried mother and her baby, which included government, churches, social service agencies, hospitals, and medical professionals. Although the name "home" suggests a place where comfort and support would be offered, Regina Kunzel describes the segregation of unmarried mothers in these facilities in terms of power relations: "attempting to create surrogate homes for the unmarried women both 'naturalized and disguised' the relations of power" (29). The "homelike" atmosphere promoted in newspapers and church publications did indeed naturalize and disguise relational power systems. Maternity homes were not homes per se, but quasi-incarceral facilities with an authoritarian power structure—one in which the unmarried mother was confined, powerless, and subjected to punitive treatment, similar to that of a jail. And, although maternity homes were disguised and promoted as comfortable homelike settings, stratified power relations within them left expectant mothers powerless not only over their daily lives but also, more importantly, over their future plans. The following excerpt describing St. Monica House in Kitchener illustrates that this home is, in fact, more of a penal institution disguised as a home. As well, it shows how the design of the home acts as a kind of camouflage and purposefully conceals the true nature of the facility: "Unlike many others, the maternity house is more like a comfortable suburban home than a penal institution. Elaborately broadloomed, cheerily and artistically decorated, it helps to soften the traumatic experience and create an atmosphere of warmth" (ACC/GSA, *Trend* 12).

Unmarried mothers residing in maternity homes occupied a place that was "explicitly disciplinary and implicitly incarcerational" (Kunzel 91). Residents were subject to strict rules and regulations. Freedom of movement, speech, and interaction with outsiders by mail, telephone, or visitation was restricted. Most homes had "sign out" forms, and "special permission to stay out for dinner must be secured" (SPCMT 46). As in the Magdalen Asylums of the nineteenth century, men were mostly prohibited, including the fathers of the babies (Carlson "The Fathers"). Some did allow putative fathers to visit, usually with permission. At the Halifax Infant's Home, unmarried mothers were not permitted to leave the premises after their eighth month of pregnancy (Morton, "Managing" 118), and at the Bethany Home in Halifax, putative fathers[122] were received only through arrangements with Children's Aid Society or the Department of Public Welfare (Morton, "Managing" 123). Many women felt as if they had been incarcerated for an offence: "I really felt like I was in jail ... I looked at it like it was some type of sentence" (qtd. in Petrie 55). This was compounded by the fact that the women were pregnant, resourceless, and fully dependent on the home not only for their own survival but that of their unborn child. These facilities epitomized ambiguity not only with their quasi-voluntary and quasi-coercive nature but with their hierarchical arrangement of power as well (Kunzel 91).

Being removed from their home, family, and community, often for the first time, had a significant impact on the girls and young women in residence. The isolation of unmarried mothers in maternity homes made them susceptible to authority and processes upon which they were now completely dependent for food, shelter, and other necessities of life. The restrictions on outside contacts disconnected the expectant mother from advice, familiar comradery, and social support; her ability to fully evaluate her situation was severely compromised.

The isolation also created the need to conform so as to be reinstated as a "good girl." Being sent away by one's family for committing what

---

122 "Putative father" was the name used widely across Canada by social service agencies for the "alleged" father of the illegitimate child as identified by the unmarried mother.

appeared to be a socially fatal act was an intensely shameful experience—one that created a need for reacceptance. Therefore, there was no rebellion evident on the part of most women by the time they were placed in a maternity home. In addition, in *Deviant Anonymous*, Andrée Lévesque alludes to the fact that the mothers themselves were socially conditioned to abhor their own state. In other words, they were themselves products of the same society that condemned them and so they condemned themselves. Believing that the punishments and atrocities heaped upon them were deserved, they accepted their fate without resistance (181).

Another way to create a sense of powerlessness was the removal of identity. Upon admission to a maternity home, the resident was either assigned a pseudonym as was done in the Magdalen Laundries of the nineteenth century or was addressed by her first name only (Dexter). Anne Petrie describes her own experience at the Salvation Army Maywood Home in Vancouver: "I had to give up my last name for the length of my stay. Now I would just be Anne. My only other identifying feature was my due date" (53). Petrie also describes the experience of Loretta with the Miséricordia Sisters in Edmonton in 1956: "The issue of her name came next, and Loretta was left with of nothing of her own. She had to give up not only her last name—that was standard in every home—but at the Miséricordia the rule in 1956 was no real first names, either. Loretta was told she would be Rose—just Rose—for the rest of her stay" (Petrie 63).

Not only were names either obscured or changed, but there were also rules in place around appropriate topics of conversation. Personal topics—including where one came from, former pursuits, family, or any other personal information about oneself—were either banned outright or strongly discouraged: "Nobody made close friends there. It was very much drilled into your head that no close contact was allowed. Anyway, if you did get to know somebody, she would just be going off soon and you'd never see her again. And, of course, you wouldn't know her real name anyway" (qtd. in Petrie 109).

Talk about pregnancy, birth, and babies was discouraged. The justification for this was to protect the privacy of the resident and to keep the girls calm. However, the result was to isolate them from others and to lull women into a kind of disassociation from their condition, their babies, and their overall situation. Although it may be difficult to imagine twenty pregnant women together in a room not talking about pregnancy, birth, and babies, this was often the reality in Canada's maternity homes. Nonetheless, hushed conversations about delivery, labour pains, water breaking, or someone leaving overnight often took place at breakfast or in the smoking room; tidbits of information about pregnancy, stretch marks, toxemia, or ways to bring on labour were passed along in surreptitious conversations. In at least two of Toronto's maternity homes in 1958, conversations at mealtime were regulated by the presence of staff at each table in the dining room (SPCMT, v). In the United Church Burnaby home the dining room consisted of: "four round tables with a staff member acting as "hostess" at each, the better to keep the seemingly rebellious girls under control and help them become comfortable with adults, Mrs. Packam [maternity home matron] reported. Intentional or not, staff presence discouraged any dinnertime conversation about babies." (Temple-Jones 22).

Another form of language regulation was to create dissociation from their babies. When matrons, social workers, and medical professionals talked about babies, it was limited to "that baby" or "the baby," never the personal "her baby," "my baby," or "your baby." This language served to create the baby as an object, to interrupt the forming maternal identity, to erode the mother's maternal expressions, and to encourage disassociation with one's growing baby during pregnancy, ostensibly to create a form of detachment in the mother. Young impressionable girls and women would have had no idea they were being manipulated in this way.

In addition to being entirely dependent on the home for the necessities of life, women's movements, contacts, activities, and discourse were restricted. In addition, maternity home matrons—who by the 1960s were frequently social workers as well—often adopted a mother role in relation to residents which generated disingenuous interactions, since residents were often unaware of the social work status of the matron. As a result of their dependence and constraints while pregnant, these women were indeed disempowered.

Coercive Psychological Systems II: Control Environment and Time

Maternity homes ran on schedules that did not vary widely from home to home. Maternity home daily schedules in the postwar years continued to reproduce those of nineteenth-century Magdalen Laundries and other institutions to house the fallen (See Appendix A). After breakfast and chapel, the making of beds, and the cleaning of rooms was followed by the work details: food preparation, washing dishes, setting tables, general cleanup or cleanup of the officers' dining room,[123] washing floors, dusting, vacuuming, bathroom detail, or laundry. An article on Armagh, which appeared in the *Presbyterian Record*, illustrates the work details there: "She took her turn on the kitchen team—got up at 7:30 am, helped with the meals, set tables, did dishes, and kept the dining room and kitchen clean. There were other teams too. One had to wash the sheets and towels, and another had to clean the bathrooms and halls. Of course, the girls had to clean their own rooms" (PCC, November, 1957, 17). Work details were mandatory. Work assignments were described as being "light, therapeutic, and assigned with consideration of the girls' physical condition" (SPCMT, ix); nonetheless, some of the work was demanding for heavily pregnant women. Although maternity homes were paid a per diem rate by the provinces,[124] residents did unpaid work as had been done in earlier institutions; only this time, no negative newspaper articles appeared about their unpaid labour.

Pregnant girls and young women continued to be expelled from Canadian high schools well into the 1970s.[125] Students in maternity homes mostly concentrated on independent work sent from their school; they were supervised by either a maternity home matron, tutor, or, in some instances, a qualified teacher. Teachers were introduced beginning in the 1940s, and by the 1960s, most homes had some arrangement for the continuance of studies. A 1969 Armagh newsletter reports that although the teacher Mrs. Allison Jones had her doctorate in education she preferred to be addressed as "Mrs.", and "that all students who wrote Grade XIII exams at the home successfully passed" (Armagh, *Newsletter*, May 1969). The Victor Home in Toronto was

123 These were in Salvation Army homes.
124 See the Department of Social Services Reports for all provinces.
125 This date varies across the country.

happy to report in 1966 that the Board of Education of Metropolitan Toronto had consented to provide teachers from the Home Instruction staff (UCA, Victor Home, *Annual Report 1966*). Prior to that, the home had encouraged the continuance of studies and supplied tutors,[126] suggesting that "girls bring their textbooks with them" (UCA, Victor Home, *Pamphlet,* 1962). A 1967 report from Humewood House in Toronto comments that: "the Department of Education has continued to supply teachers for most of the high school subjects and arrangements were made for girls from university to grade IX to write their examinations in house" (ACC/GSA, Humewood House, *Report* 1967).

School work in most homes was conducted during the morning hours. The physical classroom varied. Some had formal classrooms with desks and chalkboards, while others had a more casual arrangement. Anne Petrie describes her experience with the schoolroom at Maywood: "my professors sent my exams over to the home so I wouldn't lose any courses. One of the Army officers invigilated. In the school room there were rows of wooden desks and chairs. Along the back and sides of the room stood rickety metal typing tables topped with clunky old Underwoods" (Petrie 160).

As in the nineteenth century, domestic arts such as sewing continued to be the main activity for women. Early in the twentieth century, some homes had a laundry or sewing room onsite to produce revenue similar to the Catholic Magdalen Laundries. For example, the United Church Victor home in Toronto had operated a laundry service and a sewing operation, where the residents produced aprons (UCMF 7). A report upon the visit of one Salvation Army Officer to the Glenbrook Maternity Home in St. John's Newfoundland describes the activities there: "Do the girls employ themselves at needle-work?" I inquired. In a trice out came a heap of lovely sewing and I was introduced to 'huck weaving' and a tasteful selection of towels and cushions done in this colorful manner" (Salvation Army, *War Cry*, 12 September, 1953, 5).

By the 1960s, sewing and craft rooms continued as a mainstay, and residents spent much of their time knitting, making dolls, aprons, paper flowers, and other crafts.[127] In most homes, creating baby things was strongly discouraged, and the residents were kept busy several

---

126 This was reported as early as 1939.

127 At Catholic, Rosalie Hall, Scarborough girls did sewing and crafts such as ceramics. (Petrie 71).

hours a day creating frivolous items unrelated to maternity. However, some mothers report being encouraged to knit layettes in which to dress their babies for use at hospital discharge.[128] In any case, items lovingly made by an unmarried mother would rarely, if ever, be transferred to adoptive parents (Transue-Woolston).

Most of the homes had smoking rooms and during the 1950s and 1960s, it was the smoking room where residents often congregated (Petrie 101). As previously alluded to, it was in the maternity home smoking room that tidbits of information about birth and babies was exchanged, and for some, friendships were made. As Suzanne Morton explains: "the general importance of smoking in maternity home culture was supported by the evidence of the sister superior at the Home of the Guardian Angel [Halifax], who included a cigarette allowance in the list of expenses a resident might anticipate" (Morton, "Managing," 118).

Medical appointments were usually held at a prenatal clinic of a nearby hospital. The Salvation Army and Catholic Miséricordia Sisters ran both maternity homes and hospitals across Canada. Women residing in the maternity homes of these churches would usually receive prenatal care and give birth at one of the affiliated hospitals. Other homes had arrangements with independent hospitals. Inmates[129] were either driven to or took public transit to prenatal appointments. Some homes dictated that girls must travel in groups on "clinic days," and some even offered imitation wedding rings for the inmates to wear while on these trips (UCMF 33). Some residents continued to see their own private family doctor and did not use the hospital clinics sanctioned by maternity homes. Most homes required inmates to use side or back doors, never the front door of the home, when leaving or entering the home.[130]

128 Mother at Humewood House in 1963 reports she was strongly encouraged to knit a layette for her baby (Origins Canada, "A Way Forward").

129 Maternity home residents were referred to as "inmates" in Ontario provincial reports.

130 At Rosalie Hall, "everyone entered and left by the back door" (Miséricordia Sisters 8). At Bethel Home in Toronto once a girl entered the home she was not allowed to use the main door until she left. They would be picked up at the side door for doctor's appointments. (Petrie 60). The *Winnipeg Free Press* indicates women used the *back* door only as opposed to the front, in Winnipeg homes (*Winnipeg Free Press*, November 1, 1963).

Table 1. Daily Maternity Home Schedule

Time	Sunday	Monday	Tuesday	Wednesday	Thursday	Friday	Saturday
8:00am	Breakfast	Breakfast	Breakfast	Breakfast	Breakfast	Breakfast	Breakfast
9:00am	Chapel	Chapel	Chapel	Chapel	Chapel	Chapel	Chapel
10:00am	Modified	Assigned	Work	Duties	Assigned	Work	Modified
11:00am	Free	School or Crafts	School or Crafts	School or Crafts	School or Crafts	School or Crafts	Free
12:00pm	Dinner	Dinner	Dinner	Dinner	Dinner	Dinner	Dinner
1:00-2:00pm	Free	Pre-Natal Clinic	Lecture	Chaplain Visits	Social Work Visits	Prenatal Clinic	Free
2:00-3:00pm	Rest	Rest	Rest	Rest	Rest	Rest	Rest
4:00pm	Free	Social Work Visits	Sewing	Crafts	Social Work Visits	Crafts	Free
5:00pm	Assigned	Laundry	Crafts	Sewing	Crafts	Assigned	Laundry
6:00pm	Supper	Supper	Supper	Supper	Supper	Supper	Supper
7:00pm	Chapel	Chapel	Chapel	Chapel	Chapel	Chapel	Chapel
10:00pm	Lights	Out	Lights	Out	Lights	Out	Lights

(Salvation Army Bethany Home, Toronto, 1969)[131]

Unmarried mothers report being routinely used as teaching tools in hospital clinics, as several students would probe and check all in one visit,[132] "there were three case rooms for unwed Mothers...each and every one of these students would give you an internal examination...I would be so sore afterwards" (qtd. in Petrie 188). Others report an inability to ask questions. Kathryn, who stayed in the Victor Home in 1968, reports that she "was troubled by the extreme insensitivity she experienced at Wellesley Hospital ... doctors refused to answer even basic questions during their check-ups" (UCMF 32). These young, unmarried, pregnant girls and women were often treated with disdain and lack of respect by medical professionals.

131 As recalled by the author. Also see Armagh, *Report of the Director* (1961), which outlines a similar schedule. Also see Humewood House, *Information Sheet*, which also outlines a similar schedule.

132 Mother reports being used as a 'teaching tool' at Grace Hospital in Toronto while at Salvation Army Bethany Home in Toronto, 1969 (Origins Canada, "A Way Forward"). Petrie reports a steady stream of doctors including a group of eager young students (183).

Illus. 6.1. Armagh Maternity Home, Presbyterian, Clarkson, Ontario, ca. 1960s, PAA.

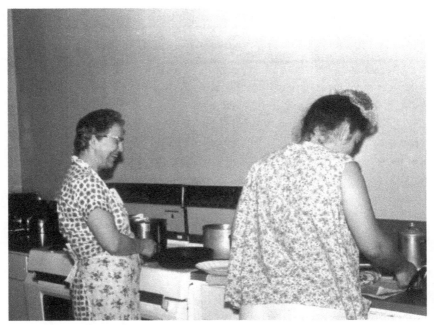

Illus. 6.2. Armagh Maternity Home, Presbyterian, Clarkson, Ontario, ca. 1960s, PAA.

Illus. 6.3. Armagh Maternity Home, Presbyterian, Clarkson, Ontario, ca. 1960s, PAA.

Those residing in Canada's maternity homes occupied shared rooms with few exceptions. The more modern ones were semi-private; older ones had dormitories. Washrooms were usually shared and institutional in type. An article titled "Overcrowded Conditions Hamper Work" about overcrowded dormitories and plans for renovations at the Anglican Humewood House in 1958 states:

> One of the major problems at the house is the crowded conditions. Cramped dormitories do not offer them any privacy .... Sleeping accommodations will be transformed from dormitories to single and double bedrooms. At present the 25 girls at the House are sleeping in two dormitories and four beds are set up each night in the recreation room and other girls are using the sunroom as a bedroom (The Toronto Star, 12 June, 1958, 57).

A more modern establishment, St. Monica House in Kitchener, boasted about the quality of its accommodations: "bedrooms are private or semi-private and there is no hint of dormitory life" (ACA, *Trend* 12).

Coercive Psychological Systems III: Keep Person Unaware

Social workers either met in person or spoke with their assigned resident during pregnancy. Some homes provided a scheduled time for social work visits. Others, such as Armagh in Clarkson, Ontario, drove residents to the offices of social service agencies "when there are vacancies in the station wagon and appointments can be arranged" (Armagh, *Report of Gwen Davenport*, 1961 33). Although there were meetings with social workers, mothers report being kept unaware of their rights and choices concerning their out-of-wedlock pregnancy. Very little information was given to unmarried mothers about labour, delivery, child welfare services, and, specifically, resources that would assist them in mothering. A Department of Social and Family Services memorandum sent by Victoria Leach, adoption coordinator in Ontario, to Miss Betty Graham, Director, Child Welfare, states:

> Yesterday afternoon Helen Allen[133] and I spoke to the girls at Armagh ... during our discussions it became very apparent that many of these young ladies have had little casework or even explanation from their social workers. They are unaware of court proceedings, some are unaware they could ask for short term wardship, they were uninformed about the appeal period and had other concerns ... I have also visited other maternity homes and found an equal lack of understanding. (AO. Dept. of Social and Family Services, *Correspondence* 1)

In this memo, Leach goes on to suggest that the Social and Family Services Branch should prepare a booklet, which "would outline in detail some of the avenues open to them in planning for their unborn

---

133 Helen Allen, a reporter with the *Toronto Telegram* launched 'Today's Child", a newspaper feature advertising children to be adopted which started in the *Toronto Telegram* in 1964 and expanded to other papers including the *Toronto Star*. Allen was also instrumental in the launch of a television version in 1968 on CFTO-TV titled *Family Finder* hosted by Dave Duvall, a program where children were showcased for adoption (Hilborn).

children" (1). However, an initialled handwritten note at the bottom of the letter directed to "Betty", presumably from Graham's superior, or Mr. Magder, who was copied on the letter, states that the Children Aid Societies should be responsible for such a booklet, and goes on to say that "in any case, if the Branch prepared it, I am sure there would be undue criticism of the contents"[134] (AO. Dept. of Social and Family Services, *Correspondence* 1). This letter illustrates that keeping mothers within maternity homes uninformed about their rights and choices with respect to their babies was an intentional policy of the Ontario government (See Appendix C). In addition, expectant mothers were not apprised of the fact that they could avail themselves of legal services. A report of the Child Welfare League indicates that "legal counsel to unmarried mothers in Maternity homes is very limited and that the laws protecting children give Children's Aid Societies extraordinary power and authority" (SPCMT 51). Keeping mothers unaware of their rights as mothers, and their rights with respect to their unborn babies was the norm in Canada's maternity homes. Most mothers believed that adoption was their only option since this was the only option provided to them by social workers, maternity home matrons, and others.

By the 1960s, some homes offered prenatal classes. Others gave lessons on reproduction. At Armagh, in 1962, the film *Human Reproduction* was viewed and Nurse Anderson was to explain it with the aid of an explanatory chart (Armagh, *Annual Report 1962*). Other homes offered limited prenatal lectures—such as the Church Home for Girls in Winnipeg where a Public Health Nurse conducted these sessions during the 1960s (UCMF 16). At Humewood House in Toronto, the Victorian Order of Nurses provided a course of prenatal classes (ACC/GSA, Humewood House, *Annual Report 1967-68*). Nonetheless, a review of annual reports of many homes shows that these types of sessions were often criticized by boards of directors, priests, or others (Humewood House, *Annual Reports*; Sisters of Rosalie Hall). In general, information regarding reproduction, birth control, labour, and delivery was in scant supply in Canada's maternity homes. Adoption activists

---

134 The author could not identify the author of the handwritten response written directly on the letter. Although it appears to have been written by a superior of Betty Graham, it does not appear to be the signature of John Yaremko, the Ontario Minister of Social and Family Services in 1970.

consider keeping residents unaware of their rights within the maternity home setting was a human rights violation.

Coercive Psychological Systems IV: Rewards and Punishments to Inhibit Behaviour Reflecting Former Identity and to Promote Group's Beliefs

Magdalenism continued to be the basis of inmates' religious reform. Chapel was attended in most homes daily, although some had two chapel services, one in the morning and one in the evening (Dexter). In some homes, ministers or priests would periodically visit to administer communion or meet with residents. Saving the souls of those who had sinned was an important goal in many of these homes, which were, after all, run by Christian churches. Evangelical and Salvation Army matrons often reported their joy in the spiritual transformation of residents within these homes. As in the nineteenth century, unmarried mothers were still seen as sinners in need of penance and repentance. However, penance now took the form of the loss of their child to adoption, a harsh penalty indeed. It was made abundantly clear to young mothers in the maternity home system that the symbolic punishment for "the mistake" was the surrender of their baby for adoption. In some cases this, was overtly stated; in others, intimated. Considered an expert on women's health at the time, Dr. Marion Hilliard, chief of the Department of Obstetrics and Gynecology at Women's College Hospital from 1947 to 1956 weighed in on the punishment of unmarried mothers: "When she renounces her child for its own good, the unwed mother has learned a lot. She has learned an important human value. She has learned to pay the price of her misdemeanour and this alone, if punishment is needed is punishment enough" (*The Telegram*, 22 November, 1956, 35).

Harsh treatment has been reported by unmarried mothers who resided in maternity homes in postwar Canada ("Unwed Mother"). Women report being verbally, psychologically, and sexually abused[135] in religious-based maternity homes and hospitals in Canada. Punishment and redemption remained an integral part of the maternity home program, as Magdalenism had been deeply embedded in maternity home theory since the late nineteenth century. In the 1961 work

---

135 One mother recalls how a priest would fondle the residents when visiting to administer communion (Alward).

Unmarried Mothers, Clark Vincent refers to the covert punishment that surrender might embody:

> It is quite possible that in the near future, unwed mothers will be "punished" by having their children taken from them right after birth. A policy like this would not be executed nor labeled explicitly—as "punishment." Rather, it would be implemented through such pressures and labels as "scientific findings," "the best interests of the child," "rehabilitation of the unwed mother," and "the stability of family and society." (199)

Harsh treatment ensured that only one mistake took place, since "repeaters" were not easily tolerated. Muriel Mulligan, a director in an Ontario Children's Aid Society states in a 1964 *Toronto Star* newspaper article that "We get very few repeaters ... they seemed to have learned their lesson" (6 April, 1964, 40). One mistake by a white middle-class girl might be overlooked if she was duly repentant and made a "realistic plan," but repeaters were different.[136] Many maternity homes would not allow repeaters as a policy of admission. The United Church Victor Home in Toronto had strict guidelines concerning repeaters: "repeaters, married women, mental defectives, and venereal disease cases shall not be admitted" (The Victor Home, *Policy Statement* 1). A report of Armagh states that the percentage of repeaters among unmarried mothers was high and that some agencies suggested it was around 25 percent. This report indicates that repeaters occurred because the mother was dissatisfied with the plan made for her first child and would want to make a different plan for a subsequent child or that she had failed to solve her personal problems at the time of her first pregnancy (Armagh, *Report of Director,* 1961). In part two of a series by Michelle Landsberg titled "Society's Smooth System for the Disposal of Unwanted Babies," Landsberg, upon interviewing a maternity home matron, exposes the matron's attitude toward second offenders: "the Director unwittingly revealed her attitude as quasi-criminal when she

---

136 In 1953 a Toronto Star article states that "Rev. A.W.Downer, P.C. Dufferin-Simcoe told the legislature's special committee on reform institutions yesterday that women who have two or more illegitimate children should be sterilized" (Toronto Star 20 November, 1953, 7). Also, in 1959 a Timmins welfare officer suggested "it should be made a criminal offence for unwed mothers to bear more than two children (Toronto Star, 18 June 1959, 3).

said that, 'second offenders, of course, are not admitted. It would be unfair to have the younger girls exposed to them'" (*Globe and Mail*, 13 September, 1963, 9). This comment echoes the nineteenth and early twentieth-century practice of separating the innocent from the delinquent.

Coercive Psychological Systems V: Use Logic and Authority that Permits No Feedback

In maternity facilities, those mothers who complied with the punishment—that is, adoption—and who rejected their former lives and behaviour were well looked upon by matrons, social workers, and others, thereby reinforcing the behaviour desired by the maternity home. Mothers that rebelled against the rehabilitation process were out of favour. By the late 1950s, talk of 'keeping'[137] in maternity homes was heavily discouraged. Those who did talk about keeping their babies were often ostracized, chastised, and considered the most pathological by maternity home matrons and social service agencies, as the following examples attest:

> In our experience in the Children's Aid Society of Metropolitan Toronto over the past few years, we have found that the more emotionally healthy unmarried mothers are the ones likely to relinquish their children. (Sutherton 7)

> Most of the girls who are financially and intellectually able to keep their babies decide not to. It's the "other kind of girl" who is more apt to make the decision to keep her baby. (Sister St. Augustine, Director, Rosalie Hall, *Toronto Star*, 20 December, 1965, 39)

> Generally the most unstable want to keep their child, the more stable gives the infant for adoption. (Captain Scoville, Booth Hospital, *Toronto Star*, 16 March, 1965, 44)

> Rosalie Hall advises against the girls keeping their babies 'they think they are taking a doll home to play with," Sister Tremblay said bluntly." Some Maternity Home Directors feel that it is the more immature girls who keep

137 That is, keeping one's baby, and not surrendering for adoption.

their babies, and the more mature girls who put the children up for adoption. (*Toronto Star*, 7 June, 1972, 77)

The large number of adoptions speaks of both the health and intelligence of the mothers. (Superintendent, United Church Home for Girls, UCMF 14)

Mothers who expressed a desire to keep were often ostracised within the maternity home environment; they were labelled by matrons as "that kind of girl" and were considered unintelligent. At the United Church Burnaby Home, "a resident who openly decided to keep her baby was moved immediately to a private room and seen only at monitored meal times" (UCMF 33) At the Salvation Army Bethany Home in Toronto a resident who openly stated she was keeping her baby left the home quietly after only two days in residence.[138] Not only were mothers who expressed a desire to keep constructed as the most pathological, but were also considered selfish. "Susan" Victor Home 1967 states the following: "Throughout her stay, she says, she received the same message repeatedly from home staff and her social worker; that giving up her child was the only option and that keeping her child would be extremely selfish and reckless" (UCMF 31). In Landsberg's article on illegitimacy, one agency director states that: "we emphasize that they're doing the right thing for the baby, that it's the best and most unselfish decision" (*Globe and Mail*, 3 September, 1963, 9).

Mothers were counselled to be unselfish. Teaching selflessness was discussed in the 1962 Annual Report for Armagh, the Presbyterian home located on the outskirts of Toronto: "We are ... most happy that we found ways by which the girls can do something for other less fortunate people and by doing so lose some of their selfishness" (Margarete Herrig, Director, Armagh, *Annual Report* 1962). In maternity homes, the term "unselfish" was a euphemism for surrendering a newborn baby as a gift to more worthy parents. The concept of unmarried mother selfishness stemmed from the idea that bringing a child into a one-parent home would be detrimental to the child and,

---

138 The writer, upon learning her new roommate was 'keeping' her baby, a possibility previously unknown to her, went to Brigadier Davies at Bethany Home to request that she keep her baby too. She was chastised, told she was selfish, and sent back to her room. The new roommate left the home mysteriously two days later. Forty-three years later, the writer received an apology from the Salvation Army for the treatment she received surrounding this incident.

therefore, would be a selfish choice. The executive director of Origins Canada[139] states that "only in an adoption context would a mother expressing the desire to nurture her newborn baby be considered selfish" (Andrews, "Flip"). Nonetheless, this characterization of young unmarried mothers continues in contemporary adoption transactions. Surrendering mothers in modern adoption culture continue to be constructed as good, mature, brave, selfless, and courageous[140]—a legacy of the adoption mandate and a powerful tool of coercion for unsupported and resourceless mothers in the twenty-first century (Andrews, "Modern"). The notion of unmarried mother unselfishness has taken root in wider discourse. In a study done in 2006 titled "Reinforcing the Motherhood Ideal: Public Perceptions of Biological Mothers who Make an Adoption Plan" Karen March and Charlene Miall found that 74 percent of males and 76 percent of females considered biological mothers who chose adoption as "unselfish."[141]

Already suffering from eroded self-esteem, shame, and isolation, most maternity home residents were averse to further notoriety and capitulated to the pressure to conform. The incentive of reinstatement to that of a "good girl" was a powerful influence for a young woman isolated in a maternity home in postwar Canada; especially considering the stigmatization and the spoiled identity of "unwed mother." It was strongly reinforced that the right kind of girl would make a "realistic decision." Conforming to the adoption mandate was constructed as a path to the return of respectability.

139 This is a Canadian federal non-profit organization that supports those separated by adoption.

140 This rhetoric intensified after the supply of domestic white newborns dried up after the 1970s. Today in domestic adoption culture, "birthmothers" are constructed and groomed to be "'brave", "selfless", and "courageous" rhetoric that is rooted in the adoption mandate (Andrews, "Modern").

141 Graph shows 74 percent of males and 76 percent of females considered biological mothers who chose adoption as "unselfish," whereas 72 percent of males and 80 percent of females believed they were "responsible" (March and Miall 377).

Babies: Then No Babies

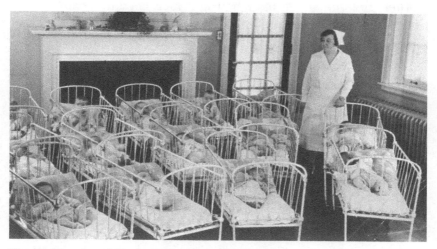

Illus. 7. Humewood House. Babies in Nursery.

Prior to and during WWII, most maternity homes not only housed unmarried mothers but cared for their babies in onsite nurseries. Some homes hired nurses and other trained staff. Prior to the 1930s, adoptions were uncommon within Canada's maternity homes. Karen Murray illustrates the practices at Humewood House, the Anglican maternity home in Toronto: "Adoptions were rare. In 1917 Humewood managers 'gladly' recorded 'only a few' adoptions" (265). In 1921, the Adoption Act was enacted in Ontario.[142] However, at that time, adoption was not widely prescribed for unmarried mothers: "Despite the new adoption law, many people were convinced of the 'naturalness' of keeping a mother and child together and supported an unwed mothers right to raise her child. Some social workers shared the conviction of managers of religious maternity homes that keeping illegitimate families together would prevent moral relapse" (Murray 273).

The stated ideal of those who ran the earliest maternity homes was to keep mother and child together (Petrie 139). Encouraging unmarried mothers to keep and mother their babies in the early twentieth century was known as "redemptive maternity" (Kunzel 27). Redemptive maternity was based on the theory that once an unmarried woman

142 Until 1921, adoption had only been possible through Private Members Bills in the provincial legislature (Chambers, *Misconceptions*).

became a mother she would mature, and mend her ways. Now a mother, the unmarried mother would turn her life towards more productive, useful, and morally decent endeavours for the sake of motherhood and her child:

> It is a dangerous thing to take an infant away from a mother of this type, asserted Lillian Clarke in 1913. It is saving her reputation at the expense of her character. If deprived of this powerful motive and influence toward an upright life, a daily safeguard from temptation, the empty craving heart is like the house swept and garnished, ready for the evil spirits to come in and take possession. (Kunzel 33)

The Salvation Army and other evangelists encouraged redemptive maternity. During the 1920s and 1930s, when the eugenics campaign was at its height, the Salvation Army in the United States required prospective residents to sign a contract promising to keep their child before being admitted to one of their homes (Kunzel 33). Redemptive maternity was also encouraged as a way to reduce infant mortality through breastfeeding. Unmarried mothers were encouraged to "take responsibility" for their children: "Agencies have advocated mothers keeping their babies on the grounds that the children would be a stabilizing influence if the mothers were forced to take responsibility for them" (Wimperis 242).

Babies were still cared for in Canadian maternity home nurseries well into the late 1950s. A study in 1958 reports that all five maternity homes in Toronto provided temporary care for infants for up to six weeks in some homes, although it was acknowledged that group care for infants was known to have damaging effects (SPCMT, x). Upon her visit to the Glenbrook Maternity Home in St. John's, Newfoundland in 1955, a Salvation Army officer observed: "The home is beautifully kept. Shiny floors, furniture and windows, but everywhere there are babies, babies, babies! I peeped into a 'frig' to find it full of bottles of formula— one feeding only. Every single inch of space is sure to have a tiny cot there (Wigh, Salvation Army, *War Cry*, 22 October, 1955,7). The annual report of Humewood House for 1955 reports that 32 babies were admitted during the year, with 33 discharged (ACC/GSA, Humewood House, Annual Report 1955). In 1950, the Ontario Welfare Council reported that in the previous year, 156 girls were admitted to St. Mary's Infant's Home in Toronto; they lived on the third floor of the home, and their babies were kept in a large nursery on the second floor (Miséricordia Sisters 10). At the Miséricordia in Edmonton in 1955, babies were kept in a third floor nursery, and the residents were on the second floor: "the babies were kept in the nursery until they were adopted or sent off to an orphanage ... the new girls took care of the babies of the girls who had preceded them" (Petrie 102). In Montreal, in 1932, the *filles-meres* at Hopital de la Miséricorde were required to work off their debt to the nuns with a six month stay after confinement to tend babies in the nursery, including wet-nursing (Lévesque 176). In a report to the Board of Armagh maternity home in the 1950s, Miss Mohan conveys that all maternity homes had nurseries and that babies stayed there for a longer or shorter period of time depending on the plan for the child (Armagh, *Miss Mohan*). Until the end of WWII, the Catholic Home of the Guardian Angel in Halifax continued with the theory of redemptive maternity, requiring six months compulsory residence after confinement:

> Until 1945 the policy of both the Catholic Home of the Guardian Angel and the Protestant Halifax Infant's Home was based on compulsory residence for mothers for six months after confinement with the purpose of breast feeding infants and cementing a bond between mother and child, which would entrench a sense of responsibility for the infant and redeem the wayward woman through the power of mother love. (Morton, "Nova Scotia" 337)

However, this practice changed quickly following WWII, and mothers were expected to leave within two weeks of birth (Morton, "Managing" 112). Most maternity homes not only cared for babies in their nurseries, but as trends to adoption increased, some also organized and facilitated adoptions directly from their premises, such as the United Church Victor Home, Toronto[143]: "While in previous decades the majority of residents had kept their children, the trend began to

143 The United Church Victor Home facilitated adoptions directly from the home until 1958 when the Board of Missions ruled that all adoptions would be arranged by the Children's Aid Society (UCMF 10).

reverse in the 1940s, and by the 1950s ... Victor Home's adoption service was in full force ... preference was given to United Church families" (UCMF 10). It is unknown if adoptions took place directly from the Evangeline Home in New Brunswick, although adoption records can be found in the collection of the Salvation Army for this home at the Provincial Archives of New Brunswick (PANB, Salvation Army, *Finding Tool*). The Home of the Guardian Angel in Halifax facilitated adoptions as a private adoption agency in Nova Scotia up until 2012 (Jones).

In the immediate postwar decades, a major shift took place in maternity homes. This change was influenced by the profession of social work and the previously discussed psychoanalytic and sociological theories emerging in postwar Canada. New practices managed and implemented by social service agencies working with the cooperation of hospital authorities and maternity homes worked to separate the unmarried mother and her baby through adoption. In the United States, the National Florence Crittendon Mission[144] changed its policy of keeping mother and child together—"signalling the end of an era and the victory of the professional ethos of social workers over the founding ideals of evangelical women reformers" (Kunzel 169).

The new practice was clean break. Infants were removed immediately from their mothers at delivery and either adopted or taken into the care of social services directly from hospital: "the babies themselves were no longer the responsibility of the maternity homes ... from 1961 on, the infants were taken directly from the hospital to a foster home 10 days after birth" (Miséricordia Sisters 14).[145] This policy not only increased the number of adoptions taking place but significantly decreased the number of babies being cared for in maternity homes. A study undertaken by the United Church in referring to the United Church Home for Girls in Burnaby, British Columbia states: "adopting directly from the hospital dramatically decreased the number of babies cared for in the home in the 1950s, yet those children who did return to the home were almost always kept by their mothers" (UCMF 14).

144 National Florence Crittendon Mission was one of the largest providers of maternity homes in the USA.

145 This is in reference to Catholic Rosalie Hall, Scarborough.

Board of Missions for the United Church ruled that all adoptions would now be arranged by the Children's Aid Society (UCMF 10). A Canadian Welfare Council report refers to this trend reversal from maternity home management to that of social service agencies: "It is also relevant that as late as 1946 fully 75% of all legal adoptions in Nova Scotia resulted from private placements made by doctors, lawyers, maternity homes etc. with only 25 per cent made by social agencies; whereas for the current year the figures will be almost reversed with 70 per cent of all legal adoptions resulting from agency placements" (The Canadian Welfare Council, "Trends").

By the 1960s, maternity home matrons routinely dropped their wards off at hospital admitting departments and left them there to labour alone.[146] By this time, mothers were being discouraged from returning to maternity homes after a birth, as it was thought they might reveal their experiences to other inmates: "there are a lot of impressionable girls who become very apprehensive and very frightened as a result of mingling with the girl who has had her baby and wants to come [back to the maternity] home and tell tall tales about it" (Armagh, Miss Mohan 12). Many homes no longer offered the service, and those that continued to accommodate mothers after birth did not offer the same hospitality to their babies. At the Armagh home outside Toronto, mothers in 1961 were allowed a maximum postpartum stay of seven days in accordance with an Ontario government grant implemented in 1960 (Armagh, Annual Report 1961). A 1961 report—which shows the number of babies that returned to the home from hospital with their mothers from 1955 to 1961—explains how the babies were cared for:

> 1955-0 1956-0 1957-3 1958-2 1959-5 1960-1 1961-0
> The babies were housed in the mother's room and cared for by her with the help of one girl who wished to do this, under the supervision of the nurse. This service has been of dubious value. Having a baby back at Armagh ... is a profoundly disturbing event for the other twenty-one girls. (Armagh, Report of Director 1961)

---

146 They were "sent to the hospital unescorted, as was the home's policy at the time" (UCMF 34). Also, the author was accompanied in a taxi by a matron from Salvation Army Bethany Home who, upon arrival at Toronto Grace Hospital, left her alone at admitting.

When interviewed for an article by the *Toronto Star* in 1963, Olivia Langford, the Executive Director at Toronto's Anglican Humewood House, described their policy quite succinctly: "At Humewood the girls return to the home for 10 days, but do not bring their babies with them. They are taken for adoption without the mothers seeing them" (Schill, *Toronto Star*, 11 September, 1963, 59). In 1951, the Superintendent of the Burnaby Home for Girls in British Columbia reported that "many residents have not returned to the Home after confinement owing to the policy of the Welfare Agencies in placing the baby – in many instances – direct from the hospital for adoption" (United Church Home for Girls, *Annual Report, 1951*). According to a United Church study about Elizabeth House, a United Church home that opened in 1968 to address the need for a Protestant, English language service in Montreal: "although residents were welcome to return to the facility for a period of convalescence following the birth, the home did not accommodate babies" (UCMF 19).

Babies were no longer provided for in Canada's maternity homes because unmarried mothers had become subject to clean break and the adoption mandate. In this climate, maternity home matrons began to groom mothers for adoption:

> At every maternity home and agency one thing is hammered home from the start: the baby must be given up for adoption. (Landsberg, *Globe and Mail*, 13 September, 1963, 9)

> We emphasize that they're doing the right thing for the baby, that it's the best and unselfish decision. So they start to regain their self-esteem and are buoyed up by the idea that they're making a wise decision. (Maternity Home Director as reported by Landsberg, *Globe and Mail*, 13 September, 1963, 9)

> Mrs. L.H. Doering, Executive Director of the United Church's Victor Home for Unmarried Mothers says they are counselling their girls not to keep their babies. (*Toronto Daily Star*, 20 December, 1965 39)

> I think we have moved into the area of adoption slowly with many of us having a good many qualms about it

originally and gradually coming to the realization that this is a good plan, so that we can help the unmarried mother accept this plan. We don't impose the plan on her, but we can guide and direct her in moving towards this. (Armagh, *Miss Mohan* 11)

Mothers from United Church maternity homes were interviewed for a report on maternity homes in 2013, a report initiated by concerns from groups advocating for former residents. The following quotes are from mothers who resided in United Church homes:

"Sheri"[147] United Church Victor Home, 1963:

She says the message she and other residents received from the home staff, the Chaplain and her social worker was consistent and clear: giving up their babies was best for all concerned; in fact, it was the only option given. (UCMF 29)

"Anne P" United Church Victor Home, 1964:

She says the moment she arrived in her room and met the other residents, she was warned about the strict atmosphere and necessity of following orders ... Anne said the staff made it clear that adoption was the only option for resident's babies. (UCMF 30)

"Kathryn B" United Church Victor Home, 1968:

Kathryn says that not only was she given no emotional support from professionals during this time, but she and other residents also were not adequately informed of their options and were led to believe that adoption was the only available choice. (UCMF 32).

Although most churches continue to minimize their role, these homes were integral to the success of the adoption mandate. In fact, within Canada's maternity homes in postwar Canada, surrender rates were as high as 95 percent, whereas statistics show that overall, unmarried mothers released their children for adoption at an average rate

147 Pseudonyms were used in the report and are, therefore, reproduced here.

of approximately 74 percent during the 1960s (See Table 2).[148] Adoption rates are not available for all homes. However, a 1961 report from Armagh states that since its inception in 1955, out of the 391 mothers who bore a live child or did not marry 358 babies were adopted, which is 92 percent (Armagh, *Annual Report 1961*). Further statistics for Armagh in 1965, show that almost all of their babies were adopted (95 percent), except for 4 "undecideds" and 3 who "kept baby" (Armagh, *Statistics 1965*).

When mothers left these homes, they were encouraged to forget their experiences, which resulted in mothers keeping their traumatic experiences secret for years, some for the rest of their lives[149] (Alton). Prudence Rains writes: "when you have completed your stay at Kelman Place, you must sever your connections and not return for visiting. This is for your own good—when you leave, you close the door on your experience" (qtd. in Rains 222). There was little if any aftercare given to the unmarried mother who resided in a maternity home. Social work casework terminated upon the discharge of the mother from hospital or the signing of adoption consents. No counselling or other type of aftercare was provided to the mother who was expected to return to her community, keep the secret, and carry on as if nothing had taken place.

In postwar Canada, maternity home practice had capitulated to psychoanalytic and social work theories of unmarried motherhood; in fact, they worked in tandem with social service agencies and hospitals to create the "smooth system" (Landsberg 9) to separate unmarried mothers from their newborn babies. Social work casework in maternity homes often included counselling mothers not to see or hold their babies in hospital, grooming them for the clean break—the violent act of separation of mother and her newborn baby[150] in Canada's delivery rooms.

Maternity home matrons were complicit with the practice and theory advanced by social service agencies, and applied them within the controlled environment of maternity homes. Canada's maternity homes operated as a sort of baby assembly line from admittance to drop off at the hospital. Not only did maternity homes serve to emphasize the

---

148 See Chapter Five for a more in-depth study of unmarried mothers and adoption statistics

149 See film that aired on CBC Passionate Eye, Forty Year Secret (Alton).

150 This was usually the firstborn.

futility of pursuing motherhood to the unmarried expectant mother, but they disempowered her; distorted her reality; controlled her environment; cast her desire to mother her own baby as selfish; kept her ignorant of her rights and choices and of the lifelong consequences; and pressured her to conform—thereby fulfilling the requirements of a coercive psychological system. An unmarried mother entering a maternity home in postwar Canada had very little chance of leaving the experience with her baby. Contrary to the insistence of many churches that they simply provided a home for those who needed one, maternity homes were essential to the success of the adoption mandate. Considering the coercive nature of these "charged sites" (Kunzel 8), and the statistics, it can be reasonably stated that the majority of women who resided in Canada's maternity homes did not make a choice or a decision for adoption.

Chapter Five

Maternalism, the Postwar Mother Imperative, and the Phenomenon of Mass Surrender

"Healthy white babies were in demand. The CAS was chronically short of money and 'adoption' was the cheapest solution to the 'problem' of unmarried pregnancy. The case files produced under the act disprove the idea that women exercised free and unfettered choice in releasing their infants for adoption"—Chambers, Misconceptions 85

Illus. 8. Women's magazines soon replaced the WWII working girl with a loving mother who became the reigning cover girl for years thereafter. McCall's Cover 1942; (R) Ladies Home Journal cover 1946 illustration Al Parker (L). Sally Edelstein Archives.

This chapter sets forth the powerful postwar climate of maternalism and the mother imperative, a period that emphasized the return of women to the private sphere who had worked in the war effort; reinforced the construction of good Canadian women as white stay-at-home mothers; and promoted nuclear families and heteronormativity—all major influences contributing to the adoption mandate. Lara Campbell writes that, "Maternalism has been defined by Sonya Michel and Seth Kovan as an exaltation of women's natural capacity to mother applied to state policies concerned with the interests of women and children" (101). The work of women, including reproduction, was used politically in nation building, particularly after WWI and WWII.

Section I of this chapter elaborates on gender and examines the powerful social construct of the postwar mother imperative, concerned only with white women. Section II explores race as it relates to the adoption mandate in Canada. Institutional prescriptions for Black and Indigenous unmarried mothers are briefly assessed in contrast to those for white women. Section III illustrates, with statistics, the phenomenon of mass infant surrender. In addition, a surplus of babies for adoption is identified in the early 1960s, and the phenomenon of babies of unmarried mothers crossing borders is also examined.

Section I: Postwar Mother Imperative. A Maternalism Ideology for Whites Only Please

In the interwar period, Victorian ideals of maternalism observed during and after WWI lost vibrancy, as new scientific models of motherhood emerged through social reformers. Victorian ideals of motherhood were viewed as overly sentimental and outdated. However, a renewed thrust of maternalism emerged after WWII. This was expressed through the postwar mother imperative, described by Nina Leibman as "the dominant social imperative of postwar America with its emphasis on the importance of nuclear family life, the proper role of the sexes, the superiority of suburbia" (173). According to Cynthia Comacchio, "maternalism became the central strategy of a politics of regeneration that would uplift both family and nation" (90). The essentialism inherent in maternalistic ideology posited white mothers as morally superior; with the ability to effect political change and nation building through their natural attributes as mothers.

Fears and tensions associated with the Cold War were soothed with consumerism and a stable home life in the suburbs. Gender roles reverted to former traditional inside and outside spheres for men and women in the new context of suburbia and the family car. By 1945, approximately 80,000 Canadian women who had served in the armed forces or worked in highly skilled jobs in the war industry had been discharged (Prentice et al. 350). Women were encouraged to return to the private sphere by governments, authorities, and local experts (Strong-Boag, *Home Dreams* 486). Incentives that had been instituted during the war to assist women to work outside of the home were discontinued, such as government day nurseries, competitive wages, and access to equal opportunities. Women were literally sent home. Mass media—including advertising, newspapers, magazines, radio, film, and increasingly, television—portrayed the good woman as a white stay-at-home wife and mother. By the 1960s, despite their war time experiences, "the majority of women were rarely visible on the public stage" (Strong-Boag, *Home Dreams* 497); their lives now played out in suburban homes, taken up with childrearing.

In the postwar social climate of maternalism, the age of brides decreased, and birth rates dramatically increased. In 1940, the median age for a woman's first marriage had been 23.2 years, but by 1965, it was 21.1 years (Canada, Stats Can., *Marriage Statistics 1921-1990*). This meant that many married women became teen mothers. However, due to their marital status, the age of these women did not emerge as a major societal concern. Since married teen mothers did not contravene norms, there was no societal preoccupation with age. This was in contrast to unmarried mothers, whose age did become a major concern for social workers and others. Sharon Wall states that "Canadian social work students were, likewise, increasingly preoccupied with the experience of 'adolescent unmarried mothers' and the phenomenon of 'child mothers'" (51).

The annual number of births in Canada rose from 252,577 in 1940 to over 478,551 in 1960 (Canada. Stats Can., *Series B1-1*). This increase in births became known as the postwar "baby boom"[151] (Canada, Stats Can., *The Baby Boom*). Although ex-nuptial pregnancy[152] had previously been associated with the lower classes (Farrar 53), increasing birth rates in the postwar climate also contributed to escalating rates of out-of-wedlock pregnancies within the white middle class. During the 1920s, illegitimate births had accounted for approximately 2.2% of all live births in Canada (Canada, Stats Can., *Series B1-1*). In the 1930s, this figure rose to around 4.0%, although Nova Scotia "had the dubious distinction of being the province with the highest illegitimacy rate in Canada ... an as yet unexplained demographic phenomenon ... ranged from 8% in the mid-1940s to 10% in the late 1960s" (Morton, "Managing" 112). Illegitimacy rates across Canada remained fairly stable until the late 1960s, when they rose to an average of 9.6% in 1970, the highest national rate of ex-nuptial pregnancy in the immediate postwar decades (Canada. Stats Can., *Series B1-1*).

Increasing rates of illegitimacy within the white middle-class contributed to the major shift in the way unmarried mothers were viewed and treated. Rickie Solinger explains: "it became increasingly difficult for parents and the new service professionals, with middle-class affiliations themselves, to sanction treating 'our daughters' as permanently ruined" (Solinger 15). Although the white unmarried mother had transgressed cultural norms, the intrinsic cultural capital of her whiteness gave her the opportunity to reclaim her standing through adoption. The adoption mandate then, operated as a "'safety valve' to

151 The postwar baby boom describes the period of increased birthrates from 1950-1970.
152 This is pregnancy outside of nuptials or marriage.

release the White single woman from motherhood thereby restoring her status as a woman of White-defined privilege and performance" (Pietsch, "Good Mothers" 36).

The postwar mother imperative and its emphasis on the nuclear family were powerful social constructs. These constructs of normative womanhood also impacted married women who sought to form families through adoption to conform to the ideals of the nuclear family. Racialized and gendered ideals of normative womanhood and good motherhood strongly influenced social policy and practice pertaining to unmarried mothers.

Section II: Race and the Adoption Mandate

Black Women: Not Real and Valuable Women

Given that this book concentrates on the white unwed mother, it is crucial to examine the basis for contrasting ideologies and prescriptions for out-of-wedlock pregnancy for women of colour and Indigenous women in Canada. Due to racist immigration policies, the Black population in postwar Canada remained relatively low in the postwar decades. For the period 1941 to 1971, the Black population averaged approximately 0.2% of the population or 18,000 in 1951 (Statistics Canada, *Trends*). This is in contrast to the Black population in the United States, which was reported to be 15 million in the same period (Gratton; Gutmann). Even though the basis for Black exclusion from the adoption mandate was essentially the same in both countries, it was not as widespread or embedded throughout Canada as it was in the United States. By 1961, the Black population in Canada had risen to 32,100. Most Black families were reported as being settled in Nova Scotia[153] and Ontario (Statistics Canada, *Trends*).

As both Solinger and Pietsch suggest, the social prescription of adoption for unmarried mothers was predominately for "whites only." Black women and other women of colour were excluded from the mandate, an exclusion that ultimately served to augment the value of the white mother and child. White supremacist assumptions interpreting and appropriating Black out-of-wedlock pregnancy imposed Eurocentric values on the Black unmarried mother. Postwar constructions of race and illegitimacy were used jointly as evidence of "individual pathology on the part of the white woman and cultural pathology on the part of the Black—[ideas that] were developed and articulated by a new set of experts interested in out-of-wedlock pregnancy" (Kunzel 165). These new experts included psychologists, psychiatrists, social workers, sociologists, and policymakers. Proponents of this prevailing view of Black unmarried mothers agreed that she should, in most cases, keep her baby (Solinger 188).

Unmarried mothers were categorized according to race. White unmarried mothers and Black unmarried mothers were separated physically, ideologically, and politically. Pietsch explains:

---

153 Black people had been living in Nova Scotia since the 16th century as slaves, freemen, or as Black Loyalists (Perreaux).

> If Black mothers were treated in the same way as white unmarried mothers, then white women would be cast as ideologically the same as Black women; and this coalescing of categories would create a socio-political crisis ... dominant adoption discourse from the postwar period separated Black unwed mothers physically, ideologically and politically from White unwed mothers. (*Good Mothers* 35)

As suggested by Pietsch, white and Black unmarried mothers were separated physically. Physical separation was exemplified in Canada's maternity home practice. As we have seen, although maternity home policies professed to be racially and culturally inclusive, the reality was that it was predominantly if not exclusively the white unmarried mother who was treated in Canada's maternity homes. Black and white unmarried mothers were separated ideologically as well:

> For some analysts white girls were products of complex, cultural patterns, refined community and gender mores, and traditional family structures. Aberrations within any of these entities ... could cause psychiatric problems, such as unwed pregnancy. Black girls, on the other hand were, according to this view, products of no such higher-order structures. Their behaviour was unmediated, natural, biological. (Solinger 43)

Black unmarried mothers were also characterized as being natural mothers in line with the racist idealization of the "Black Mammy."[154] Therefore, they needed no redemption or rehabilitation: "by becoming mothers, even unwed mothers, Black women were simply doing what came naturally" (Solinger 189).

By Eurocentric standards, Black unmarried mothers were considered to be culturally different in their attitudes to out-of-wedlock pregnancy. A 1945 study of Black unmarried mothers found that "for culturally determined reasons, the morality codes of many Negroes do not include a prohibition against illegitimacy" (Kunzel 157). The

---

154 Although the "mammy's mothering role is to nurture white Children ("good"), but she cannot meet the criterion for "White saintly motherhood ("bad") (Harris 13, 20; Pietsch, "Good Mothers" 37).

argument that Black illegitimacy was culturally accepted in Black communities led social workers to dismiss it as a problem before the 1940s (Kunzel 157). Nonetheless, white interpretation of Black unmarried mothers as accepting of illegitimacy due to a morality code negated the fact that mothering, motherhood, and othermothering were, and continue to be, valued in Black culture and that mothering represents a site of power and resistance for Black women (O'Reilly 100).

Feminist Patricia Collins identifies various concerns of racial ethnic mothers that differ from mothers in the dominant culture—the first of which is "keeping the children born to you" (O'Reilly 97). The legacy of slavery in the context of reproduction and mothering cannot be overlooked when discussing the Black unmarried mother and her baby in postwar Canada. During slavery, Black children were considered commodities and were routinely removed from their mothers to be sold as slaves. In view of this, and the prevailing racist policies that failed to create social services for Black unmarried mothers, it is unsurprising that traditional practices of informal adoption and other-mothering continued as part of the fabric of life in Canada's Black community: "White women had the option of formal adoption, but no such institutions existed for the children of African Nova Scotian women, who therefore turned to their communities for support ... these children became the responsibility of their extended families and of the community" (Bernard and Bonner 163). These informal support systems within the community resisted racist social policies, protected children from racism and violence, gave mothers power as mothers of their own babies, and preserved the Black community (O'Reilly 100).

Another factor that may have contributed to Black unmarried mothers keeping their babies was the tradition of the Black matriarchal family structure. Racial oppression was not congruent with the nuclear family, and less strict gender roles were the norm for Black families. Economic and other factors meant that Black women often worked outside the home: "it was the Black woman who more often chose to raise her child alone ... by doing so, these women simultaneously subverted patriarchal, heterosexual, and social mandates" (Pietsch, "Un/titled" 96). A November 1969 study titled "Negro-White Differences in Decisions Regarding Illegitimate Children" reveals that Black unmarried mothers were overwhelmingly advised by their parents to keep their out-of-wedlock child; 86% of their mothers and 88% of their fathers advised them to do so (Pope 760). This was in stark contrast to advice given and action taken by white families.

Black unmarried mothers in postwar Canada would have understood that their devalued social status would transfer to their babies, and, in fact, Black and mixed race babies in postwar Canada were not considered valuable commodities for adoption purposes. Racialized babies were classified as "unadoptable," "difficult to adopt," and often labelled "special needs" (Guyatt 14), or even "handicapped." This is illustrated in a 1967 article in the *Globe and Mail* that addresses the issue of unwanted Black children being shipped abroad for adoption due to a lack of adoption homes in Canada: "The Catholic Children's Aid Society of Toronto classifies colored babies as handicapped along with children who are mentally or physically abnormal" (Lawson 1).

Physiological and race matching were prominent in adoption practice during the postwar decades, and it was thought that "proper matching was key to the cohesion of the adoptive family" (Balcom 32). This encompassed matching religion, intelligence, hair, skin, and eye colour to ensure an adopted child that could appear as if born to the adopters; thus, "care is taken to place the children with parents with characteristics similar to the child" (Alberta, *Dept. of Public Welfare 1959-1960* 24). Racism and its resulting economic factors together with low rates of Black population in general contributed to extremely low rates of agency-approved non-white adoptive homes.

Although there were a few transracial adoption transactions in postwar Canada, it was still considered an anomaly. It wasn't until 1958 in Montreal that Margaret Edgar and her husband became "among the first white parents to adopt legally non-white children in North America" (Dubinsky 61). The Edgars and other adoptive parents founded the Open Door Society, a support and lobby network for interracial adoption. Other advances in Quebec through the Children's Service Centre (CSC) worked to re-categorize Black children as "adoptable". However, according to Dubinsky the numbers were small: "my best estimate is that there were about 350 children who were labelled non-white placed for adoption by the CSC in Montreal between 1955 and 1969 ... 300 of whom were adopted by whites" (63). Michele Landsberg also reported on this topic in Toronto. In an article titled "Families Experiment in Integration," Landsberg writes:

20 other Toronto families have adopted children of mixed
racial background this year. The unprecedented number of
mixed adoptions has been spurred by a joint project of the
Metropolitan Toronto Children's Aid Society and the
Social Planning Council, who are working together to
spread enlightenment and find homes for these children
who, until recently, were considered unadoptable. (*Globe
and Mail*, 23 August, 1963, 10)

It was the prevailing view that Black mothers needed no rehabilitation to reinstate them as good mothers within Canadian society
since, as pointed out by Pietsch: "in order to be a good mother, one first
must be a real and valuable woman, and in effect, White" ("Good
Mothers" 29). As a result Black unmarried mothers in postwar Canada
were excluded from the same social work practices, processes, and
social prescriptions as white unmarried mothers because they did not
fit the hegemonic norms of (white) motherhood in Canadian society,
and, as such, their babies were not considered to be valuable commodities.[155] In fact, Black unmarried mothers were "actively discouraged
from relinquishing their children for adoption, even during the period
when white women were pressured in the opposite direction" (Balcom
33).

The Indigenous Sixties Scoop

The "Sixties Scoop" is a term coined by Patrick Johnston in 1983 to
describe the widespread "scooping" of Indigenous children in Canada
from their homes and reserves by child welfare authorities from the
1960s to the 1980s and their adoption into primarily non-Indigenous
homes. According to Raven Sinclair, Johnston's term "Sixties Scoop" is
appropriate for two reasons:

First, Johnston observed in the statistics that adoption as
the mechanism to address problematic child welfare issues

---

155 Outside of the parameters of this study, later in the 20th and 21st century, Black unmarried
mothers would be recast once again as "welfare moms," and constructed as "the single most
destructive social pathology in modern American society" (493). Black women and their
children would increasingly become political targets by governments and social service systems
in Canada and the USA. As Morton states, "the moral issue was transformed from a women's
sexual history to her dependency on the taxpayer" ("Nova Scotia" 342).

had resulted in notable increases in Aboriginal child apprehensions in the decade of the 1960s. Secondly, in many instances, Aboriginal children were literally apprehended from their homes and communities without the knowledge or consent of families and bands. ("All My" 66)

The actual number of children "scooped" by social service agencies will probably never be known, since many status[156] children were never recorded as such. Some Indigenous children were recorded as "Métis" or "French" in child welfare documents (Sinclair, "All My" 20). Inaccurate records often led to the loss of tribal identities in the adoption transaction (Fournier; Crey; Sinclair). With reference to the actual number of children taken, Sinclair reports that "statistics from the Department of Indian Affairs indicate a total of 11,132 status Indian children adopted between the years of 1960 and 1990. However the actual numbers are believed to be much higher" ("All My" 20). It is estimated that approximately 70 percent of Indigenous children taken from their mothers during the Sixties Scoop were taken in disproportionate numbers and were eventually adopted into non-Indigenous homes in Canada, the United States and overseas ("All My" 66).

In the overall context of bourgeoning adoption statistics in Canada during the 1960s, it is unsurprising that Indigenous adoption statistics also increased dramatically during this period. In postwar Canada, the adoption mandate, fuelled by social workers, had posited adoption as the social response to any pregnancy that fell outside the norms and ideals of traditional white motherhood. Black women had been mostly excluded from the mandate due to racialized notions concerning culture and biology, but Indigenous women were located in a separate category of nonconformity and were, therefore, subject to the changing adoption policies and practices embraced by child welfare agencies. Although there are similarities and connections to the white mandate, the context and purpose of the Indigenous Sixties Scoop was founded on very different principles.

156 See Government of Canada, Department of Indigenous and Northern Affairs. A Status Indian is a person is recognized by the Government of Canada as a registered Indian (commonly referred to as a Status Indian). Status Indians may be entitled to a range of benefits, rights, programs and services offered by federal agencies, and provincial or territorial governments, https://www.aadnc-aandc.gc.ca/eng/1100100032463/1100100032464.

Targeting kinship and family systems was a strategy used by successive Canadian governments to oppress, assimilate, and destroy Indigenous people, and by the 1960s, separating Indigenous children from their families through forced assimilation policies already had a long history in Canada. Canada's residential schools had been removing Indigenous children from their homes since the mid-nineteenth century as a policy to suppress traditional knowledge and language and to "kill the Indian in the child."[157] Residential schools operated to indoctrinate and assimilate Indigenous children into Christian, Euro-Canadian culture. Suzanne Fournier and Ernie Crey observe the following:

> This deliberate policy to separate and forcibly assimilate aboriginal children into the mainstream has pervaded every era of aboriginal history in Canada and profoundly injured of [sic] First Nations people both historically and today. Each era saw a new reason to take aboriginal children away from home, placing them in residential schools, foster care or non-aboriginal adoptive families. (17)

Indigenous traditional mothering was not based on Eurocentric ideals and values; it was, therefore, viewed as substandard by Euro-Canadian culture. As well, during this period Indigenous communities were in disarray, states of poverty, and social chaos due to continuous oppressive and racist government policies over time (Sinclair, "All My" 38). This is further exemplified by Fournier and Crey: "In many cases, children were taken from parents whose only crime was poverty–and being aboriginal. Finding a grandmother caring for several small children in a home without a flush toilet, refrigerator or running water was enough to spur a social worker to seize the children and take them into the care of the state" (85). Instead of investing in infrastructure and social programs to assist Indigenous people, government policy and practice endorsed removing children for adoption into mostly non-Indigenous families. Fournier and Crey further observe: "The white social worker, following hard on the heels of the missionary, the priest, and the Indian agent was convinced that the only hope for the salvation

157 This quote is commonly attributed to Duncan Campbell Scott, Department of Indian Affairs. For another viewpoint, see Sniderman.

of the Indian people lay in the removal of their children" (84). Indigenous mothers lost their children to adoption in the 1960s, as did the white unmarried mother; not because they were considered candidates for rehabilitation to the ideals and norms of Canadian motherhood. Instead, the Indigenous mother was deemed unfit, and her child was taken for adoption because of institutionalized racism targeting her community, her family, and her traditional mothering practices. Embedded government policies of cultural genocide and assimilation meant that the Indigenous mother had little if any opportunity to mother her child, especially in the context of the rise of adoption culture in postwar Canada.

The loss of Indigenous children through residential schools and forced adoptions left an entire generation of Indigenous people—many of whom lost their Indian Status through adoption—with a deep sense of loss and grief. Intergenerational trauma from the Sixties Scoop still impacts the lives of Indigenous people. Fournier and Crey give an example of how these policies affected one family, that of Wayne Christian, a former Spallumcheen chief, who was "taken away as a child along with his younger siblings":

> They were split up and assigned to separate non-Indian homes. At seventeen Christian returned to Spallumcheen. His mother had almost been destroyed by the removal of her children; although she had not been alcoholic before, she had turned to drinking as a release...one morning Wayne found his beloved younger brother [who had also returned home] dead. He had shot himself in the head. (88)

Although in 1976 the Supreme Court found that Indian Status was not negated by adoption, the adoptee can only claim that status upon reaching the age of majority (Chambers, *Legal*). This was and remains problematic. As Lori Chambers explains, "if a child retained his or her status, but had no knowledge of, or contact with, his or her birth parents, or Indigenous community how would this status be recognized?" (*Legal* 122). In other words, an Indigenous adoptee would have to know: first of all, that they were adopted, secondly that they were Indigenous, and finally, the name of their family of origin, in order to be repatriated. To compound matters, adoption records remain sealed and partially sealed in all provinces and territories in Canada, which limits full access to original birth registrations or other paperwork that would facilitate status attainment for those reaching the age of majority. Despite the fact that the Supreme Court, in 2016, expanded Indian status to include over 600,000 Métis not previously granted status, for Métis adoptees, parentage will be difficult to prove in many cases (Blanchfield).

Many Indigenous Sixties Scoop survivors remain marginalized, resourceless, and unaware of their rights. This is slowly changing as Indigenous adoptees who suffered loss of family, community, and culture have started to organize and come together to promote a sense of belonging and healing, and to seek justice for the illegal, unethical, and human rights abuses they suffered and continue to suffer under Canada's Child Welfare policies.[158] In early 2017, a judge ruled in favour of Sixties Scoop survivors in Ontario for "failing to prevent on-reserve children from losing their Indigenous identity after they were forcibly taken from their homes" (CBC News, February 14, 2017). This ruling has led to an agreement between the Federal government and Sixties Scoop survivors across Canada that includes financial reparations for those impacted.[159]

158 See National Indigenous Survivors of Child Welfare Network, an Indigenous activist group.
159 Not all Sixties Scoop survivors support the agreement.

Section III: The Phenomenon of Mass Surrender

Prior to WWII, adoption had been used as a social prescription for out-of-wedlock pregnancies on a limited basis, as the trend had been toward redemptive maternity. This changed dramatically in the immediate postwar decades when babies from unmarried mothers were adopted in numbers never seen prior to, or since, in Canadian history. I refer to this as the "phenomenon of mass surrender."[160] The following statistics illustrate the number of babies from unmarried mothers that were adopted in Canada during the postwar decades, a phenomenon that has not been previously quantified.

Adoptions are facilitated by and statistics kept, by the provinces. There are few directly comparable adoption statistics available by province since, historically individual provinces often recorded different data.[161] Some provinces—such as Ontario, Alberta, New Brunswick, and Newfoundland—kept separate data for unmarried mother adoptions, while others reported only provincial wards and non-wards.[162] Some provinces recorded adoptions by religion, gender, and age of child, and others simply recorded a total number of adoption transactions completed during the year with no category breakdown. In addition, provincial records changed their format over the years, so there is little consistency in data collection and reporting for comparison purposes. Nevertheless, by studying the adoption statistics provided in provincial government social services reports, some interesting patterns and trends emerge in the data.

By the 1940s, adoptions began to escalate and continued to increase until the early 1970s. For example, in Ontario in 1948, there were 2,536 adoptions, and in 1968, there were 7,157, almost three times as many (Table 2). In New Brunswick in 1948, 261 children were adopted, but by 1968, that figure had almost doubled to 545 (New Brunswick, Department of Health, *Thirty-First Annual*; New Brunswick, *Adoption Statistics*). In British Columbia, adoptions completed in 1945 totalled

---

160 Although I have used the term "surrender" and "surrender rates" in this chapter to denote adoptions from unmarried mothers, it is important to note that it is not assumed that all unmarried mothers "surrendered," rather than willingly "relinquished," as there are mothers who assert that they did choose adoption. Furthermore, the use of these terms is not to totalize or regulate alternative unmarried mother narratives.

161 Adoption statistics are still not standardized by provinces in order to obtain vital national information.

162 A ward is a child of the state.

292, but by 1967, there were 2,183 adoptions (British Columbia, *Social Assistance Branch 1945*; British Columbia, *Vital Statistics 1967*).

Babies from unmarried mothers accounted for the majority of adoptions that took place in postwar Canada. As reported in Alberta in 1955: "The total number of births registered out of wedlock is one thousand, three hundred and thirty-two for the fiscal year, and it will be noted that a large percentage of those babies are surrendered by transfer of legal guardianship for adoption purposes" (Alberta, *Dept. of Public Welfare 1954-55*). To illustrate this point in the data, total adoptions in Ontario from 1960 to 1965 inclusive were 32,724, and adoptions from unmarried mothers[163] represented 24,222 of these, or 74.0% showing that the vast majority of adoptions were babies from unmarried mothers (Table 2). Rates of adoption of illegitimate[164] children in New Brunswick expressed as a percentage of total adoptions for the same period in New Brunswick appear to be higher as total adoptions were 2,983 and adoptions of illegitimate children were 2,813, or 81% (New Brunswick, *Adoption Statistics*). In New Brunswick, in the year 1968 alone, adoption of illegitimate children represented 87% of total adoptions (New Brunswick, *Adoption Statistics*).[165] Reports from British Columbia from 1965 and 1966 show total adoptions of 4,323 with adoptions of illegitimate children representing 3,193 of these, or 74% (British Columbia, *Vital Statistics 1965-1966*). Alberta government reports for the same period, that is, 1960-1965 inclusive, show that unmarried mother adoptions represented 63.4% of total adoptions (Alberta, *Dept. of Public Welfare 1960-1965*).[166] Nova Scotia reports reveal that from 1954 to 1957 inclusive, total adoptions were 1,543, with adoptions from unmarried mothers representing 1,288 of these or, 83.5% (Nova Scotia, *Child Welfare Annual Reports 1954-1957*).

Although maternity home surrender rates recorded in annual reports are reported to be from 85-95%, surrender rates outside of maternity homes are more difficult to determine. One way to calculate a raw surrender rate by province is to express unmarried mother

163 Adoptions from unmarried mothers were recorded as a separate category in Ontario

164 "Illegitimate" is the language used in the report to denote a child born out of wedlock

165 Information about the 13% not accounted for is unknown.

166 This lower rate of unmarried adoptions as a percentage of total adoption in Alberta might be due to the fact that Alberta recorded only those unmarried mothers who surrendered through Surrender and Indenture. These statistics do not include babies that may have been apprehended due to the marital status of the mother.

adoptions as a percentage of the total number of illegitimate births by province.[167] This is only possible in a few provinces, as not all provinces recorded unmarried mother adoptions separately. However, some trends do emerge. For example, from 1960-1964 inclusive in Ontario, the total number of illegitimate births were 29,927,[168] and adoptions from unmarried mothers for this period were 19,507 (Table 2), representing a total surrender rate of 65.1%. In New Brunswick for the same period, the total number of illegitimate births were 3,805; and unmarried mother adoptions were recorded as 2,316, or a surrender rate of 61% (New Brunswick, *Adoption Statistics*). So, from 1960–1964 in Ontario and New Brunswick rates appears to be show an average of around 63%. It appears from this data that approximately two-thirds of unmarried mothers were surrendering their babies for adoption in postwar Canada. This trend is further exemplified by a Department of Social Welfare report from British Columbia and is suggestive of a surrender rate of approximately 66 percent:

> Judging from the number of unwed mothers who sought help for themselves and child from a Children's Aid Society or the Department of Social Welfare, and the comparatively small number who placed their baby for adoption through channels other than an authorized agency this year, it would appear that less than one-third of the total 2,484 children born out of wedlock remained with their parent or parents or were placed by them in a home of a blood relative. (British Columbia, Dept. of Social Welfare, 1959, 50)

Surrender rates in Newfoundland appear to be low in comparison. Reports from the 1960s show surrender rates from anywhere between 29.1 and 34.9%. It is difficult to determine the reason as to why surrender rates appear to be lower in Newfoundland. It is unclear if all data was recorded. However, one hypothesis may be that many unmarried mothers remained in their own homes during pregnancy rather than being sent to maternity homes. In 1965, at the peak of the

---

167 It is difficult to access Quebec adoption statistics and surrender rates outside of maternity homes since, child welfare was enacted by, and records kept primarily by the Catholic Church in that province until the first consolidated Children's Protection Act in 1977 (Balcom).

168 See État Civil/Vital Statistics, annuaire du québec/Québec yearbook 1966-67, Department of Industry and Commerce, Québec Bureau of Statistics.

adoption mandate, while churches across Canada were upgrading their maternity home facilities, building more homes, and increasing capacity, the Salvation Army Glenbrook home in St. John's, Newfoundland closed its doors. The Newfoundland Annual Report of the Department of Public Welfare for 1969 states that: "During the year under review 613 unmarried mothers sought the services provided by the Department through the field staff. The majority of those remained in their own homes but for the very limited number who were unable to do this accommodation was available in private boarding homes" (*Annual Report, 31 March, 1970*).

The fact that unmarried mothers were remaining in their own homes, suggests that they may not have been subjected to child welfare policies, and also may have enjoyed family support, factors that may have increased the likelihood of these mothers keeping their babies. Another explanation for the lower surrender rates in Newfoundland could be due to the protection of the unique identity and culture of the people of Newfoundland, a province that did not enter Confederation until 1949. Moreover, much of Newfoundland's economy relied on the work of families and fisheries; therefore, an illegitimate child might have been seen as a welcome addition to a fishing family to assist in this work.

Another province that suggests lower surrender rates is Saskatchewan. Even though legislation required that illegitimate births be reported by hospitals and that every unmarried mother be interviewed about plans for her child (Saskatchewan, *Dept. of Social Welfare, 1963-64*) out of the illegitimate children recorded as being born in Saskatchewan from 1960-1964 inclusive, only 2,257 are recorded as being admitted to care from unmarried mothers out of a total of 7,380,[169] an average surrender rate of 30.5%. This rate is similar to that which is found in Newfoundland. This may also be due to the rural nature of the province and its postwar economic dependence on agriculture, which relied on families to carry on the tradition of working on family farms. The *Annual Report of 1965-66* comments on the disparity between Saskatchewan and other jurisdictions with respect to out-of-wedlock births, although no explanation for this difference was offered:

---

169 Unmarried mother statistics were recorded separately in the Province of Saskatchewan.

> During the fiscal year 1965-66, the number of unmarried
> mothers in Saskatchewan remained basically the same as
> in the previous year. This represents a different situation
> than in some sections of Canada and the United States
> where Social Agencies are expressing concern bordering
> on alarm at the increased incidence of out-of-wedlock
> births. (Saskatchewan, *Dept. of Social Welfare, 1965-66*)

From 1945 to 1971 inclusive,[170] there were 581,488 illegitimate births recorded in Canada (Canada, Stats Can., *Series B1-1 Live Births/Illegitimate Births*). Using a conservative national surrender rate of 60%[171] it can be reasonably estimated that approximately 350,000 babies were surrendered for adoption across Canada by unmarried mothers during the postwar mandate. This is a rather conservative estimate considering provincial surrender rates varied and also considering that in Ontario alone 92,080 (or approximately one third of this estimate) were recorded as adoptions being from unmarried mothers for that same period (Table 2). Moreover, these statistics are restricted to the years between 1945 and 1971, even though adoptions of the babies of unmarried mothers occurred well before these dates, and continued well afterwards.

In addition, although adoption statistics for Quebec[172] are not available, statistics for illegitimate births are. Based on the number of illegitimate births in Quebec, which closely resemble the number of illegitimate births in Ontario,[173] and considering the large number of maternity homes operating in Quebec and the predominance of the Roman Catholic religion, it can be reasonably estimated that Quebec adoption surrender rates for the period are quite likely to have equally or even surpassed those of Ontario. Quebec rates may then, easily represent

170 This is the period recognized by most scholars as that of the postwar adoption mandate. The year 1973 was the last year that the federal government recorded illegitimate births.

171 See Wolfish, Canadian Family Physician, Vol. 30, April 1964 which states that "in Ontario the proportion of single mothers who chose to keep their babies rose from 30% in 1968 to 88% in 1977" suggesting that 70% of unmarried mothers surrendered their babies for adoption in Ontario in 1968, which is consistent with government reports showing an average rate of 74% during the mandate period (904). Also see Table 1.

172 Adoption records in Quebec were primarily maintained by the Church, private agencies and court systems (Griffith).

173 From 1960-1964 illegitimate births inclusive. See État Civil/Vital Statistics, *annuaire du québec/ Québec yearbook 1966-67*, Department of Industry and Commerce, Québec Bureau of Statistics. Quebec 26653, Ontario 29927.

another 100,000 adoptions. This would mean that the two provinces of Quebec and Ontario were responsible for approximately 200,000 unmarried mother adoptions within the overall figure of 350,000.

Table 2. Adoptions from Unmarried Mothers 1942-1971—Province of Ontario

Year	Total Adoptions	Unmarried Mother	%
1942	1706	1392	81.5
1943	1775	1436	80.9
1944	1744	1459	83.5
1945	2048	1695	82.7
1946	2075	1160	55.9
1947	2136	1646	77.0
1948	2536	1866	73.5
1949	2560	1941	75.8
1950	2598	1943	74.8
1951	3678	2721	74.4
1952	3957	2888	72.9
1953	3319	2402	72.4
1954	3411	2462	72.2
1955	4073	2945	72.0
1956	4085	2869	70.2
1957	4135	3100	75.0
1958	4334	3225	74.4
1959	5278	3837	72.7
1960	5056	3506	69.3
1961	5103	3754	73.6
1962	5109	3900	76.3
1963	5493	4077	74.2
1964	5718	4270	74.7
1965	6245	4715	75.5
1966	6543	4841	74.1
1967	6884	5428	78.8
1968	7157	5242	73.2
1969	7679	5826	75.9
1970	7740	5772	74.6
1971	7126	4049	56.8
TOTAL	131301	96367	73.3

Source: Raw data retrieved from 1942-1964 Inclusive Reports of the Minister of Public Welfare
Raw data retrieved from 1965-1971 Inclusive Reports Minister of Social and Family Services

After 1970 adoption rates dropped dramatically (See Table 1). Some reasons were due to changing norms, better access to abortion, the birth control pill, less stigma placed on unmarried mothers, and women asserting their right to mother as a sole parent. Unmarried mothers or unwed mothers became known as "single parents" or "single mothers." Suzanne Morton describes this change as follows: "A 1970 study of maternity homes by the newly formed Halifax Women's Bureau ... signalled a change in attitudes towards unmarried mothers...the study, which adopted the term 'single mother' ...represented a departure from past practices and interpretations" (Morton, "Managing" 132). A report compiled by the Victor Home in 1973 states that by 1973, 62% of unmarried mothers were now raising their children (Maternity Homes Association of Canada, *Brief by Victor Home*). This was a relatively quick flip in statistics from just four years earlier when 74% of unmarried mothers in Ontario surrendered their children to adoption. A report in Canadian Family Physician in 1984 states: "more young mothers are keeping their babies today. This trend appears to be worldwide. In Ontario, the proportion of single mothers who chose to keep their babies rose from 30% in 1968[174] to 88% in 1977" (Wolfish 904).

Although there is no direct comparable for Canada, data from the United States suggest that by 1988, surrender rates by unmarried mothers had fallen to approximately 2% (Sobol and Daly 494). In June 1995, a United States think tank, Child Trends Inc., reported that: "currently only about two percent of premarital births are relinquished for adoption" (Moore et al. vi). In 2005, the U.S. Department of Health and Human Services reported that "less than 1% of children born to never-married women were placed for adoption from 1989-1995 ... the percentage is higher for white never-married women (1.7 percent, than for Black never-married women (near 0 percent)" (U.S. *Dept. Health and Human Services* 1).

Something was going on in postwar Canada...unmarried mothers surrendered their babies for adoption in staggering numbers from 1940-1970 and beyond, a phenomenon that has never been seen before, or since, in the history of Canada. It was the adoption mandate, also referred to as "forced adoption" by governments and by many in the adoption reform movement.[175]

---

174 This figure is indicative of a 70% surrender rate in 1968.

175 See Commonwealth of Australia. Prime Minister Julia Gillard. National Apology for Forced Adoptions. Also see Canada. Senate of Canada "The Shame is Ours: Forced Adoptions of the Babies of Unmarried Mothers in post-war Canada".

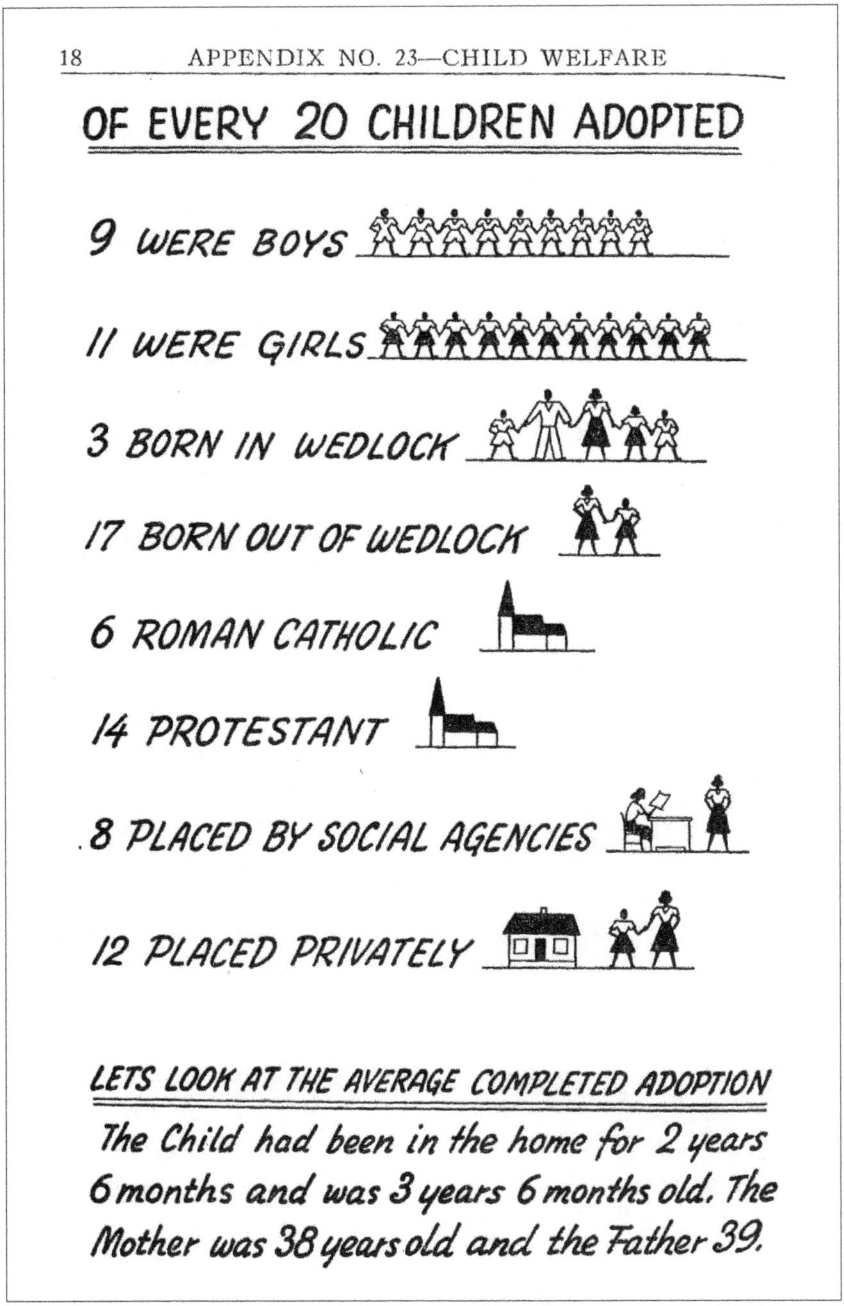

18 APPENDIX NO. 23—CHILD WELFARE

OF EVERY 20 CHILDREN ADOPTED

9 WERE BOYS

11 WERE GIRLS

3 BORN IN WEDLOCK

17 BORN OUT OF WEDLOCK

6 ROMAN CATHOLIC

14 PROTESTANT

8 PLACED BY SOCIAL AGENCIES

12 PLACED PRIVATELY

LETS LOOK AT THE AVERAGE COMPLETED ADOPTION

The Child had been in the home for 2 years 6 months and was 3 years 6 months old. The Mother was 38 years old and the Father 39.

Figure 4. Nova Scotia. Department of Public Welfare. *Annual Report 1956*, 22.

Cross Border Babies

Within a discussion of statistics concerning the adoption of babies of unmarried mothers during this period, it is important to include those babies adopted outside of Canada. Babies of unmarried mothers were sent as far afield as France, but most of the babies that left Canada went to the United States. Determining the exact number of children adopted from Canada into the United States in the immediate postwar decades is almost impossible, since some provinces provide statistics for out of country adoptions and others do not. In *The Traffic in Babies: Cross Border Adoption and Baby Selling Between the United States and Canada, 1932-1972,* Karen Balcom suggests that: "between 1930 and the mid-1970s, several thousand Canadian-born children were adopted by families in the United States. The adoptions originated from every province and territory, and children went to almost every U.S. state. Most of the children were very young infants the majority of whom were born to unwed mothers" (3). Although cross border adoptions had been taking place since the early twentieth century—including illegal and black market adoptions most notably from Nova Scotia, Quebec, and Alberta (Balcom)—it was not until 1966 that a formal network was developed to facilitate this type of adoption. The Adoption Resource Exchange of North America (ARENA) was an inter-state and international network developed to assist in placing "hard to place" children. Children were often placed outside the country due to disability, race, or religion.

In February 1968, the Catholic Children's Aid Society of Toronto reaffirmed its policy of placing children only in Catholic homes and defended the practice of placing Catholic children outside Canada. Although citizenship was important, it was thought to be secondary to a good Catholic family life (British Columbia, *Dept. of Social Welfare, 1960,* 42). In 1968, Ward Markle, executive director of the Catholic Children's Aid Society of Toronto, confirmed that the society had placed approximately 400 children outside of Canada between 1958 and 1968 ("400 Homes"). The organization appeared to be confident that sending children outside of Canada was a reasonable act on its part. However, I have not found any evidence that unmarried mothers were apprised of the fact that their child might leave or had left the country. Markle states the following: "We must be acutely conscious that the decision to surrender a child is a conditional, voluntary act on the part of an unmarried mother and whether it be by law or assumption, we have an implied responsibility in endeavouring to find a home of the same religious faith ("400 Homes").

The province of Alberta recorded 308 adoption placements outside of Canada from 1956 to 1965, and in 1966, it reported that "the number of children placed in the United States has continued to decrease, partly because of legal difficulties in completing the adoption and partly because of the increased availability of children in various States (Alberta, *Dept. of Public Welfare, 1965-66,* 15). Newfoundland reported that between 1958 and 1965, court orders for adoption were granted for 315 children to be adopted into the United States. Newfoundland reports show a high number of these were due to the United States Air Force base located in Newfoundland: "Over the past year 41 new applications for adoption of children were received in this office ... of these 41 new applications 22 were from the United Air Force personnel. The announcement in January of the phase out of Pepperrell Air Force Base has created a most difficult situation for both our clients and staff" (Newfoundland, *Dept. of Public Welfare, 1960*). Prince Edward Island routinely sent babies to the United States. Sister Mary Henry explains how and where the placements were made in 1953:

> Placements [were] made in Minnesota, New York, New Jersey, and Massachusetts. Over one hundred children could be placed in Minnesota alone ... The placements are made with the cooperation of the accredited agencies within the areas chosen for the children. Final decisions are then approved by the State Departments of Welfare and permission for placements granted. These agencies do the follow-up supervision and the legal proceedings are carried out in the U.S. courts. (qtd. in MacDonald 382)

In an oral history project interview conducted with Sister Mary Henry in 1984, she relates that it was difficult to place children for adoption on Prince Edward Island since most already had large families and they were poor (Hill 45:00). In this interview the Sister talked about the Prince Edward Island "American Adoption Program": "from 1954 on, we placed the bulk of our children [from Prince Edward Island] in the United States from that to 1977 ... we took children from them [Nova Scotia] and placed them in the United States too" (Hill 45:00).

A series of articles concerning children being adopted outside the country appeared in the *Globe and Mail* on 3 October 1967. One of them, titled "Quebec Babies Adopted in France, US," states that "fewer than 100 per year" have been adopted in the United States and into other countries as far away as France. Another article that appeared on the same day—with the headline "Unwanted Negro Children Shipped Abroad for Adoption, Agencies Say" explains that from 1964 to 1967 the Catholic Children's Aid Society "shipped out 48 unwanted children to foreign homes and the non-Roman Catholic CAS has done the same with about 25 more" (1). In the same issue of the *Globe*, the editorial was also devoted to the topic and questions the policy of sending Canadian babies out of the country.

It is impossible to know the exact number of Canadian infants of unmarried mothers that were sent to the United States and other countries for adoption. Many of these now adult adoptees seek their lost Canadian roots and citizenship. Others may still have no idea they were born in Canada. This also applies to their Canadian mothers, who, even if they somehow become aware that an international adoption took place, are constrained, as are their children, by the closed records systems in most U.S. states.

Too Many Babies

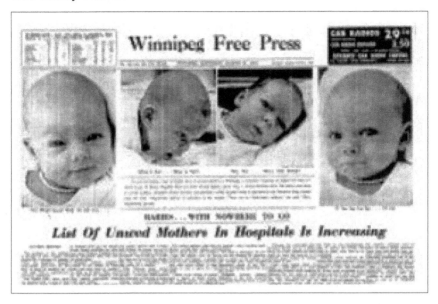

Illus. 9. A front page article in the *Winnipeg Free Press* reports that "an ever increasing 'crop' of babies born to unwed mothers in Winnipeg is creating a backlog of babies who have nowhere to go" (Telpner1).

By the mid-1960s, articles began to appear nationwide suggesting that the number of prospective adoptive homes were not keeping pace with the number of babies available. There were several reasons for this surplus in white newborns available for adoption. Illegitimacy rates during the 1960s were increasing, and white unmarried mothers continued to be convinced by social workers and others that adoption was the realistic plan for their child. As well, prospective adopters had been primarily born during the Great Depression when birth rates were low, whereas unmarried mothers in the 1960s were part of the "baby boom," causing a disparity in the numbers of adopters versus babies for adoption. In addition, by the 1960s, medical advances in fertility treatment increased childbearing choices for women who might have adopted in the past. Another reason for the surplus, according to the *United Church Observer*, was that potential adopters were scared off by what had been "stiff standards" for adoptive homes: "we've been a bit snooty in the past", admits Laurie Charleson, adoption consultant for Ontario" (Clarke 12). Conversely, in the same article, Margaret Goodman of the Western Manitoba Children's Aid Society argues that the relaxing of standard was a crisis: "We're gambling with the lives of these children ... we're putting them in homes we would have rejected ten years ago, but we can't have them sleeping in the streets" (Clarke 12).

At a conference entitled "Out of Wedlock"—arranged by United and Anglican churches in Toronto in November 1965 that included social workers, superintendents, and boards of directors of homes for unmarried mothers—social worker Mary Taylor spoke about the surplus of babies and the policies and practices that had driven social workers and others:

> This afternoon we were told there were 600 children born out of wedlock in B.C. for whom there were not adopting homes available ... for a generation, social workers, and to a degree, clergymen and parents and other people had been strongly encouraging girls who were pregnant to place their children for adoption ... we are faced at this moment with the need to re-evaluate this advice because of the realties that face us ... but, until we find some other alternatives, we'd better not separate children from their mothers, with no assurance that we will have any other mother to give them. (ACC/GSA 13)

In February 1966, Walter W. Blackburn, the assistant director of the Children's Aid Society of Metropolitan Toronto stated that "adoption has become almost a panacea for unwed mothers ... if this trend continues there will not be adoption homes for all our illegitimate babies" (*Toronto Daily Star*, February 17, 1966). Although Blackburn's concerns about adoption homes were echoed throughout Canada by various social workers, social service agencies, and maternity home directors, the "smooth system" (Landsberg 9) for adopting babies from unmarried mothers continued.

A 1965 article published in the *Toronto Star* reveals how adoption was entrenched as the dominant prescription for out-of-wedlock pregnancy during this period (Stapleton). The article refers to a speech made by Allan Sherlock, head of the Unmarried Parents Department of the Catholic Children's Aid, wherein he states that unmarried mothers may have to mother their own children due to lack of adoption homes.

Sherlock's statements came as a surprise to some including Sister St. Augustine of the Toronto Catholic Home for Unwed Mothers, Rosalie Hall who in the same article states that "we hope we won't have to resort to encouraging girls to keep their own children" (Stapleton 39). In another article that appeared in the *United Church Observer*, Allan Sherlock laments the situation, while at the same time, stating explicitly that the policy had been to encourage unmarried mother to surrender their babies: "This is a blow to ministers and social workers who, for a generation, have told girls that giving up their babies was the unselfish thing, best for them, for the babies, and for the childless couples begging for them" (Clarke 13). Another maternity home matron, Mary Dale, the president of Humewood House Association in Toronto states in her 1967 report that "As a gap between adopting parents and the number of babies available for adoption becomes more evident, it is possible that in the not too distant future, emphasis on the service provided [by maternity homes] may have to change" (ACC/GSA, Humewood House Association, *Report* 1967). An inter-office correspondence from the Board of Evangelism and Social Service department of the United Church of Canada regarding the United Church Victor Home in Toronto validates this as well:

> Mrs. Doering reported concerning the critical situation developing in the Home owing to the fact that the Children's Aid Society is no longer able to find foster homes for newborn children one baby is still waiting for placement at the age of five months. Mrs. Doering reports that during recent conversations with Children's Aid Workers she has been advised by them no longer to counsel a girl that the unselfish thing for her to do is place her child in a suitable home as the Society can no longer assure placement. (UCA, *Correspondence*, 7 June 1965, 2)

However, Mrs. Doering and the overwhelming majority of social workers and maternity home matrons did not tell unmarried mothers that there would likely be no homes for their babies, nor did they stop telling unmarried mothers that surrendering their babies for adoption would be unselfish. Instead, as shown in earlier chapters, maternity homes continued to renovate and increase their capacities and Children's Aid Societies continued to hire and grow based on the number of children in care. Although the problem of surplus infants had been flagged by social workers as early as 1963, adoptions from white unmarried mothers in Canada increased at even higher rates in the latter half of the 1960s (See Table 1).

A review of newspaper and other articles during this period reveals information about the babies of unmarried mothers languishing in hospitals, receiving homes, foster homes, and other locations due to the lack of adoptive homes. Meanwhile, social workers were telling mothers that their children would languish in these types of institutions if they *did not* sign consents as soon as possible after birth. A 1963 article the *Winnipeg Free Press* in 1963 illustrates that babies were often held in hospital as long as 50 days: "But babies don't often leave the hospital after 14 days if they are born to unwed mothers. This is because there are not enough foster homes available and more children available than there are people here who wish to adopt them. Brigadier Everett explains 'some of the babies we have here now have been in hospital as long as 50 days'" (31 August, 1963, 1).

In this chapter, we saw how the ideology of maternalism, which reemerged after WWII in Canada, was another major factor contributing to the "perfect storm," which was the adoption mandate—a period when heteronormativity and nuclear families were powerful constructs, and good womanhood and motherhood were increasingly entrenched as raced and gendered.

The sheer number of babies taken for adoption—or the "phenomenon of mass surrender" from unmarried mothers—was identified and quantified, mostly through government reports. My estimate of 350,000 babies is conservative. However, not only does this number illustrate the vast number of babies adopted from unmarried mothers during the mandate, it also speaks to the systemic and institutionalized systems at play in the separation of the white unmarried mother and her baby—a phenomenon that continued even after a surplus of babies for adoption had been identified by social workers in the early 1960s.

Conclusion

"Friends, as the time for birth came, these babies would be snatched away before they had even held them in their arms ... sometimes consent was achieved by forgery or fraud. Sometimes women signed adoption papers whilst under the influence of medication. Most common of all was the bullying arrogance of a society that presumed to know what was best ... the hurt did not simply last for a few days or weeks. This was a wound that would not heal ... you were not legally or socially acknowledged as mothers and you yourselves were deprived of care. You were forced to endure the coercion and brutality of practices that were unethical, dishonest and, in many cases, illegal."—Commonwealth of Australia. Gillard, J., Prime Minister, National Apology for Forced Adoptions, Canberra, Australia, 21 March 2013)

The overriding purpose of this work was to define, substantiate, and uncover evidence of the postwar adoption mandate as a social prescription for white unmarried mothers in Canada, and to quantify the associated phenomenon of mass infant adoption. This work is critical to the feminist pursuit of foregrounding subjugated knowledges, as it uncovers a hidden history for women in Canada. Without this research, the adoption mandate in Canada and related phenomenon of mass surrender would remain a secreted knowledge that continues to subjugate the women impacted, insofar as they are often portrayed as free agents who actively relinquished their children to adoption.

Contrary to a dominant discourse that centres choice for these mothers, I have argued, and the research indicates, that the vast majority of white unmarried mothers in Canada, particularly those who resided in maternity homes, had negligable if any choice in the surrender of their newborn infants for adoption in the immediate postwar decades. In addition, the research shows that those mothers who assert that they actively chose adoption would also have been impacted by the prevailing unmarried mother characterizations and adoption policies and practices of the period. The phenomenon of mass surrender, over 350,000 babies surrendered for adoption in the postwar decades, is one that has not previously been quantified. The mandate was a formidable force, particularly as it affected mostly young, isolated, and marginalized women.

This study explored key historical, social, and political elements that converged, informed, and led to the adoption mandate, to demonstrate that mass infant adoption was the result. It sought to illustrate the ways in which adoption can operate or effectively function as a form of violence against women and the maternal body. Through the use of primary and secondary sources, I have attempted to identify and contextualize the factors that coalesced into a "perfect storm" to produce a unique set of institutional forces at a particular historical moment.

Despite the fact that the adoption mandate operated mostly post-WWII—a period when the social emphasis for women was the mother imperative—the roots of the mandate were in Magdalenism, a religious theory broadly based on the redemption of Mary Magdalene. Without the previously embedded set of social ideals that supported the separation, incarceration, and rehabilitation of unmarried mothers, it may not have been possible for the mandate to succeed in mainstream twentieth-century Canada. Canada's Magdalen Laundries and other similar institutions provided not only the moral framework but the foundation of practices through daily schedules, rehabilitative structures of penance, religious instruction, and domestic work that facilitated the mandate in Canada over 100 years later in those "charged sites" (Kunzel 8) that were Canada's maternity homes. The most comprehensive list of maternity homes in Canada thus far, together with many images of the mostly Victorian-type homes, illustrates the enormity of the practice nationwide.

Through an examination of the evolution of the major re-characterizations of white unmarried mothers during the twentieth century up to 1970—first as a threat to communities, then as feeble-minded, and later as sex delinquent—the white unmarried mother emerges in postwar Canada defined by psychoanalytic theory as a pathological subject in need of a cure. With each new characterization, corresponding prescriptions were imposed on these subjects ranging from "redemptive maternity" to the "clean break." These prescriptions exemplify how unmarried mother characterizations and social prescriptions worked interdependently to regulate and subjugate the bodies and offspring of these mothers. In other words, the white unmarried mother was subject to various cures depending on the distinct and popular portrayal of her character as such a woman at the time.

The profession of social work, which currently promotes itself as an anti-oppressive body (Baines) was the antithesis of anti-oppression when—entrenched in its own doctrine while attempting to legitimize the social work profession within the emerging social science community—its members, even when they knew that adoption and clean break would affect these women for the rest of their lives, ignored this fact—and continued to threaten, lie, trick, pressure, force, coerce, and counsel unmarried mothers to surrender their babies as the unselfish and realistic choice—even after a surplus of babies was identified in the mid-1960s. The adoption policy and practices introduced by social workers and implemented in collusion with maternity home matrons and the medical community caused trauma and violence against women in Canadian hospitals—a trauma and material loss from which most never recovered.

Race and gender were integral to the mandate. Corresponding social prescriptions emanating from distinctive characterizations of white, Black, and Indigenous women emerged. Racism resulted in lack of services for Black women, which, in this instance, led to many Black mothers keeping their babies or having them raised through othermothering practices within the community. The loss of Indigenous children to non-Indigenous adopters was in the context of cultural genocide. However, the white mother, even the unmarried one, retained cultural capital. It was the innate value in her whiteness that made her a candidate for rehabilitation for normative womanhood and motherhood. Through the relinquishment of her child, and the secret, she was made whole and marketable once again for marriage and legitimate motherhood in keeping with the ideals of "good" Canadian motherhood.

Empirical data gleaned from maternity home annual reports, provincial government reports, and other resources estimates the number of babies of white unmarried mothers surrendered for adoption in Canada post WWII at approximately 350,000. The fact that approximately 98% of unmarried mothers today choose to mother their children as opposed to 5% of mothers in postwar maternity homes forces us to reflect on what mothers of the mandate might have chosen, given choice. All of the factors leading up to and contributing to the mandate did, indeed, create a unique locus in time.

Mother Activism

The timeliness of this work is crucial, since many of the women impacted are now in their 60s, 70s and 80s. Canadian mothers and adult adoptees lobby for adoption reform and for church and government inquiries into the illegal and unethical practices, as well as human rights abuses, in adoption policy and practice during the adoption mandate. Spearheading this activism in Canada is Origins Canada, a federal non-profit organization supporting those separated by adoption. Mothers, adoptees and families are telling their secrets and governments and churches are beginning to listen ("Unwed Mothers"; Galloway; Andrews, "Inquiry"). Several years of lobbying efforts and MP meetings included a meeting organized by Origins Canada in May 2016 titled "Adoption Policies and Practices in Non-Indigenous and Indigenous Contexts." This meeting, held on Parliament Hill, was attended by over fifty Members of Parliament and Senators along with representatives from the Prime Minister's Office. Success for these efforts came in December 2017, when the Senate Social Affairs Committee adopted a motion to study these issues.

The senate study sought by Origins Canada was modelled on the inquiry that was held in Australia. The Australian *Senate Inquiry into Forced Adoptions*[176] resulted in several recommendations, including a national apology to those separated by adoption, which was given by

176 See The Commonwealth of Australia, Senate Committee Report, Community Affairs Reference Committee, Commonwealth Contribution to Former Forced Adoption policies and practices, February 2012.

then Prime Minister Julia Gillard[177] in 2013. The Australian Inquiry also resulted in apologies from Australian state governments[178] and various Australian churches and hospitals[179]—including the Sisters of the Good Shepherd,[180] Sisters of Mercy, Perth (Emerson) The Roman Catholic Church (Malkin), the Uniting Church (Rosenbaum), The Salvation Army,[181] the Australian Nursing Federation, Victoria Branch, Benevolent Society, Royal Hospital for Women, Brisbane, St. Anne's Hospital, Perth, Catholic Health Australia. All of these groups apologized for their role in the policy of forced adoptions and the impact those policies had on the lives of those affected.

In March of 2018, the Standing Senate Committee on Social Affairs, Science and Technology (SSCSAST) in Canada heard the testimony of witnesses in a series of hearings over three days. The Senate Report was released on 19 July, 2018 and was titled "The Shame Is Ours: Forced Adoptions of the Babies of Unmarried Mothers in Post-war Canada." Recommendations in Canada's senate report echo those of the Australia; they call for a national apology to those impacted; to develop training programs for professional counsellors and counselling to those impacted at no cost; and to develop a consensus position regarding

---

177 On 21 March 2013, Prime Minister Julia Gillard apologized on behalf of the Australian Government to people affected by forced adoption or removal policies and practices. The national apology was delivered in the Great Hall of Parliament House, Canberra, Australia (Commonwealth of Australia).

178 Australian states are similar to Canada's provinces. All six Australian states apologized for forced adoptions, including New South Wales (NSW), September 2012, Western Australia (WA), South Australia (SA), June 2012, Victoria (VIC), October 2012, Queensland (QLD), November 2012, and Tasmania (TAS), October 2012.

179 See Rosenbaum, A, 24 January 2012, Hospitals Sorry for forced adoptions, in which the Royal Women's Hospital apologizes for their role in forced adoptions. The Age, Victoria, Australia. See also apologies of St. Anne's Hospital, Perth, Royal Brisbane Hospital, Catholic Health Australia, and the Australian Nursing Federation.

180 See Sisters of the Good Shepherd Australia. Upon the 150th birthday of the Good Shepherd Sisters in Australia, Sister Anne Manning, province Leader of Australia and New Zealand stated that "girls and women were placed with Good Shepherd through various sources: courts, government agencies, child welfare organizations, parents or guardians. Some stayed for very short periods of time and others for longer. In relatively few cases, women chose to remain for many years ... we acknowledge, however, that for numbers of women, memories of their time with Good Shepherd are painful. We are deeply sorry for acts of verbal or physical cruelty that occurred: such things should never have taken place in a Good Shepherd facility. The understanding that we have been the cause of suffering is our deep regret as we look back over our history." (Catholic Religious Australia 1).

181 Salvation Army, Australia, September 19, 2012. The Salvation Army Apologises to People Affected by Forced Adoption. Communications and Public Relations Department, Sydney (Salvation Army, Australian Eastern Territory).

accessibility to adoption records that acknowledges a person's right to know their identity. Furthermore, it calls for religious organizations that operated maternity homes to accept responsibility and to acknowledge the harm that resulted from their actions, and for child welfare organizations to examine their roles in forced adoption practices with a view to issuing apologies. This report will now go to the Parliament of Canada, which has 150 sitting days to respond to the recommendations.

For the most part, churches continue to insist they had nothing to do with adoption but simply provided housing for those who needed it. A statement from the Salvation Army in the United States still defends maternity homes, and the Salvation Army in Canada also remains intransigent. In a brief submitted to the Senate Social Affairs Committee in March 2018, the Salvation Army states that "the Salvation Army regrets the prejudices and harsh attitudes of a society that led families friends and others to convince young mothers that they must place their children for adoption ... the Salvation Army has never supported the deliberate breaking of, or any attack on the bond between a mother and child." Although the Salvation Army in Canada and the United States continues to be uncompromising, the Salvation Army in Australia did apologize:

> The Salvation Army Australia Eastern Territory ... would like to offer its most sincere apology to the many mothers, fathers, and babies who are now adults, for the role we played in the policy of forced adoptions in the past and the continuing impact this policy may have had in the lives of those affected. We are aware forced adoption practices did occur previously in homes and hospitals operated by the Salvation Army. (Salvation Army, Australia Eastern Territory, 19 September, 2012)

Adoption activists have met with the Catholic, Anglican, and Presbyterian churches in Canada, and although these churches were invited to speak at the Senate Hearings on this topic in March 2018, they did not appear, nor did they provide a brief. The Catholic Church and Church of England have apologized for these events in the United Kingdom and Australia. The Catholic Church in the United Kingdom apologized to those impacted following the airing of a documentary on BBC titled *Britain's Adoption Scandal: Breaking the Silence*, which related the accounts of women impacted by the adoption mandate there

(Sherwood). However, the Catholic and Anglican churches in Canada remain silent. On his recent visit to Ireland, Pope Francis met with Paul Redmond[182] and other adoption activists and expressed concern about the Magdalen Laundries and Mother Baby Homes in that country and assured mothers that seeking their lost children was not a mortal sin, as they had been told.

The response of the majority of mainstream Canadian churches is in contrast to that of the United Church of Canada, which has worked with the mothers and adoptees impacted. The United Church of Canada invested in a study to uncover its role in past forced adoption practices, formed an "Adoption Task Group," created a liturgy of remorse, and attended the Senate Hearings, where they offered the following statement: "we believe that forced or coerced adoption is unethical... we sincerely regret the role the church has played in unethical adoption" (The United Church of Canada, Rev. D. Hayward, 3).

Adoption and Feminism

This research is original in scope and contributes to the wider discipline of critical adoption studies as an emerging body of work within women's studies, law, history, social work, and psychology. Adoption as a form of violence against women and gender injustice remains mostly unchallenged by feminist scholars, and in fact, mothers are often criticized. For example, within a critical analysis of the writings of mothers of the mandate Barbara Melosh critiques the term "lost to adoption", a term used by many mothers of the mandate to describe the loss of their babies to an institutionalized power system:

> Most portray themselves as powerless victims of circum-stance, pressured by parents and social workers, brain-washed by the rhetoric of the best solution...some birth mothers describe their relinquished children as "lost" to adoption as if they had unaccountably wandered off—a choice of words that obscures the actual scene of relinquishment, in which birth mothers themselves sign papers to execute their voluntary termination of parental rights. (256)

---

182 See Redmond, Paul. *The Adoption Machine: Dark History of Ireland's Mother and Baby Homes.*

Although feminists approach critical adoption studies from various perspectives and competing narratives are acknowledged, some writings limit the interpretation of the postwar unwed mother as either essentialist or as a consequence of the social construction of gender or maternity (Strong-Boag, *Finding* 228). This is problematic since these types of categorizations serve to dismiss the lived experience of these mothers. Furthermore, due to the secrecy and shame entwined in past adoption practice and the systemic silencing of those impacted, a culture of appropriation of adoption narratives has flourished for the past eighty years. This has led to unevenness in voices represented in modern adoption discourse. The categorization and reframing of the lived experience of the postwar unwed mother by others is an appropriation of knowledge and creates an environmental discourse within which those women are re-victimized and re-silenced.

One of the tenets of feminist scholarship is to forefront and to validate the lived experiences of women, and to unearth subjugated knowledges (Hesse-Biber, 3). As suggested, feminist theoretical debates and literature in critical adoption studies is an emerging field. There is much work yet to be done in the area of feminism and adoption. As Twila Perry points out, "the subject of adoption has received little attention from feminists in general, but there are many reasons why this important subject requires further exploration" (102). This research uncovers a history and knowledge that will hopefully add to and further the discussion of adoption within feminism and also contribute to the development of critical adoption studies as a field of study within academic feminism in Canada.

Epilogue

This work is not meant to imply that there are no positive adoption outcomes or that there are no mothers who implicitly state that they actively relinquished their babies in postwar Canada. However, when one considers the powerful processes at play during the mandate it is clear that the majority of the 350,000 unmarried mothers that surrendered their babies for adoption in postwar Canada made no informed decision or choice for adoption. Many women are still held in the grip of the powerful messages with which they were indoctrinated; they believe they gave a gift, or they were unselfish, or they made the realistic choice, or that it was "God's will." Some mothers cling to these adoption myths as a way to cope with the trauma. I know I did. These dominant narratives—impressed so forcefully upon a young girl or woman, compounded by the power of the shame, and the secret they were groomed to keep, and might have kept for fifty years or more—still prevent many mothers from telling, or from pursuing or accepting reunion.

The Universal Declaration of Human Rights of 1948 states that "Motherhood and childhood are entitled to special care and assistance," but that did not apply to the unmarried mother and her baby in postwar Canada (UN, Article 25, 2). Notwithstanding the realities of sole parenthood that these mothers may have faced, the fact remains that the majority of these women and girls were not only victims of violence, but also of illegal and unethical adoption policies and practices, and human rights abuses that were so *at the time*, and not simply through the retrospective lens of today. These mothers now in their senior years, and their adult children, are entitled to the special care and assistance they were denied so many years ago.

Works Cited

"400 Homes Found Outside Canada for Children, Catholic CAS Says." *Globe and Mail*, 28 Feb. 1968.

Alberta. An Act to Amend the Sexual Sterilization Act. *Statutes of the Province of Alberta*, 1937, http://www.ourfutureourpast.ca/law/page.aspx?id=2968369. Accessed 25 Oct.2018.

Alberta. Department of Public Welfare. *Eighth Annual Report of the Department of Public Welfare, 1951-1952*. Edmonton, 1952.

Alberta. Department of Public Welfare. *Tenth Annual Report of the Department of Public Welfare*. Edmonton, 1954.

Alberta. Department of Public Welfare. *Twelfth Annual Report of the Department of Public Welfare, 1955-1956*. Edmonton, 1956.

Alberta. Department of Public Welfare. *Thirteenth Annual Report of the Department of Public Welfare, 1956-1957*. Edmonton, 1957.

Alberta. Department of Public Welfare. *Fourteenth Annual Report of the Department of Public Welfare, 1957-1958*. Edmonton, 1958.

Alberta. Department of Public Welfare. *Fifteenth Annual Report of the Department of Public Welfare, 1958-1959*. Edmonton, 1959.

Alberta. Department of Public Welfare. *Sixteenth Annual Report of the Department of Public Welfare, 1959-1960*. Edmonton, 1960.

Alberta. Department of Public Welfare. *Seventeenth Annual Report of the Department of Public Welfare, 1960-1961*. Edmonton, 1961.

Alberta. Department of Public Welfare. *Eighteenth Annual Report of the Department of Public Welfare, 1961-1962*. Edmonton, 1962.

Alberta. Department of Public Welfare. *Nineteenth Annual Report of the Department of Public Welfare, 1962-1963*. Edmonton, 1963.

Alberta. Department of Public Welfare. *Twentieth Annual Report of the Department of Public Welfare, 1963-1964*. Edmonton, 1964.

Alberta. Department of Public Welfare. *Twenty-First Annual Report of the Department of Public Welfare, 1964-1965*. Edmonton, 1965.

Alberta. Department of Public Welfare. *Twenty-Second Annual Report of the Department of Public Welfare, 1965-1966*. Edmonton, 1966.

Alberta. Department of Public Welfare. *Twenty-Third Annual Report of the Department of Public Welfare, 1966-1967*. Edmonton, 1967.

Alberta. Department of Public Welfare. *Twenty-Fourth Annual Report of the Department of Public Welfare, 1967-1968.* Edmonton, 1968.

Alberta. Department of Public Welfare. *Twenty-Fifth Annual Report of the Department of Public Welfare, 1968-1969.* Edmonton, 1969.

Alberta. Department of Social Development. *1st Annual Report of the Department of Social Development 69-70.* Edmonton, 1970.

Alberta. Department of Social Development. *Annual Report 1970-1971.* Edmonton, 1971.

Alberta. Department of Health and Social Development. *Annual Report 1971-1972.* Edmonton, 1972.

Alberta. Department of Health and Social Development. *Annual Report 1972-1973.* Edmonton, 1973.

Alberta. Department of Health and Social Development. *Annual Report 1973-1974.* Edmonton, 1974.

Alberta. Department of Health and Social Development. *Annual Report 1974-1975.* Edmonton, 1975.

Alberta. Department of Health and Social Development. *Annual Report 1975-1976.* Edmonton, 1976.

Alberta. Department of Health and Social Development. *Annual Report 1976-1977.* Edmonton, 1977.

Alberta. Department of Health and Social Development. *Annual Report 1977-1978.* Edmonton, 1978.

Alberta College of Social Workers. *Alberta College of Social Workers,* http://www.acsw.ab.ca/site/about?nav=sidebar. Accessed 25 Oct. 2018.

Allen, Richard. *The Social Passion: Religion and Social Reform in Canada 1914-1928.* University of Toronto Press, 1973.

Alexander, Ruth M. *The "Girl Problem", Female Sexual Delinquency in New York 1900-1930.* Cornell University Press, 1995.

Alton, Mary Anne, dir. *The 40 Year Secret.* Prod. Deborah Parks, Narr. Sarah Polley, Dundas Productions Inc., 2009, DVD.

Alward, Sharon, dir. *Exiled Mothers.* 2015, DVD.

Andrews, Valerie J. "#Flip the Script on Teen Mothers." *Mothers, Mothering, Motherhood in 21st Century: Culture, Society, Literature, and the Arts.* Motherhood Initiative for Research and Community Involvement (MIRCI) Conf., 21-23 October 2015, Heaslip House, Ryerson University, Toronto.

Andrews, Valerie J. "Inquiry into Postwar 'Baby Scoop Era' Can Start Healing Process." *Toronto Star,* 24 May 2016: A11.

Andrews, Valerie J. "Modern Domestic Adoption." *Adoption Experience,* Origins Canada Conf., 19-20 October 2012. Hilton Garden Inn, Toronto.

Andrews, Valerie J. "Motherhood Denied: Canada's Maternity Homes." *Mothers, Mothering, Motherhood in Today's World: Gala Conference Celebrating MIRCI's 20th Anniversary.*

Motherhood Initiative for Research and Community Involvement (MIRCI) Conf., 14-16 October 2016, Pantages Hotel, Toronto.

Andrews, Valerie J. "Sales and Marketing in Modern Domestic Adoption." *Sleeping Giants in Adoption: Power, Privilege, Politics and Class,* 8th Biennial Adoption Initiative Conf., 19-21 May 2014. St. John's University, New York.

Anglican Church of Canada, Diocese of Toronto. *Anglican Social Services: What They Are, How You Can Help.* Pamphlet. General Synod Archives. M82-15 Diocesan Publications Collection. Series 530: Diocese of Toronto, Diocesan Publications. File 8, Diocesan Council for Social Service, 1946-1956.

Anglican Church of Canada. *Annual Report of the Humewood House Association, 1955.* General Synod Archives. M82-15 Diocesan Publications Collection. Series 530: Diocese of Toronto, Diocesan Publications. File 12. Humewood House Association, 1943-1956.

Anglican Church of Canada. *Humewood House, Anglican Home for Unmarried Mothers.* Pamphlet. General Synod Archives. M82-15 Diocesan Publications Collection. Series 530: Diocese of Toronto, Diocesan Publications. File 12, Humewood House Association, 1943-1956.

Anglican Church of Canada. *Humewood House, 1912-1962.* Pamphlet. 1962. General Synod Archives. M82-15 Diocesan Publication Collection. Series 530: Diocese of Toronto, Diocesan Publications. File 12. Humewood House Association, 1943-1956.

Anglican Church of Canada. *Annual Report of the Humewood House Association, 1946.* General Synod Archives. M82-15 Diocesan Publications Collection. Series 530: Diocese of Toronto, Diocesan Publications. File 12. Humewood House Association, 1943-1956.

Anglican Church of Canada. *Humewood House Association. Information Sheet* [195?]. M82-15 Diocesan Publications Collection. Series 530: Diocese of Toronto, Diocesan Publications. File 12. Humewood House Association, 1943-1956.

Anglican Church of Canada. *Humewood House Association Report, 1967.* General Synod Archives. M82-15 Diocesan Publications Collection. Series 530: Diocese of Toronto, Diocesan Publications. File 12. Humewood House Association, 1943-1956.

Anglican Church of Canada. *Out of Wedlock.* CSS Bulletin No. 193, 1965. Proceedings of Conference of Superintendents and Boards of Directors of Homes for Unmarried Mothers. Arranged by United and Anglican Churches at Toronto, ON. 12-13 November, 1965. General Synod Archives. GS75-106 Council for Social Service (CSS) Fonds. Marriage and Family Life Bulletins 1966-1968.

Anglican Church of Canada. *The One Parent Family.* Pamphlet. 1969. General Synod Archives. GS75-106 Council for Social Service (CSS) Fonds. Marriage and Family Life Bulletins 1966- 1968.

Anglican Church of Canada. "Trend." *The Canadian Churchman*, March 1969. General Synod Archives. Periodicals Collection.

Anglican Church of Canada. *Welfare Resources, 1951.* General Synod Archives. Series 530: Diocese of Toronto, Diocesan Publications. File 8, Diocesan Council for Social Service, 1946-1956.

Anglican Church of Canada. "Marion Hilliard House to Close its Doors." Photograph. *The Central Interior Link,* September 2002:8. Territory of the People Diocese. General Synod Archives.

Archives of Ontario. Department of Social and Family Services. Correspondence dated 17 June, 1970 from Victoria Leach to Betty Graham. File RG29-31-1-122, Box 50.

Archives of Ontario. Jacobson, S. "The Unmarried Mother: Notes Concerning some Psychological Factors of Importance to Caseworkers Summarized from Important Literature, Agency Records and Casework Practice." National Committee for Mental Hygiene Canada, 1947. RG10-30-1-6.07.

Archives of Ontario. Maternity Homes Association of Ontario. Correspondence dated 9 March, 1974 from Mrs. A.C. Gerrard, Secretary Treasurer of the Maternity Homes Association of Ontario to the Honourable R. Brunelle, Ministry of Community and Social Services, with Attachment of Briefs Submitted by Ontario Maternity Homes in Preparation for a Delegation to the Minister on Wednesday, 13 March 1974. RG29-1, Box 50.

Archives of Ontario. Guardianship and Adoption Records, Research Guide 223, November 2013, http://www.archives.gov.on.ca/en/access/documents/research_guide_223_guardianship_ and_adoption.pdf. Accessed 25 Oct. 2018.

Archives of Ontario. Industrial House of Refuge. Rules and Regulations of the Industrial House of Refuge for Females, [Toronto Magdalen Laundry], Toronto, 1855. CHIM 1549.

Archives of Ontario. Juvenile and Family Court Judges Association. Papers, Speeches 1961-1966. F819, MU 5090, Box 19.

Archives of Ontario. The Canadian Welfare Council. "New Trends in Adoption Planning, 1954." RG 29-31.

Archives of Ontario. The Canadian Welfare Council. "Report of the Committee on Services to Unmarried Parents." December, 1955. RG 29-31.

Archives of Ontario. The Toronto Magdalene Asylum. Report of the First Annual Meeting of the Toronto Magdalene Asylum, 20 March, 1854. CIHM 1549, 1854.

Archives of Ontario. The Toronto Magdalene Asylum. Twenty-Second Annual Report. The Toronto Magdalene Asylum: Industrial House of Refuge, January 1877, Toronto, CIHM 01277.

Anzaldúa, Gloria E. *Borderlands/La Frontera: The New Mestiza.* Aunt Lute Books, 1987.

Archbishop John Joseph Lynch, C.M, http://www.archtoronto.org/archives/bishops. Accessed 25 Oct. 2018.

Armagh. *Annual Report 1957.* The Presbyterian Church in Canada Archives.

Armagh. *Annual Report 1958.* The Presbyterian Church in Canada Archives.

Armagh. *Annual Report 1959.* The Presbyterian Church in Canada Archives.

Armagh. *Annual Report 1960.* The Presbyterian Church in Canada Archives.

Armagh. *Annual Report 1961.* The Presbyterian Church in Canada Archives.

Armagh. *Annual Report 1962.* The Presbyterian Church in Canada Archives.

Armagh. *Annual Report 1963.* The Presbyterian Church in Canada Archives.

Armagh. *Annual Report 1966.* The Presbyterian Church in Canada Archives.

Armagh. *Annual Report 1970.* The Presbyterian Church in Canada Archives.

Armagh. *Annual Report 1971.* The Presbyterian Church in Canada Archives.

Armagh. The Presbyterian Church in Canada Archives. May 1969, Newsletter.

Armagh. Report of Director Gwen Davenport, 1961. The Presbyterian Church in Canada Archives.

Armagh. *Residents in Maternity Home.* Series 1259-FC. The Presbyterian Church in Canada Archives. Photographs.

Armagh. Miss Mohan Report to Armagh Board on Maternity Home Study. The Presbyterian Church in Canada Archives.

Askwith, K. G. "Illegitimacy and Research." *Ontario Association of Children's Aid Societies,* vol. 13, no. 1, 1970, pp. 9-13.

Askren, Holly Ann and Kathaleen C. Bloom. "Post-adoptive Reactions of the Relinquishing Mother. A Review." *Journal of Obstetric, Gynecological and Neonatal Nursing,* vol. 28, no. 4, July 1999, pp. 395-400.

"Babies for Export." Editorial. *Globe and Mail,* 3 October 1967.

Backhouse, Constance. *Petticoats and Prejudice: Women and Law in Nineteenth- Century Canada.* Women's Press, 1991.

Baines, Donna, ed. *Doing Anti-Oppressive Practice: Social Justice Social Work.* 2nd ed. Fernwood Publishing, 2011.

Balcom, Karen A. *The Traffic in Babies: Cross Border Adoption and Baby-Selling between the United States and Canada 1930-1972.* University of Toronto Press, 2011.

Barnhill, Gretchen H. "Fallen Angels: Female Wrongdoing in Victorian Novels." Master of Arts Thesis. University of Lethbridge, 2005.

Begg, Dorothy R. "Psychiatric Problems of Unmarried Mothers." Master of Social Work Thesis. McGill University, 1951.

Bernard, Wanda Thomas, and Claudine Bonner. "Kinship and Community Care in African Nova Scotian Communities." *Journal of the Motherhood Initiative,* vol. 4, no. 1, 2013, pp. 155-167.

Bernstein, Rose. "Are We Still Stereotyping the Unmarried Mother?" *Social Work,* vol. 5, 1960, p.117.

Bernstein, Rose. "Are We Still Stereotyping the Unmarried Mother?" *The Unwed Mother,* edited by Robert W. Roberts, Harper & Row, 1966, pp. 105-117.

Black, Debra. "Immigration Laws Welcome Many, But Not Everyone." *Toronto Star*, 16 February 2013: GT1.

"Blame Movie Morality for Unwed Mothers." *Toronto Daily Star,* 6 April 1964: 40.

Blanchfield, Mike. "Landmark Supreme Court Ruling Extends Rights to 600,000 Métis, 'Non-status' Indians." *National Post*, 14 April 2016.

Blanton, T. & Deschner, J. "Biological Mother's Grief: The Postadoptive Experience in Open Versus Confidential Adoption." *Child Welfare*, vol. 69, 1990, pp. 525-535.

Bowlby, John. "Maternal Care and Mental Health." *Bulletin of the World Health Organization*, no. 3, 1951.

Boyd, Susan B., et al. *Anonymous Motherhood? A Socio-Legal Study of Choice and Constraint.* University of Toronto Press, 2015.

Braydon, Kâté. Photograph. Evangeline Home. In Cunningham, April. "A Daughter's Search Reaches Into a Darker Past." *The Telegraph Journal*, 3 February 2014: C1.

Briggs, Laura. *Somebody's Children: The Politics of Transracial and Transnational Adoption.* Duke University Press, 2012.

British Columbia. Department of Health Services and Hospital Insurance. *Vital Statistics of the Province of British Columbia, Eighty-Ninth Report for the Year 1960.* Victoria, 1960.

British Columbia. Department of Health Services and Hospital Insurance. *Vital Statistics of the Province of British Columbia, Ninetieth Report for the Year 1961.* Victoria, 1961.

British Columbia. Department of Health Services and Hospital Insurance. *Vital Statistics of the Province of British Columbia, Ninety-Fourth Report for the Year 1965.* Victoria, 1965.

British Columbia. Department of Health Services and Hospital Insurance. *Vital Statistics of the Province of British Columbia, Ninety-Fifth Report for the Year 1966.* Victoria, 1966.

British Columbia. Department of Health Services and Hospital Insurance. *Vital Statistics of the Province of British Columbia, Ninety-Sixth Report for the Year 1967.* Victoria, 1967.

British Columbia. Department of Health Services and Hospital Insurance. *Vital Statistics of the Province of British Columbia, Ninety-Seventh Report for the Year 1968.* Victoria, 1968.

British Columbia. Department of Health and Welfare. Social Welfare Branch. *Annual Report of the Social Welfare Branch of the Department of Health and Welfare for the Year Ended March 31st, 1948.* Legislative Assembly, Victoria, 1948.

British Columbia. Department of Health and Welfare. Social Welfare Branch. *Annual Report of the Social Welfare Branch of the Department of Health and Welfare for the Year Ended March 31st, 1951.* Victoria, 1951.

British Columbia. Department of Health and Welfare. Social Welfare Branch. *Annual Report of Social Welfare Branch of the Department of Health and Welfare for the Year Ended March 31st, 1958.* Victoria, 1958.

British Columbia. Department of Social Welfare. *Annual Report of the Department of Social Welfare for the Year Ended March 31, 1959.* Victoria, 1959.

British Columbia. Department of Social Welfare. *Annual Report of the Department of Social Welfare for the Year Ended March 31, 1960.* Victoria, 1960.

British Columbia. Department of Social Welfare. *Annual Report for the Year Ended March 31, 1961.* Victoria, 1961.

British Columbia. Department of Social Welfare. *Annual Report for the Year Ended March 31, 1962.* Victoria, 1962.

British Columbia. Department of Social Welfare. *Annual Report for the Year Ended March 31, 1963.* Victoria, 1963.

British Columbia. Department of Social Welfare. *Annual Report for the Year Ended March 31, 1964.* Victoria, 1964.

British Columbia. Department of Social Welfare. *Annual Report for the Year Ended March 31, 1965.* Victoria, 1965.

British Columbia. Department of Social Welfare. *Annual Report for the Year Ended March 31, 1966.* Victoria, 1966.

British Columbia. Department of Social Welfare. *Annual Report for the Year Ended March 31, 1967.* Victoria, 1967.

British Columbia. Department of Social Welfare. *Annual Report for the Year Ended March 31, 1968.* Victoria, 1968.

British Columbia. Department of Social Welfare. *Annual Report for the Year Ended March 31, 1969.* Victoria, 1969.

British Columbia. Department of Social Welfare. *Annual Report of the Department of Social Welfare for the Year Ended March 3, 1971.* Victoria, 1971.

British Columbia. Department of the Provincial Secretary. *Annual Report of the Welfare Field Service for the Fiscal Year 1938-39.* Victoria, 1939.

British Columbia. Department of the Provincial Secretary. *Annual Report of the Superintendent of Neglected Children for the Year Ended March 31st, 1942.* Victoria, 1942.

British Columbia. Department of the Provincial Secretary. The Social Assistance Branch. *Annual Report of the Department of the Provincial Secretary for the Year Ended March 31, 1945.* Victoria, 1945.

British Columbia. Department of the Provincial Secretary. The Social Assistance Branch. *Annual Report of the Social Assistance Branch of the Department of the Provincial Secretary for the Year Ended March 31st, 1945.* Victoria, 1945.

British Columbia. Provincial Board of Health. *Sixty-Seventh Report of Vital Statistics for the Province of British Columbia for the year 1938.* Victoria, 1938.

British Columbia. Provincial Board of Health. *Sixty-Eighth Report of Vital Statistics for the Province of British Columbia for the Year 1939.* Victoria, 1939.

British Columbia College of Social Workers. *British Columbia College of Social Workers,* www.bccollegeofsocialworkers.ca/about-us/history/. Accessed 25 Oct. 2018.

Brock, Margaret. "A Hospital's Adoption Policy." *Canadian Welfare,* 1957, pp. 126-129.

Budin, Pierre. *The Nursling.* Caxton Publishing, 1907.

Cahill, Betty. *Butterbox Babies.* McClelland-Bantam Inc., 1992.

Campbell, Lara. "'Respectable Citizens of Canada': Gender, Maternalism and the Welfare State in the Great Depression." *Maternalism Reconsidered: Motherhood, Welfare and Social Policy in the Twentieth Century* edited by Marian van der Klein et al, Berghahn Books, 2012, pp. 99-120.

Canada. Canada Assistance Plan. *Annual Report, Year Ended March 31,* 1969.

Canada. Department of Indigenous and Northern Affairs. *Indian Status,* https://www.aadnc-aandc.gc.ca/eng/1100100032463/1100100032464. Accessed 25 Oct. 2018.

Canada. Department of Justice. *Custody, Access and Child Support: Findings from the National Longitudinal Survey of Children and Youth.* Ottawa, 1999.

Canada. Senate of Canada. Standing Senate Committee on Social Affairs, Science and Technology. *The Shame Is Ours: Forced Adoptions of the Babies of Unmarried Mothers in Post-war Canada.* July 2018.

Canada. Statistics Canada. *Blacks in Canada: A Long History.* Canadian Social Trends, Milan, A., and K. Tran., Catalogue No. 11-008, 2004. https://sites.ualberta.ca/~jrkelly/blacksinCanada.pdf. Accessed 25 Oct. 2018.

Canada. Statistics Canada. *Chart A. The Baby Boom,* http://www.statcan.gc.ca/pub/75-001-x/2007108/c-g/4096851-eng.htm. Accessed 25 Oct. 2018.

Canada. Statistics Canada. *Life After Teenage Motherhood,* Ottawa, 2008.

Canada. Statistics Canada. *Live Births.* Series B1-1, Ottawa.

Canada. Statistics Canada. *Selected Marriage Statistics, 1921-1990.* Catalogue 82-552, Occasional. Ottawa, 1990.

Canada. Statistics Canada. *Year Book 1967.* Ottawa, 1967.

Canadian Association of Social Workers. *Oral History Project. Interview with Sister Mary Henry.* Mount St. Mary, Charlottetown, Prince Edward Island, February 10, 1984.

Canadian Association of Social Workers. "Services for Unmarried Mothers." *The Social Worker,* vol. II, no. 4, May 1943.

Canadian Association of Social Workers. "The Unmarried Mother in Manitoba: A Study Made by the Manitoba Branch of the Canadian Association of Social Workers, July 1937." *The Social Worker,* vol. 5, no. 9, 1937, pp. 2-7.

Canadian National Committee for Mental Hygiene. "Mental Hygiene Survey, Province of Saskatchewan." *Canadian Journal of Mental Hygiene,* vol. 3, no. 2, July 1921, pp. 315-399.

Carlson, Kathryn Blaze. "The Fathers Had No Say." *National Post,* 14 March 2012: A1

Carlson, Kathryn Blaze. "Women Coerced into Surrendering Babies Years Ago Find Support in Ottawa." *Globe and Mail,* 22 October 2013.

Carlson, Kathryn Blaze. "Your Baby Is Dead: Mothers Say Their Supposedly Stillborn Babies Were Stolen from Them." *National Post,* 24 March 2012: A1.

Carr, Mary Jo. "Birthmothers and Subsequent Children: The Role of Personality Traits and Attachment History." *Journal of Social Distress and the Homeless*, vol. 9, 2000, pp. 339-348.

Catholic Religious Australia. "Good Shepherd's 150 Years," 9 May 2013, http://www.catholicreligiousaustralia.org.au/index.php/news-a-views/news/item/1024-good-shepherd-s-150-years. Accessed 25 Oct. 2018.

Cattell, James P. "Psychodynamic and Clinical Observations in a Group of Unmarried Mothers." *American Journal of Psychiatry*, vol. 111, 1954, pp. 337-342.

CBC News. "Judge Rules in Favour of Indigenous Survivors of Sixties Scoop." 14 February 2017, http://www.cbc.ca/news/canada/60s-scoop-ruling-aboriginal-1.3981771. Accessed 25 Oct. 2018.

CBC News. "Manitoba Social Work Staff Escape Scrutiny Thanks to Loophole, Says College." 6 April 2015, http://www.cbc.ca/news/canada/manitoba/manitoba-social-work- staff-escape-scrutiny-thanks-to-loophole-says-college-1.3022672. Accessed 25 Oct. 2018.

CBC News. "Nova Scotia Again Urged to Open Adoption Records." 30 March 2015, http://www.cbc.ca/news/canada/nova-scotia/nova-scotia-again-urged-to-open-adoption- records-1.3015351. Accessed 25 Oct. 2018.

Chambers, Lori. *A Legal History of Adoption in Ontario, 1921-2015*. Osgoode Society for Canadian Legal History, University of Toronto Press, 2016.

Chambers, Lori. "Adoption, Unwed Mothers and the Powers of the Children's Aid Society in Ontario, 1921-1969." *Ontario History*, vol. 98, no. 2, 2006, p. 161.

Chambers, Lori. *Misconceptions: Unmarried Motherhood and the Ontario Children of Unmarried Parents Act 1921-1969*. University of Toronto Press, 2007.

Champagne, J. "Sisters Built First Hospitals: They Came From Afar to Meet Health Care Needs of Pioneers, Natives." *Western Catholic Reporter*, 5 September 2005.

Chodorow, Nancy. *The Reproduction of Mothering: Psychoanalysis and the Sociology of Gender*. University of California Press, 1978.

Claman, A. David et al. "Reaction of unmarried girls to Pregnancy." *Canadian Medical Association Journal*, vol. 101, 1969, pp. 328-334.

Clarke, Charles Kirk. "Juvenile Delinquency and Mental Defect." *Canadian Journal of Mental Hygiene*, vol. 3, no. 1, April, 1921. Clarke, Patricia. "Crisis in Adoptions." *United Church Observer*, 1 February 1966, pp. 12-15.

Clothier, Florence. "Psychological Implications of Unmarried Parenthood." *American Journal of Orthopsychiatry*, vol. 13, no. 3, 1943, pp. 531-549.

Collins, Patricia H. *Black Feminist Thought: Knowledge, Consciousness, and the Politics of Empowerment*. Routledge, 1990.

Comacchio, Cynthia R. *The Infinite Bonds of Family: Domesticity in Canada, 1850-1940*. University of Toronto Press, 1999.

Commonwealth of Australia. Department of Families, Housing, Community Services and Indigenous Affairs. *Impact of Past Adoption Practices: Summary of key issues from Australian research.* A Report to the Australian Government Department of Families, Housing, Community Services and Indigenous Affairs by the Australian Institute of Family Studies. Canberra, 2010.

Commonwealth of Australia. Department of Families, Housing, Community Services and Indigenous Affairs. *Past Adoption Experiences: National Research Study on the Service Response to Past Adoption Practices*, Research Report No. 21. Canberra, 2012.

Commonwealth of Australia. Parliament. Senate. Community Affairs Reference Committee. *Commonwealth Contribution to Former Forced Adoption Policies and Practices.* Canberra, 2012.

Commonwealth of Australia. Prime Minister Julia Gillard. *National Apology for Forced Adoptions*, 21 March 2013, Canberra https://www.ag.gov.au/About/ ForcedAdoptionsApology/Documents/Nationalapologyforf orcedadoptions.PDF. Accessed 25 Oct. 2018.

Crawford, Susan. "Public Attitudes in Canada toward Unmarried Mothers, 1950-1996." *Past Imperfect,* vol. 6, 1997, pp. 111-132.

Dalby, Diny. "Mother Needs to Know the Sacrifice She Makes." *Winnipeg Free Press*, 27 June 1966.

Daly, Kerry J., and Michael P. Sobol. "Adoption in Canada." *Statistics Canada, Canadian Social Trends,* no. 32, 1994, pp. 2-5.

Daniels, Phyllis D. *The Plan the Unmarried Mother Makes for Her Baby: A Study of the Psychological Factors in the Current Life Situation that Influence the Plan the Unmarried Mother Makes for Her Baby.* Master of Social Work Thesis. McGill University, 1960.

Demerson, Velma. *Incorrigible.* Wilfred Laurier University Press, 2004.

Deutsch, Helene. *The Psychology of Women A Psychoanalytic Interpretation: Volume Two Motherhood.* Grune & Stratton, 1945.

Dexter, Susan. "Maternity Home is Shield from Society." *Winnipeg Free Press,* 1 November 1963: 20.

Drew, L. R. H. "The Psychiatrist and the Unwed Mother." *International Journal of Social Psychiatry,* vol. 11, no. 2, 1965, pp. 123-130.

Dubinsky, Karen. *Babies Without Borders: Adoption and Migration across the Americas.* University of Toronto Press, 2010.

Duschinsky, Robert. "Tabula Rasa and Human Nature." *Philosophy,* vol. 87, no. 4, 2012, pp. 509-529.

Emerson, D. "Nuns Sorry for Forced Adoption." Australian newspaper.

"Fallen Women." Editorial. *The Ladies Repository,* vol. 4, no. 3, September 1869, pp. 219-222.

Farrar, Patricia D. "Abject Mothers: Women Separated from their Babies Lost to Adoption: Reading Kristeva" *Unbecoming Mothers: The Social Production of Maternal Absence* edited by Diana L. Gustafson, The Haworth Clinical Practice Press, 2005, pp. 51-72.

Ferenc, Leslie. "Turning Shame to Empowerment for 100 Years." *Toronto Star*, 10 April 2012: G2-56.

Fessler, Ann. *The Girls Who Went Away: The Hidden History of Women Who Surrendered Children for Adoption in the Decades Before Rose v. Wade.* Penguin Books, 2006.

Fingard, Judith, and Janet Guildford, eds. *Mothers of the Municipality: Women, Work and Social Policy in Post-1945 Halifax.* University of Toronto Press, 2005.

Finnegan, Frances. *Do Penance or Perish: Magdalen Asylums in Ireland.* Oxford University Press, 2001.

Fournier, Suzanne, and Ernie Crey. *Stolen from Our Embrace: The Abduction of First Nations Children and the Restoration of Aboriginal Communities.* Douglas & McIntyre, 1997.

Freundlich, Madelyn. *Adoption and Ethics: The Market Forces in Adoption.* Child Welfare League of America, 2000.

Friedlander, Walter A. *Concepts and Methods of Social Work.* 2nd ed. Prentice-Hall, 1976.

Galloway, Gloria. "Former 'Unwed Mothers' Renew Request for Public Inquiry into Forced Adoptions." *The Globe and Mail*, 18 May 2016: A1.

Glasbeek, Amanda. *Moral Regulation and Governance in Canada: History, Context, and Critical Issues.* Canadian Scholars' Press, 2006.

Glover, Craig/QMI Agency. Photograph. Bethesda Home. In Martin, Chip. "Bethesda Land on Selling Block." *London Free Press*, 11 October 2012.

Goldson, Jill. "Adoption in New Zealand: An International Perspective." *Adoption: Changing Families, Changing Times* edited by Anthony Douglas and Terry Philpot, Routledge, 2003, pp. 246-250.

Goodman, Annekathryn et al. "The Long-Term Effects of In Utero Exposures: The DES Story." *The New England Journal of Medicine*, vol 364, no. 22, 2011, pp. 2083-2084.

"Good Shepherd Home - Inmates Not Paid for Work in Laundry." *The Toronto Telegram*, 16 September 1927: 1, 3.

Gratton, Brian and Myron Gutmann. *Historical Statistics of the United States: Millennial Edition.* Cambridge University Press, 2006.

Griffith, Keith C. *The Right to Know Who You Are.* K.C Griffith and Kimball Publishers, 1991.

Gripton, James, and Allan Irving. "Social Work and Social Welfare Research in the Post-War Years 1945-1960." *Canadian Social Work Review/Revue canadienne de service social*, vol. 13, no. 2, 1996, pp. 205-220.

Guyatt, D. E. "Adoption in Ontario." *Journal Ontario Association of Children's Aid Societies*, vol. 10, no. 9, 1967, pp. 12-15.

Haraway, Donna. "Situated Knowledges: The Science Question in Feminism and the Privilege of Partial Perspective." *Feminist Studies*, vol. 14, no. 3, 1988, pp. 575-599.

Harlow, Harry F. "The Nature of Love." *American Psychologist*, No. 13, 1958, pp. 573-685.

"Harry F. Harlow, Monkey Love Experiments." *Adoption History Project*. University of Oregon, http://darkwing.uoregon.edu/~adoption/studies/HarlowMLE.htm. Accessed 25 Oct. 2018.

Harstock, Nancy. "The Feminist Standpoint: Developing the Ground for a Specifically Feminist Historical Materialism." *The Second Wave: A Reader in Feminist Theory*, edited by Linda Nicholson, Routledge, 1997, pp. 216-240.

Haslanger, Sally, and Charlotee Witt eds. *Adoption Matters: Philosophical and Feminist Essays*. Cornell University Press, 2005.

Heiman, Marcel, and Esther Levitt. "The Role of Separation and Depression in Out-of-Wedlock Pregnancy." *American Journal of Orthopsychiatry*, vol. 30, no. 1, 1960, pp. 166-174.

Hess, E.H. *Imprinting: Early Experience and the Developmental Psychobiology of Attachment*. Van Nostrand Reinhold Co., 1973.

Hesse-Biber, Sharlene, ed. *The Handbook of Feminist Research: Theory and Praxis*. 2nd ed. Sage Publications, 2012.

Hick, Steve. *Social Work in Canada: An Introduction*. 2nd ed. Thompson Educational Publishing, 2006.

Hilborn, Robin. "Adoption Crusader, Helen Allen dies at 99." Adoption News Central, Family Helper, 2006. http://www.familyhelper.net/news/061124Allen.html

Hill, Karen. Principal Investigator. Canadian Association of Social Workers Oral History Project. Interview with Sister Mary Henry, 10 February, 1984, Mount Saint Mary, Charlottetown, Prince Edward Island. Published by McMaster School of Social Work Leadership Archive, https://www.youtube.com/watch?v=rKyRh-z9PUs. Accessed 25 Oct. 2018.

Hooks, bell. *Feminist Theory: From Margin to Center*. South End Press, 1984.

Horstmann, H. *Consular Remembrances*. J. B. Lippincott Co., 1886.

Houlihan, Lindsey Grey. *Child Attachment at Adoption and Three Months*. Dissertation. Case Western Reserve University, 2010.

Howard, Frank. "Quebec Babies Adopted in France, U.S." *Globe and Mail*, 3 October 1967.

Howarth, Dorothy. "Mothers Not All Unhappy." *The Telegram*, 22 November 1956: 35.

Humewood House. "100 Stories—An Experience," http://www.humewoodhouse.com/2012/04/26/an-experience/. Accessed 25 Oct. 2018.

Indigenous and Northern Affairs Canada. *Indian Status*, http://www.aadnc-aandc.gc.ca/eng/1100100032374/1100100032378. Accessed 25 Oct. 2018.

Irving, Allan. "The Scientific Imperative in Canadian Social Work: Social Work and Social Welfare Research in Canada, 1897-1945." *Canadian Social Work Review/Revue canadienne de service social*, vol. 9, no. 1, 1992, pp. 9-27.

Isserman, Betty Kobayashi. "The Casework Relationship in work with Unmarried Mothers." *The Social Worker*, vol. 17, no. 1, 1948, pp. 12-17.

"Issues Writ Against Good Shepherd Home." *Toronto Daily Star*, 28 February 1919: 2.

Iwanek, Mary. "Healing History: The Story of Adoption in New Zealand." *Social Work Now*, no. 8, 1997, pp. 13-17.

Jarvie, Sandra. "Silenced, Denigrated and Rendered Invisible: Mothers Who Lost their Babies to Adoption in the 1960s and 1970s." *Home/Bodies: Geographies of Self, Place and Space* edited by Wendy Schissel, University of Calgary Press, 2006, pp. 69-82.

Jarvie, Sandra. Witness. Senate Standing Committee on Social Affairs, Science and Technology, Forced Adoption Hearings, 20 March 2018.

Jennissen, Therese, and Colleen Lundy. "Keeping Sight of Social Justice: 80 Years of Building CASW." *Canadian Association of Social Workers*, April 2006, 201, p. 1, http://www.casw-acts.ca/sites/default/files/attachements/CASW%20History.pdf. Accessed 25 Oct. 2018.

Johnson, Daniel and Edith Fein. "The Concept of Attachment: Applications to Adoption." *Children and Youth Services Review*, vol. 13, 1991, pp. 397-412.

Johnson, Brian D. "Joni's Secret: Mother and Child Reunion." *Maclean's Magazine*, 21 April 1997.

Johnston, Patrick. *Native Children and the Child Welfare System: The Canadian Council on Social Development*. James Lorimer Limited Publishers, 1983.

Jones, Lindsay. "Home of the Guardian Angel ends Adoption Program After 125 Years." *The Chronical Herald*, 12 June 2012.

Josie, Svanhuit. "Public Opinion of Social Work." *Social Worker*, vol. 15, no. 2, 1946, pp. 17-20.

Josie, Svanhuit. "The American Caricature of the Unmarried Mother." *Canadian Welfare*, vol. 29, no. 12, December 1955, pp. 246-249.

Karch-Ackerman, Michele. "Perspectives of Innocence: Foundling." The Clay and Glass Gallery, 28 March—6 June, 2010. Exhibition.

Kelly, Judy. *The Trauma of Relinquishment: The Long Term Impact on Birthmothers who Lost Their Infants to Adoption During the Years 1965-1972*. Master of Arts Thesis. Goddard College, 1999.

Khlentzos, Michael T., and Mary A. Pagliaro. "Observations from Psychotherapy with Unwed Mothers." *American Journal of Orthopsychiatry*, vol. 35, no. 4, 1965, pp. 779-786.

Kim, Peter. Photograph. 450 Pape Avenue, Toronto. In "Filming of Stephen King's Horror Classic 'It' Becoming a Nightmare for some Residents." 22 August 2016. Global News.

Retrieved from: http://globalnews.ca/news/2896739/filming-of-stephen-kings-horror-classic-it- becoming-nightmare-for-some-residents/

Kirkwood, Leone. "Unwed Who Gives Up Child May Mourn Lifetime, Group Told." *The Globe and Mail*, 11 May 1966: 11.

Kline, L. C. "Group Living for Unmarried Mothers." *Ontario Association of Children's Aid Societies*, vol. 10, no. 8, 1967, pp. 11-14.

Kronick, Jane C. "An Assessment of Research Knowledge Concerning the Unmarried Mother." *The Unwed Mother*, edited by Robert W. Roberts, Harper & Row, 1966, pp. 233-251.

Krueger, L. "Metro's Homes for Unwed Mothers Now Have Waiting Lists." *Toronto Star*, 7 June 1972: 77.

Kunzel, Regina. *Fallen Women, Problem Girls: Unmarried Mothers and the Professionalization of Social Work 1890-1945.* Yale University Press, 1993.

Lake, Bryony E.B. *Posttraumatic Stress Disorder in Natural Mothers.* Master of Arts Thesis. City University, 2009.

Landsberg, Michele. "Are We Failing the Unwed Mother." United Church Observer, 1 August, 1966: 14-15, 29.

Landsberg, Michele. "Families Experiment in Integration." *Globe and Mail*, 28 August, 1963:10.

Landsberg, Michele. "Illegitimacy—Part II. Society's Smooth System for the Disposal of Unwanted Babies." *Globe and Mail*, 3 September, 1963: 9.

Latchford, Frances J. "Reckless Abandon: The Politics of Victimization and Agency in Birthmother Narratives." *Adoption and Mothering*, edited by Frances J. Latchford, Demeter Press, 2012, pp.73-87.

Lawson, Bruce. "Unwanted Negro Children Shipped Abroad for Adoption, Agencies Say." *Globe &Mail*, 3 October 1967: 1.

Laycock, Margaret, and Barbara Myrvold. *Parkdale in Pictures: Its Development to 1889.* Toronto Public Library, Board Local History Handbooks: No. 7, 1991.

Leibman, Nina C. "The Family Spree of Film Noir." *Journal of Popular Film & Television*, vol. 16, no. 4, Winter 1989, pp. 169-184.

Lévesque, Andrée. "Deviant Anonymous: Single Mothers at the Hopital de la Miséricorde in Montreal 1929-1939." *Historical Papers/Communications historiques*, vol. 19, no. 1, 1984, pp. 168-184.

Library and Archives Canada. *Geneology and Family History*, https://www.bac-lac.gc.ca/eng/discover/genealogy/Pages/introduction.aspx#toc3. Accessed 25 Oct. 2018.

Library and Archives Canada. *John Sandfield MacDonald Collection, 1812-1972.* Correspondence 23 January, 1871 from Sir John A. MacDonald to John Sandfield, Textual Record Microfilm Reel C-29, Archival Reference MG26-A.

Library and Archives Canada. Quebec, Birth Adoption and Orphanage Records, http://www.bac-lac.gc.ca/eng/discover/vital-statistics-births-marriages-deaths/Pages/birth-adoption-orphanage-records.aspx. Accessed 25 Oct. 2018.

Liebmann, George W. "The AFDC Conundrum: A New Look at an Old Institution." *Social Work*, vol. 38, no. 1, January 1993, pp. 36-43.

Lifton, Robert J. *Thought Reform and the Psychology of Totalism: The Study of Brainwashing in China.* University of North Carolina Press, 1989.

Littner, Ner. "The Natural Parents." *Child Welfare Conference on Adoption*. Conf. Chicago, Illinois, January 1955.

MacDonald, Heidi. *The Sisters of St. Martha and Prince Edward Island Social Institutions, 1916-1982.* Dissertation. University of New Brunswick, 2000.

Magdalen Hospital. *A List of the Governors of the Magdalen Hospital.* London, UK: W. Wilson. 1803.

Mahood, Linda. *The Magdalenes: Prostitution in the Nineteenth Century,* Routledge, 1990.

Malkin, Bonnie. "Australia's Roman Catholic Church Apologises for Forced Adoptions." *The Telegraph,* 25 July 2011.

Manitoba College of Social Workers. "About the College," https://mcsw.ca/about-the-college/. Accessed 25 Oct. 2018.

March, Karen, and Charlene E. Miall. "Reinforcing the Motherhood Ideal: Public Perceptions of Biological Mothers." *Canadian Review of Sociology,* vol. 43, no. 4, November 2006, pp. 367-386.

"Maria Monk, Affidavit of Madame D.C. McDonnell, Matron of the Montreal Magdalen Asylum." Ste. Genevieve Street, Montreal, QC, 1836, http://eco.canadiana.ca/view/oocihm.50665/2?r=0&s=1. Accessed 25 Oct. 2018.

Marie-Josephte Fitzbach. "History," http://www.soeursdubonpasteur.ca/en/info/History/. Accessed 25 Oct. 2018.

Marshall, Audrey, and Margaret McDonald. *The Many-Sided Triangle: Adoption in Australia.* Melbourne University Press, 2001.

Mawani, Renisa. "Regulating the 'Respectable' Classes: Venereal Disease, Gender, and Public Health Initiatives in Canada, 1914-1935." *Moral Regulation and Governance in Canada: History, Context, and Critical Issues,* edited by Amanda Glasbeek, Canadian Scholar's Press, 2006, pp. 145-167.

Mayes, L. C. and D. J. Cohen. "Anna Freud and Developmental Psychoanalytic Psychology." *Psychoanal Study Child,* vol. 51, 1996, pp. 117-141.

McDonald-Lawrence, Margaret. "The Intermediary System is Not the Solution." National American Adoption Conf., 4 May 1979. Washington, D.C.

McDowall, John Robert. *Magdalen Facts, Issue 1, Report of the New York Magdalen Society.* The Author, 1832.

McGahan, Florence. "Magdalens." *The Catholic Encyclopedia,* vol. 9, Robert Appleton Company, 1910, http://www.newadvent.org/cathen/09524a.htm. Accessed 25 Oct. 2018.

McLaren, Angus. *Our Own Master Race: Eugenics in Canada, 1885-1945.* McClelland and Stewart, 1990.

Melosh, Barbara. *Strangers and Kin: The American Way of Adoption.* Harvard University Press, 2002.

Miller, Susan. "History of Breastfeeding in Canada." *Island Parent Magazine,* 2011, https://islandparent.ca/index.php?kic_article_action=display&kic_article_id=684. Accessed 25 Oct. 2018.

Monk, Maria. *Awful Disclosures of Maria Monk: As Exhibited in a Narrative of her Sufferings,* Truslove and Bray Ltd. London, UK, https://publicdomainreview.org/collections/awful-disclosures-of-maria-monk-1836/. Accessed 25 Oct. 2018.

Moore, Kristen A. et al. "Beginning Too Soon: Adolescent Sexual Behaviour, Pregnancy, and Parenthood." Child Trends Inc., 1995, http://www.childtrends.org/wp-content/uploads/2013/01/Adolescent-Sexual-Activity.pdf. Accessed 25 Oct. 2018.

"More Unwed Mothers Admitted." *Globe and Mail,* 6 March 1963.

Morton, Marian J. *And Sin No More; Social Policy and Unwed Mothers in Cleveland 1855-1990.* Ohio State University Press, 1993.

Morton, Suzanne. "Nova Scotia and its Unmarried Mothers, 1945-1975." *Mapping the Margins: The Family and Social Discipline in Canada, 1700-1975,* edited by Nancy Christie and Michael Gauvreau, McGill-Queens University Press, 2004, pp. 327-348.

Morton, Suzanne. "Managing the Unmarried Mother 'Problem': Halifax Maternity Homes." *Mothers of the Municipality: Women, Work and Social Policy in Post-1945 Halifax,* edited by Judith Fingard and Janet Guildford, University of Toronto Press, 2005, pp. 110-140.

"Motherhood Interrupted." *The Current.* Prod. Kathleen Goldhar. Canadian Broadcasting Corporation. 19 September 2011. Radio.

Mulvany, Charles P., and Graeme M. Adam. History of Toronto and County of York, Ontario. C. Blackett Robinson, 1885.

Mumm, Susan. "'Not Worse Than Other Girls': The Convent-Based Rehabilitation of Fallen Women in Victorian Britain." *Journal of Social History,* vol. 19, no. 3, 1996, pp. 527-547.

Mundie, Gordon S. "The Out-Patient Psychiatric Clinic." *Canadian Journal of Mental Hygiene,* vol. 1, no.1, April, 1919.

Murray, Karen Bridget. "Governing 'Unwed Mothers' in Toronto at the Turn of the Twentieth Century." *The Canadian Historical Review,* vol. 85, no 2, 2004, pp. 253-276.

Myers, Tamara. *Criminal Women and Bad Girls: Regulation and Punishment in Montreal, 1890-1930.* Dissertation. McGill University, 1996.

Nathoo, Tasnim, and Aleck Ostry. *The One Best Way? Breastfeeding History, Politics, and Policy in Canada.* Wilfred Laurier Press, 2009.

National Indigenous Survivors of Child Welfare Network. *Indigenous Adoptee,* https://indigenousadoptee.com/. Accessed 25 Oct. 2018.

Nead, L., in Collaboration with the Foundling Curatorial Team. "The Fallen Woman." The Foundling Museum, 25 September 2015—3 January 2016, London, U.K., Exhibition.

"Needed: New 'Unwed Mother' Plan." *Toronto Daily Star,* 17 February 1966: 28.

New Brunswick. Child Welfare Division, Adoption Statistics, 1960-1969, RS571. Provincial Archives of New Brunswick.

New Brunswick. Department of Health. *Thirty-First Annual Report of the Chief Medical Officer to the Minister of Health and Social Services for the year ending October 31, 1948.* Fredericton, 1948.

New Brunswick. Department of Social Development. *Public Response Paper: Opening of Sealed Adoption Records.* 2014, http://www2.gnb.ca/content/dam/gnb/ Departments/sd-s/pdf/adoption/PublicResponsePaper.pdf. Accessed 25 Oct. 2018.

New Brunswick. Department of Social Services. *Annual Report 1 April 1974 to 31 March 1975.* Fredericton, 1975.

Newfoundland. Department of Public Welfare. *Annual Report of the Department of Public Welfare for the year ended March 31st, 1959.* St. John's, 1959.

Newfoundland. Department of Public Welfare. *Annual Report of the Department of Public Welfare for the Year Ended March 31st, 1960.* St. John's, 1960.

Newfoundland. Department of Public Welfare. *Annual Report of the Department of Public Welfare for the Year Ended March 31st, 1961.* St. John's, 1961.

Newfoundland and Labrador. Department of Public Welfare. *Annual Report of the Department of Public Welfare for the Year Ended March 31st, 1964.* St. John's, 1964.

Newfoundland and Labrador. Department of Public Welfare. *Annual Report of the Department of Public Welfare for the Year Ended March 31st, 1965.* St. John's, 1965.

Newfoundland and Labrador. Department of Public Welfare. *Annual Report of the Department of Public Welfare for the Year Ended March 31st, 1966.* St. John's, 1966.

Newfoundland and Labrador. Department of Public Welfare. *Annual Report of the Department of Public Welfare for the Year Ended March 31st, 1967.* St. John's, 1967.

Newfoundland and Labrador. Department of Public Welfare. *Annual Report of the Department of Public Welfare for the Year Ended March 31st, 1968.* St. John's, 1968.

Newfoundland and Labrador. Department of Public Welfare. *Annual Report of the Department of Public Welfare for the Year Ended March 31st, 1969.* St. John's, 1969.

Newfoundland and Labrador. Department of Public Welfare. *Annual Report of the Department of Public Welfare for the Year Ended March 31st, 1970.* St. John's, 1970.

Nova Scotia. Department of Child Welfare. *Forty-first Annual Report of the Director for the Fiscal Year ending March 31, 1954.* Halifax, 1954.

Nova Scotia. Department of Public Welfare. *Annual Report for the Year Ending March 31, 1955.* Halifax, 1955.

Nova Scotia. Department of Public Welfare. *Annual Report for the year ending March 31, 1956.* Halifax, 1956.

Nova Scotia. Department of Public Welfare. *Forty-Fifth Report of the Director of Child Welfare for the year ending March 31, 1958.* Halifax, 1958.

"Nova Scotia Survey." *Canadian Journal of Mental Hygiene,* vol. 3, no. 1, April 1921.

O'Neil, Mary K. "Casework in a Maternity Home." St. Patrick's, 1965. Report. Archives of the Roman Catholic Archdiocese of Toronto.

Ontario. Department of Social and Family Services. *Report on Adoption and Foster Care.* Toronto, 1970.

Ontario. Ministry of Community and Social Services. *Institutions for Children and Youth.* Toronto, 1973.

Ontario. Ministry of Community and Social Services. *Review of Maternity Homes in Ontario.* Toronto, 1983.

Ontario. Parliament. House of Commons. Ministers Committee on Child Welfare. *Report of Proceedings. The Canadian Conference on Social Welfare (1966-67).* Toronto, 1967.

Ontario. Department of Public Welfare. *Report of the Minister of Public Welfare for the fiscal year 1942-1943.* Toronto, 1943.

Ontario. Department of Public Welfare. *Report of the Minister of Public Welfare for the fiscal Year 1943-1944.* Toronto, 1944.

Ontario. Department of Public Welfare. *Report of the Minister of Public Welfare for the fiscal Year 1944-1945.* Toronto, 1945.

Ontario. Department of Public Welfare. *Report of the Minister of Public Welfare for the fiscal Year 1945-1946.* Toronto, 1946.

Ontario. Department of Public Welfare. *Report of the Minister of Public Welfare for the Fiscal Year 1946-1947.* Toronto, 1947.

Ontario. Department of Public Welfare. *Report of the Minister of Public Welfare for the Fiscal Year 1947-1948.* Toronto, 1948.

Ontario. Department of Public Welfare. *Report of the Minister of Public Welfare for the Fiscal Year 1948-1949.* Toronto, 1949.

Ontario. Department of Public Welfare. *Report of the Minister of Public Welfare for the Fiscal Year 1949-1950.* Toronto, 1950.

Ontario. Department of Public Welfare. *Report of the Minister of Public Welfare for the Fiscal Year 1950-1951.* Toronto, 1951.

Ontario. Department of Public Welfare. *Report of the Minister of Public Welfare for the Fiscal Year 1951-1952.* Toronto, 1952.

Ontario. Department of Public Welfare. *Report of the Minister of Public Welfare for the Fiscal Year 1952-1953.* Toronto, 1953.

Ontario. Department of Public Welfare. *Report of the Minister of Public Welfare for the Fiscal Year 1953-1954.* Toronto, 1954.

Ontario. Department of Public Welfare. *Report of the Minister of Public Welfare for the Fiscal Year 1954-1955.* Toronto, 1955.

Ontario. Department of Public Welfare. *Report of the Minister of Public Welfare for the Fiscal Year 1955-1956.* Toronto, 1956.

Ontario. Department of Public Welfare. *Report of the Minister of Public Welfare for the Fiscal Year 1956-1957.* Toronto, 1957.

Ontario. Department of Public Welfare. *Report of the Minister of Public Welfare for the Fiscal Year, 1957-1958.* Toronto, 1958.

Ontario. Department of Public Welfare. *Report of the Minister of Public Welfare for the Fiscal Year 1958-1959.* Toronto, 1959.

Ontario. Department of Public Welfare. *Report of the Minister of Public Welfare for the Fiscal Year 1959-1960,* Toronto, 1960.

Ontario. Department of Public Welfare. *Report of the Minister of Public Welfare for the Fiscal Year 1960-1961.* Toronto, 1961.

Ontario. Department of Public Welfare. *Report of the Minister of Public Welfare for the Fiscal Year 1961-1962.* Toronto, 1962.

Ontario. Department of Public Welfare. *Report of the Minister of Public Welfare for the Fiscal Year 1962-1963.* Toronto, 1963.

Ontario. Department of Public Welfare. *Report of the Minister of Public Welfare for the Fiscal Year 1963-1964.* Toronto, 1964.

Ontario. Department of Public Welfare. *Report of the Minister of Public Welfare for the Fiscal Year 1964-1965.* Toronto, 1965.

Ontario. Department of Public Welfare. *Report of the Minister of Public Welfare for the fiscal Year 1965-1966.* Toronto, 1966.

Ontario. Department of Public Welfare. *Social Laws of Canada and Ontario: Summarized for the Use of Children's Aid Societies and Social Workers.* Toronto, 1934.

Ontario. Department of Public Welfare, Child Welfare Branch. "Adoption Policy Guide, 1966." Fonds 1001, Series 538, File 35. City of Toronto Archives.

Ontario. Department of Public Welfare, Child Welfare Branch. *Report to the Minister of the Committee on Child Care and Adoption Services.* Minister of Public Welfare, Toronto, 1951.

Ontario. Department of Social and Family Services. *Report of the Minister of Social and Family Services for the Fiscal Year 1966-1967.* Toronto, 1967.

Ontario. Department of Social and Family Services. *Report of the Minister of Social and Family Services for the Fiscal Year 1967-1968.* Toronto, 1968.

Ontario. Department of Social and Family Services. *Report of the Minister of Social and Family Services for the Fiscal Year 1968-69.* Toronto, 1969.

Ontario. Department of Social and Family Services. *Report of the Minister of Social and Family Services for the Fiscal Year 1969-1970,* Toronto, 1970.

Ontario. Department of Social and Family Services. *Report of the Minister of Social and Family Services for the Fiscal Year 1970-1971.* Toronto, 1971.

Ontario. Department of Social and Family Services. *Annual Report of the Minister Report of the Minister of Social and Family Services for the Fiscal Year 1971-1972.* Toronto, 1972.

Ontario. Ministry of Community and Social Services. *Annual Report of the Minister: 1972-1973.* Toronto, 1973.

Ontario. Ministry of Community and Social Services. *Annual Report of the Minister: 1972-1973.* Toronto, 1973.

Ontario. Ministry of Community and Social Services. *Statistical Supplement 43rd and 44th Annual Reports for Fiscal Years Ending March 1974 and 1975.* Toronto, 1975.

Ontario. Office of the Inspector of the Feeble-Minded. Report Upon the Care of the Feeble- Minded in Ontario, 1907, https://archive.org/details/feebleminded-inon1907onta/page/n3. Accessed 25 Oct. 2018.

Ontario. Sessional Papers. Vol.XIX – Part V. First Session of the Sixth Legislature, 1887.

Ontario. *Seventeenth Annual Report of the Inspector of Prisons and Public Charities, House of Refuge and Orphan and Magdalen Asylums,* 1886. https://archive.org/details/n05-ontariosession19ontauoft. Accessed 25 Oct. 2018.

Ontario. The Inspector of Prisons and Public Charities. *Eighteenth Annual Report of the Inspector of Prisons and Public Charities upon the Houses of Refuge and Orphan and Magdalen Asylums aided by the Province of Ontario, Being for the Year Ended 30th September, 1887.* Warwick and Sons. Fonds 1035, Series 804. City of Toronto Archives.

Ontario. The Inspector of Prisons and Public Charities. *Nineteenth Annual Report of the Inspector of Prisons and Public Charities upon the Houses of Refuge and Orphan and Magdalen Asylums aided by the Province of Ontario, Being for the Year Ended 30th September, 1886.* Warwick and Sons.

Ontario Association of Children's Aid Societies. "Your CAS: Where Things Happen." Fonds 1001, Series 538, 1966. Brochure. City of Toronto Archives.

Ontario Association of Professional Social Workers. "Statement on Child Welfare, Presented to the Ministers Advisory Committee on Adoption and Foster Care." *Ontario Association of Children's Aid Societies,* vol. 13, no. 1, 1970, pp. 9-13.

Ontario College of Social Workers and Social Service Workers. http://www.ocswssw.org/about-us/general-information/. Accessed 25 Oct.2018.

O'Reilly, Andrea. "African American Mothering: Home is Where the Revolution Is." *Mothers, Mothering and Motherhood Across Cultural Differences: A Reader,* edited by Andrea O'Reilly, Demeter Press, 2014, pp. 93-117.

O'Reilly, Andrea. *Matricentric Feminism: Theory, Activism, and Practice.* Demeter Press, 2016.

Origins Canada. "A Way Forward." Interfaith Meeting with Churches That Ran Maternity Homes in Canada, Held at United Church of Canada, June 2012.

Origins Canada. "Adoption Experience 2012." Conf. Toronto, 19-20 October 2012, Hilton Garden Inn, Vaughan.

Origins Canada. "Past Adoption Policies and Practices: Non-Indigenous and Indigenous Contexts." Parliament Hill, 27 May 2016.

Origins Canada. "Sue's Adoption Story." *Origins Canada,* http://www.originscanada.org/resources/mothers-stories-adoption-across-canada/sue-foster-ottawa-ontario-1970/. Accessed 25 Oct 2018.

Page, Maria D. Artist/Creator. "Building for Health." YWCA Vintage Poster, ca.1914-1919. Library Company of Philadelphia, Digital Collections. WW1 Posters, Drawer 3, Oversize 1.

Pearl-McDowell, Daryle. *Ottawa's Magdalen Asylum: A Place for Penitent Prostitutes, 1866-1892.* Master of Arts Thesis. Carleton University, 2010.

Pederson, Diana. "Keeping Our Good Girls Good:" The YWCA and the 'Girl Problem,' 1870-1930." *Canadian Women Studies/Studies/Les Cahiers de la Femme,* vol. 7, no.4, 1986, pp. 20-24.

Pengilley, Heather. *Hidden Voices: The Language and Losses of Birthmothers.* Master of Social Work Thesis. McMaster University, 2003.

"Pension Abuses by Unmarried Mothers Cited." *Toronto Daily Star,* 18 June 1959: 3.

Perry, Twila L. "Transracial and International Adoption: Mothers, Hierarchy, Race, and Feminist Legal Theory." *Yale Journal of Law & Feminism,* vol. 10, no. 1, Article 5, 1998, pp. 101-164.

Petrie, Anne. *Gone to an Aunt's: Remembering Canada's Home's for Unwed Mothers.* McClelland and Stewart, 1998.

Phillips, Raylene. "Uninterrupted Skin-to Skin Contact Immediately After Birth." *Newborn and Infant Nursing Review,* vol. 13, no. 2, 2013, pp. 67-72.

Pietsch, Nicole. "Good Mothers, Bad Mothers, Not-Mothers: Privilege, Race and Gender and the Invention of the Birthmother." *Adoption and Mothering,* edited by Frances J. Latchford, Demeter Press, 2012, pp. 36-41.

Pietsch, Nicole. "Un/titled: Constructions of Illegitimate Motherhood as Gender Insurrection." *Journal of the Association for Research on Mothering,* vol. 4, no. 1, 2002, pp. 88-100.

Pope, Hallowell. "Negro-White Difference in Decisions Regarding Illegitimate Children." *Journal of Marriage and the Family,* November 1969, pp. 756-764.

Powell, Eugenia. Witness. Senate Social Affairs Committee on Social Affairs, Science and Technology. Forced Adoption Hearings. 20 March 2018.

Prentice, Alison et al. *Canadian Women: A History.* 2nd ed. Harcourt Brace & Company, 1996.

Prince Edward Island. Department of Health and Welfare. *Adoptions.* 1953.

Prince Edward Island. Department of Health and Welfare. *Adoptions.* 1954.

Prince Edward Island. Department of Health. *Adoptions.* 1955.

Prince Edward Island. Department of Health. *Adoptions.* 1956.

Prince Edward Island. Department of Health. *Adoptions.* 1957.

Prince Edward Island. Department of Health. *Adoptions.* 1958.

Prince Edward Island. Department of Health. *Adoptions.* 1959.

Prince Edward Island. Department of Health. *Adoptions.* 1960.

Prince Edward Island. Department of Health. *Adoptions.* 1961.

Prince Edward Island. Department of Health. *Adoptions.* 1962.

Prince Edward Island. Department of Health. *Adoptions.* 1963.

Prince Edward Island. Department of Health. *Adoptions.* 1964.

Prince Edward Island. Department of Health. *Annual Report of the Department of Health 1966.* Summerside, 1966.

Prince Edward Island. Department of Health. *Annual Report of the Department of Health 1967.* Summerside, 1967.

Prince Edward Island. Department of Health. *Annual Report of the Department of Health 1968.* Charlottetown, 1968.

Prince Edward Island. Department of Health. *Annual Report of the Department of Health 1969.* Charlottetown, 1969.

Prince Edward Island Social Work Registration Board. http://socialworkpei.ca/board/

Quebec. Ministere de L'Industrie et du Commerce/Department of Industry and Commerce. *Annuaire du Québec/Québec Yearbook 1962-1963.* Bureau de la statistique du Québec/Bureau of Statistics. Québec City, 1963.

Quebec. Ministere de L'Industrie et du Commerce/Department of Industry and Commerce. *Annuaire du Québec/Québec Yearbook 1964-1965.* Bureau de la statistique du Québec/Bureau of Statistics. Québec City, 1965.

Quebec. Ministere de L'Industrie et du Commerce/Department of Industry and Commerce. *Annuaire du Québec/Québec Yearbook 1966-1967.* Bureau de la statistique du Québec/Bureau of Statistics. Québec City, 1967.

Rains, Prudence Mors. "Moral Reinstatement: The Characteristics of Maternity Homes." *The American Behavioral Scientist*, vol.14, no. 2, 1970, p. 219.

Redmond, Paul Jude. *The Adoption Machine: The Dark History of Ireland's Mother and Baby Homes and the Inside Story of How Tuam 800 Became a Global Scandal.* Merrion Press, 2018.

Rich, Adrienne. *Of Woman Born: Motherhood as Experience and Institution.* W.W. Norton & Company, 1995.

Richmond, Mary E. *Social Diagnosis.* New York, NY: Russell Sage Foundation, 1917.

Ritchie, Thomas. "No Longer Forgotten or Friendless: A History of Ottawa's Protestant Orphans Home, Protestant Home for the Aged and Home for Friendless Women." Beechwood Cemetery, Funeral and Cremation Services, 2013.

Roberts, Dorothy. *Shattered Bonds: the Color of Child Welfare.* Civitas, 2002.

Roberts, Robert W. *The Unwed Mother.* Harper and Row, 1966.

Romkey, Lillian. *The Disposition of Children of Unmarried Mothers with Limited Intelligence.* Master of Arts Thesis. University of Toronto, 1951.

Rooke, Patricia T., and Rodolph. L. Schnell. *Discarding the Asylum: From Child Rescue to the Welfare State in English Canada (1800-1950).* University Press of America, 1983.

Rosenbaum, Alana. "Church Adoption Apology." *Sydney Morning Herald* 28 February 2012.

Rosenbaum, Alana. "Hospital Sorry for Forced Adoptions." *The Age.* 24 January 2012.

Salvation Army. Australia Eastern Territory. "The Salvation Army Apologises to People Affected by Forced Adoption." 19 September 2012. Communications and Public Department.

Salvation Army. Brief. Submitted to the Standing Senate Committee on Social Affairs, Science and Technology: Forced Adoption in Postwar Canada, 21 March 2018.

Salvation Army. "Evangeline Home." Saint John Records. MC 2009. Provincial Archives of New Brunswick.

Salvation Army. *Our Army on the March.* 1965. Salvation Army Archives. Pamphlet.

Salvation Army. *The Unmarried Mother and the Salvation Army.* 1958. Salvation Army Archives. Pamphlet.

Salvation Army. "Faith Haven Outgrows Itself." *War Cry,* 15 October 1938, 13.

Salvation Army. "A City Well-Served by the Army." *War Cry,* 5 September 1953, 5.

Salvation Army. "Women's Auxiliary Raises Funds for Vancouver Home." *War Cry,* 19 June 1965, 14.

Salvation Army. "The Problem of the Unwed Mother." *War Cry,* 30 November 1968, 10.

Sangster, Joan. *Girl Trouble: Female Delinquency in English Canada.* Between the Lines, 2002.

Sangster, Joan. "Incarcerating "Bad Girls" The Regulation of Sexuality through the Female Refuges Act in Ontario, 1920-1945." *Journal of History of Sexuality,* 7 (2), 1996, pp. 239-275.

Sangster, Joan. "Incarcerating "Bad Girls": The Regulation of Sexuality through the Female Refuges Act in Ontario, 1920-1945." *Moral Regulation and Governance in Canada: History, Context, and Critical Issues,* edited by Amanda Glasbeek, Canadian Scholar's Press, 2006, pp. 189-216.

Sangster, Joan. *Regulating Girls and Women: Sexuality, Family, and the Law in Ontario, 1920-1960.* Oxford University Press, 2001.

Saskatchewan. Department of Social Welfare and Rehabilitation. *Annual Report 1959-1960.* Regina, 1960.

Saskatchewan. Department of Social Welfare and Rehabilitation. *Annual Report 1960-1961.* Regina, 1961.

Saskatchewan. Department of Social Welfare and Rehabilitation. *Annual Report 1961-1962.* Regina, 1962.

Saskatchewan. Department of Social Welfare and Rehabilitation. *Annual Report 1962-1963.* Regina, 1963.

Saskatchewan. Department of Social Welfare and Rehabilitation. *Annual Report 1963-1964.* Regina, 1964.

Saskatchewan. Department of Welfare. *Annual Report 1964-1965.* Regina, 1965.

Saskatchewan. Department of Welfare. *Annual Report 1965-1966.* Regina, 1966.

Saskatchewan. Department of Welfare. *Annual Report 1966-1967.* Regina, 1967.

Saskatchewan. Department of Welfare. *Annual Report 1967-1968*. Regina, 1968.

Saskatchewan. Department of Welfare. *Annual Report 1968-1969*. Regina, 1969.

Saskatchewan Association of Social Workers. http://www.sasw.ca/site/about?nav=02. Accessed 25 Oct. 2018.

Schill, Betty. "Family Atmosphere for Unwed Moms." *Toronto Daily Star,* 11 September 1963: 59.

Schissel, Bernard and Linda Mahood. *Social Control in Canada: Issues in the Social Construction of Deviance.* Oxford University Press, 1996.

Schlumberger, Bruno. Photograph. Bethany House. In Reevely, David. "Bethany House Heritage Decision Delayed." *The Ottawa Citizen,* 8 May 2012.

Schumacher, H.C. "The Unmarried Mother: A Socio-Psychiatric Viewpoint." *Journal of Mental Hygiene,* vol. 11, 1927, pp. 775-782.

Sessional Papers. *First Session of the Sixth Legislature of the Province of Ontario,* 1887, Toronto, Warwick and Son.

Shawyer, Joss. *Death by Adoption.* Cicada Books, 1979.

Sherwood, Harriet. "Catholic Church Apologises for Role in 'Forced Adoptions' Over a 30-Year Period." *The Guardian,* 3 November 2016, www.theguardian.com/society/2016/nov/03/catholic-church-apologises-for-role-in-forced-adoptions-over-30-year-period. Accessed 25 Oct. 2018.

"Should Stop Unwed Girls Having Children-Minister." *Toronto Daily Star ,*20 November 1953:7

Sinclair, Raven. *All My Relations—Native Transracial Adoption: A Critical Case Study of Cultural Identity.* Dissertation. University of Calgary, 2007.

Sinclair, Raven. "Identity Lost and Found: Lessons from the Sixties Scoop." *The First Peoples Child and Family Review,* vol. 3. no.1, 2007, pp. 65-82.

"Sister Mary of the Good Shepherd Monastery of Our Lady of Charity to His Grace, The Most Reverend J. J. Lynch [Archbishop of Toronto]." Undated Correspondence. Archives of the Roman Catholic Archdiocese of Toronto.

Sister Maryan. "The Work of the Congregation of the Good Shepherd in Toronto, 1875-1973." *The York Pioneer.* 1974. Archives of the Roman Catholic Archdiocese of Toronto.

Sisters of the Good Shepherd. *A Short Notice on the Origin and Object of the Sisters of Our Lady of Charity Better Known as the Sisters of the Good Shepherd.* Printed at the Asylum, 1882. http://eco.canadiana.ca/view/oocihm.92555/2?r=0&s=1. Accessed 25 Oct. 2018.

Sisters of the Good Shepherd. *Fifty Golden Years: the Monastery of Our Lady of Charity of the Good Shepherd at Saint John, New Brunswick, 1893-1943.* Sisters of Our Lady of Charity of the Good Shepherd, 1943.

Sisters of the Good Shepherd Australia. "Good Shepherd's 150 Years."http://www.catholicreligiousaustralia.org.au/index.php/news-a-views/news/item/1024-good-shepherd-s-150-years. Accessed 25 Oct. 2018.

"Slave Labour: Magdalene Laundries Disgraced Irish Catholic Women." *16 x 9*. Prod. Mia Sheldon, Rep. S. Mallen. Global Television Network. February 2012. Television.

Smith, James M. *Ireland's Magdalen Laundries and the Nation's Architecture of Containment.* University of Notre Dame Press, 2007.

Smith, Marjorie J. "Education for Social Work." *Canadian Welfare*, 1949.

Sniderman, A. "The Man Wrongly Attributed to Uttering 'Kill the Indian in the Child.'" *Maclean's*. 8 November 2013.

Sobol, Michael P., and Kerry Daly. "Canadian Adoption Statistics: 1981-1990." *Journal of Marriage and Family*, vol. 56, no. 2, 1994, pp. 493-499.

Social Planning Council of Metropolitan Toronto. "A Report on Maternity Homes in Metropolitan Toronto." July, 1960.

Solinger, Rickie. *Wake Up Little Susie: Single Pregnancy and Race Before Roe v. Wade.* Routledge, 1992

Speers, Mary E. "Case Work and Adoption." *The Social Worker*, vol. 16, no. 3, 1948, pp. 18-21.

Stapleton, Betty. "One Third of Girls Now Keep Babies and in Future More Will Have To." *Toronto Daily Star* 20 December 1965: 39.

Statutes of Nova Scotia. *Passed in the Session Held in the Fifty-Fourth Year of the Reign of Her Majesty, Queen Victoria,* 1891.

Statutes of the Province of Canada. *Passed in the Session Held in the Twenty-Ninth Year of the Reign of Her Majesty, Queen Victoria,* Part 2, 1865.

Stevens, Emily E. et al. "A History of Infant Feeding." *The Journal of Perinatal Education.* vol. 18, no. 2, 2009, pp. 32-39.

Strange, Carolyn. *Toronto's Girl Problem: The Perils and Pleasures of the City, 1880-1930.* Toronto Press, 1995.

Strange, Carolyn, and Tina Loo. *Making Good: Law and Moral Regulation in Canada, 1967-1939.* University of Toronto Press, 1997.

Strong-Boag, Veronica. *Finding Families, Finding Ourselves: English Canada Encounters Adoption from the Nineteenth Century to the 1990's.* Oxford University Press, 2006.

Strong-Boag, Veronica. "Home Dreams: Women and the Suburban Experiment in Canada, 1945-1960." *Readings in Canadian History Post-Confederation,* 4th ed. Edited by R. Douglas Francis and Donald B. Smith, Harcourt Brace & Co., 1994, pp. 481-507.

Sutherton, K. "The Relationship Between Maternity Homes and Children's Aid Societies." Unmarried Parent Department, Children's Aid Society of Metropolitan Toronto, Presentation at Armagh Annual Meeting, 10 March 1959. Presbyterian Archives.

Tait, William. *Magdalenism: An Inquiry into the Extent, Causes, and Consequences of Prostitution in Edinburgh.* 2nd ed. P. Rickard, 1842.

"Talking Teen Pregnancy." *Take 30.* Int. Cameron, Anna & Margaret Norquay M., Guests Sister St. Francis Cabrini, Little Betty. Canadian Broadcasting Corporation. 8 December 1964. Television.

Temple-Jones, Chelsea. "Bernadette's Secret." *United Church Observer.* December 2012, 18-25.

Thaler-Singer, Margaret. *Cults in our Midst: The Continuing Fight against Their Hidden Menace.* Wiley, 2003.

Telpner, Gene. "Babies ...with Nowhere to Go: List of Unwed Mothers in Hospitals is Increasing." *Winnipeg Free Press,* 31 August 1963:1.

The Canada Directory for 1857-58. Religious and Benevolent Institutions.

The Historical Society of Philadelphia. Finding Aid, Collection 2016, Magdalen Society of Philadelphia Records, 1800-1874. Historical Society of Philadelphia Archives.

The Holy Bible. Revised Standard Version. Thomas Nelson & Sons, 1952.

The Miséricordia Sisters. *Choosing the Life Within: 75 Years of Caring for Single Mothers and their Babies, An Informal History of St. Mary's Infants' Home (1914-1956) and Rosalie Hall (1956-1989).* Archives of the Roman Catholic Archdiocese of Toronto, Pamphlet.

The New Brunswick Association of Social Workers. http://www.nbasw-atsnb.ca/en/about. Accessed 25 Oct. 2018.

The Presbyterian Church in Canada. *The Presbyterian Record,* LXXVIII, No. 5, May 1953, Toronto. The Presbyterian Church in Canada Archives.

The Presbyterian Church in Canada. *The Presbyterian Record,* LXXXII, No. 11, November 1957, Toronto. The Presbyterian Church in Canada Archives.

The Presbyterian Church in Canada. *The Presbyterian Record,* November 1964, Toronto. The Presbyterian Church in Canada Archives.

The Presbyterian Church in Canada. *The Presbyterian Record,* February 1968, Toronto. The Presbyterian Church in Canada Archives.

The Presbyterian Church in Canada. *The Presbyterian Record,* November 1969, Toronto. The Presbyterian Church in Canada Archives.

The Sisters of Miséricorde. *Western Catholic Reporter.* http://wcr.ab.ca/old-site/news/2005/1107/sisters110705.shtml. Accessed 25 Oct. 2018.

"Torn Apart: Stories of Forced Adoption." *16 x 9.* Prod. Mia Sheldon. Global Television Network. May 2012. Television.

Transue-Woolston, Amanda. "Something I Still Cry About." *Origins Canada Newsletter,* Spring, 2013.

Tredgold, A. F. "Mental Deficiency in Relation to Venereal Disease." *Canadian Journal of Mental Hygiene,* vol. 1, no. 2, 1919, pp. 188-193.

Truth and Reconciliation Commission of Canada. http://www.trc.ca/websites/trcinstitution/index.php?p=3. Accessed 25 Oct. 2018.

Turner, Francis J. *Encyclopedia of Canadian Social Work.* Wilfred Laurier University Press, 2005.

United Church Archives. *A Concern for People: Directory of Homes and Institutions of the United Church of Canada under the Supervision of the Board of Evangelism and Social Services.* Pamphlet. 1960. Toronto. PAM HV 530 U5B8.

United Church Archives. *A Policy Statement on Admissions and Adoptions.* The Victor Home Board/The Toronto Home Missions Council United Church of Canada. Pamphlet. May 1954. Toronto. PAM BV 2613 V5A2.

United Church Archives. *Homes and Institutions.* United Church of Canada, Board of Evangelism and Social Services. Pamphlet. 1964. HV 530.U55H66 1964 PAM.

United Church of Canada. Permanent Committee on Programs for Mission and Ministry, Adoption Task Group. *United Church Maternity Facilities: Review of Historical Adoption Policies and Practices,* Executive of the General Council, 16-18 November, 2013.

United Church Archives. *The Victor Home.* United Church of Canada. Pamphlet. March 1962. Toronto. PAM BV 2613 V5A5.

United Church Archives. United Church of Canada, Board of Evangelism and Social Services, Departments of the Work; Homes Institutions and Associations supported by the Board, Annual Report of the Victor Home for 1966. 510/2/1,1983.052C, 4-8.

United Church Archives. United Church of Canada Board of Evangelism and Social Services, Departments of the Work; Homes Institutions and Associations supported by the Board. Letter to Rev. J.R. Hord re. Consultation on Counselling, Victor Homes for Girls, 7 June, 1965. 510/2/1,1983.052C, 4-8.

United Church Archives. United Church of Canada, Board of Evangelism and Social Services, Office of the Secretary. Minutes of the Executive and Sub Executive, 10 June, 1966. 510/1/1, 1988.088C.

United Church of Canada. Rev. Dan Hayward, Witness Testimony. Senate Committee for Social Affairs, Science and Technology, *Canada's postwar Adoption Mandate for Unmarried Mothers.* 22 March 2018.

United Church Home for Girls Burnaby, B.C. Board of Directors, Annual Report, 1951. File No. 2/11-2/13, The United Church of Canada British Columbia Conference Archives.

United Church Home for Girls Burnaby, B.C. Board of Directors. Semi-Annual Report, 1970. File No. 2/11-2/13, The United Church British Columbia Conference Archives.

United Nations. Rights of the Child, United Nations, Economic and Social Council, Commission on Human Rights. Report submitted by Juan Miguel Petit, Special Rapporteur. Fifty-Ninth Session, 6 January, 2003.

United Nations. "Universal Declaration of Human Rights." General Assembly Resolution 217A, 10 December, 1948. http://www.un.org/en/universal-declaration-human-rights/. Accessed 25 Oct. 2018.

United States of America. Department of Health and Human Services. Child Welfare Information Gateway. "Voluntary Relinquishment for Adoption, Numbers and Trends, March 2005." https://www.childwelfare.gov/pubPDFs/s_place.pdf. Accessed 25 Oct. 2018.

"Unwed Mothers, Unknown Choices." Editorial. *Globe and Mail*, 31 October 2013: A14.

Valverde, Mariana. *The Age of Light, Soap and Water: Moral Reform in English Canada, 1885- 1925.* Toronto Press, 2008.

Vicedo, Marga. "The Father of Ethology and the Foster Mother of Ducks: Konrad Lorenz as an Expert on Motherhood." *The History of Science Society*, vol. 100, 2009, pp. 263-291.

Vicedo, Marga. "The Social Nature of the Mother's Tie to her Child: John Bowlby's Theory of Attachment in post-war America." *British Journal for the History of Science*, vol. 44 no. 3, 2011, pp. 401-426.

Vincent, Clark E. *Unmarried Mothers.* The Free Press of Glencoe, 1961.

Wall, Sharon. "They're 'More Children than Adults': Teens, Unmarried Pregnancy, and the Canadian Medical Profession, 1945-61." *Canadian Bulletin of Medical History/ Bulletin canadien d'histoire de la médecine,* vol. 31, no. 2, 2014, pp. 49-69.

Walton, Laurel. "Handmaids No More." *United Church Observer,* May 2012.

Ward, Lester F. "Eugenics, Euthenics, and Eudemics." *American Journal of Sociology*, vol. 18, no. 6, May 1913, pp. 737-754.

Ward, W. Peter. "Unwed Motherhood in Nineteenth-Century English Canada." *Historical Papers,* vol. 16, no. 1, 1981, pp. 34-56.

Ward, W. Peter, ed. *The Mysteries of Montreal: Memoirs of a Midwife by Charlotte Fuhrer.* University of British Columbia Press, 1984.

Watts, George Frederick. *Found Drowned.* 1867. Oil on Canvas. Watts Gallery, Compton, UK.

Waugh, Benjamin. *Baby Farming.* Kegan, Paul, Trench, Trubner & Co., 1890.

Weinberg, Merlinda. *Pregnant with Possibility: Reducing Ethical Trespass in Social Work Practice with Young Single Mothers.* Dissertation. University of Toronto, 2004.

Welbourne, Penelope. "Attachment Theory and Children's Rights." *Adoption: Changing Families, Changing Times,* edited by Anthony Douglas and Terry Philpot, Routledge, 2003, pp. 60-73.

Wellfare, Dian. *A Sanctioned Evil: A History of Illegal Adoption in Australia.* Cilento Publishing, 2016.

Wellfare, Dian. "Civil Rights Crimes in Adoption or I Will Not Live Your Lie." *6th Australian Conference on Adoption, From Separation to Reunion and Reconciliation,* Conf. June 1997, Brisbane, AUS.

Wells, Sue. "Post-Traumatic Stress Disorder in Birthmothers." *Adoption and Fostering,* vol. 17, no. 2, 1993, pp. 30-32.

Whiting, Glynis, dir. *The Sterilization of Leilani Muir*. Prods. Graydon McRae and Jerry Krepakevish. National Film Board of Canada, 1996. Film.

Wiebe, Robert H. *The Search for Order, 1877-1920*. Hill and Wang, 1967.

Wigh, Sylvia. "A Little Extra Plus". Salvation Army. *War Cry*, 22 October 1955, 7.

Williams, Frances. "Overcrowded Conditions Hamper Work." *Toronto Star*, 12 June 1958: 57.

Williams, Georgina. *Delcina's Tears*. Pemmican Publications, 2007.

Wilson-Buterbaugh, Karen. "Not by Choice." *Eclectica Magazine*. July/Aug 2001.

Wimperis, Virginia and Clifford Witting. *The Unmarried Mother and Her Child*. George Allen & Unwin Ltd., 1960.

Wolfish, Martin G. "Teenage Pregnancy." *Canadian Family Physician*, vol. 30 April 1964, pp. 903-907

Young, Leontine. *Out of Wedlock*. McGraw-Hill, 1954.

Appendix A

Rules and Regulations of the Industrial House of Refuge for Females (Magdalen Laundry)

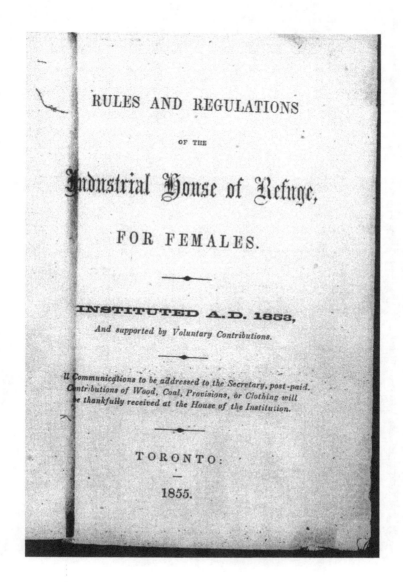

RULES AND REGULATIONS

OF THE

Industrial House of Refuge,

FOR FEMALES.

INSTITUTED A.D. 1853,

And supported by Voluntary Contributions.

All Communications to be addressed to the Secretary, post-paid.
Contributions of Wood, Coal, Provisions, or Clothing will
be thankfully received at the House of the Institution.

TORONTO:

1855.

7

who have been previously approved; but shall be kept carefully
separated from them, till the Committee shall have been fully satis-
fied of their fitness to continue in the Institution.

2. All the inmates who are in health shall rise at five a.m. in
summer, and half-past six in winter. Half-an-hour shall be allowed
dressing, private reading, and prayer. Before leaving their room for
they shall open the windows, and spread out the bed-clothes;
after that they shall assemble for family worship and breakfast,
for which one hour shall be given; then return to their rooms,
and make their beds; that done, they shall go to their daily
work, and continue at it until 12 o'clock, when they shall dine;
and, having dined, they shall rest, or take exercise and recreation, until one o'clock: at that hour they shall return to their
occupation, and remain at it until five p.m., when they shall
assemble for tea and recreation until six: from six to eight they
shall work at their several tasks. At eight there shall be family
worship; after which the inmates shall retire to rest, and every
one shall be in bed at ten o'clock.

3. While engaged in the morning and evening worship, due
decorum and attention shall be maintained; and during the
hours of work, peace and good order shall be preserved. Gos-
sip, exciting or insulting language, and any allusion to past character (except in the way of humiliation and thankfulness) shall
be most strictly prohibited.

4. Implicit obedience to the Matron, and due respect to
visitors, shall be invariably required of all the inmates of the
Asylum; and every phrase and gesture, and their whole conduct, whether towards each other or those who may come into
their presence, shall be regulated by kindness and propriety.

5. None of the inmates shall hold any intercourse with their
friends, or former associates and acquaintances, either by conversation or writing, except through the Matron, who shall hear
or read all communications that may be necessary.

6. No one shall be re-admitted who may have been previously
expelled the House, or convicted of having left it to return to
former habits, except under very special circumstances.

SECTION IV.
OF EXPULSION AND DISCHARGE.

1. The inmates shall not be permitted to leave the Asylum

Appendix B

The Unmarried Mother in Mary Richmond's
Social Diagnosis, 1917

SOCIAL DIAGNOSIS

BY

MARY E. RICHMOND

DIRECTOR CHARITY ORGANIZATION DEPARTMENT
RUSSELL SAGE FOUNDATION
AUTHOR OF
"THE GOOD NEIGHBOR," ETC.

NEW YORK
RUSSELL SAGE FOUNDATION
1917

CHAPTER XXIV

THE UNMARRIED MOTHER

WE HAVE seen earlier that the affixing of a label—even of a correct label—has no practical bearing upon prognosis and treatment, and that a classification of this sort is not a social diagnosis. This truth has been illustrated in the dealings of social agencies with the mother of an illegitimate child. There are few tasks requiring more individualization, and there are few in which there has been so little.

Mrs. Sheffield, in the questionnaire regarding an Unmarried Mother which follows, aims to bring out first, under the captions The Mother and The Father, certain facts of environment and early influence together with the outstanding traits of these two people which may throw light on their standards of conduct and habits of thought. Although, in our treatment of an unmarried woman or girl in this situation, we are liable to overlook her father, it is obvious that his characteristics and what went to mould them are quite as significant socially as those of her mother. The information may point the way not only to effective treatment in the particular case, but also to measures for mass betterment in the community.

The last part of the questionnaire calls for the more immediate explanation of the girl's or woman's situation and for facts bearing on the identity and responsibility of the man. For various reasons the child's father only too frequently escapes responsibility. Evidence of paternity may not be convincing, the man may disappear, or the social agency—occupied with many other tasks—may feel that the small amount which the mother would be likely to receive does not warrant the labor of establishing the man's whereabouts and of bringing him to trial. The question has other aspects, however. Even small sums, if required whenever paternity can be established, will have an influence in modifying

413

SOCIAL DIAGNOSIS

public opinion, will lead it to hold a man as well as a woman answerable for the support of offspring.

In making final arrangements for mother and child, their physical welfare, including the mother's fitness for giving the baby proper care, is of course of primary concern. The need of facts that bear on the choice of work and surroundings for the mother herself is indicated by earlier questions. And it should not be necessary to emphasize an unmarried mother's need for wise supervision— whether she keeps her infant with her or not.

QUESTIONNAIRE REGARDING AN UNMARRIED MOTHER[1]

This is not a schedule to be filled out nor a set of queries to be answered by a social agency's client or clients. For an explanation of the purpose of these questionnaires see p. 373 sq.

A star (*) indicates that the answer to the question may be found in, or confirmed by, public records.

The preliminary social questions regarding the husband and wife contained in the questionnaire regarding Any Family, p. 378—those regarding names, ages, nationality, religion, language spoken, length of residence in city, state, and country—may be assumed to apply to the Unmarried Mother, and (in cases in which she is sure who he is) to the father of her child.

I The Mother

Her family and home

1. Did or does she live with her own parents? Is she legitimate? Adopted? Did she ever live in an institution, and if so, when, how long, and why? What is the standing of parents in the community? Are they self-supporting, self-respecting people? Is the home clean and respectable looking? Was her parents' marriage forced? Did her mother or sisters have illegitimate children? Were these children kept with their mothers, or what became of them?

2. Are (or were) parents fond of children? Even-tempered or irritable? Faithful to church? Earnest or indifferent as to moral standards? Lax or firm in control (for instance, are they conscientious in overseeing their daughters' recreations; did the mother teach her daughters housework, instruct them in sex hygiene)? Or oversevere (for instance, are they reasonable in allowing pleasures and part of earnings)?

Her community

3. What is the character of the city quarter or town in which the girl or woman grew up—in size, race, religion, general moral standards, faithfulness to church, predominating occupation, if any, recreations and social life? Is it a factory town, farming region, or what is its industrial character? Has it distinct foreign colonies?

[1] Prepared for this volume by Mrs. Ada Eliot Sheffield.

414

THE UNMARRIED MOTHER

4. If she came from a small town or village is it within easy distance of a large city? Do her companions have local amusements or do they go to the city for them? Are their pleasures supervised?

5. Are the schools good from academic, vocational, and social standpoints?

6. Are the local police alert towards loose behavior on the streets? Are saloons dance halls, etc., regulated well? Are they numerous in proportion to the population? Is the judge in the local police court interested in the welfare of boys and girls?

7. What is the proportion of illegitimate births in the girl's or woman's native town or country?* Does custom there treat the offense as a slight one, or is ostracism relentless? Do pregnant girls frequently leave to hide their condition and dispose of the child elsewhere? Is this region equipped to care for such girls? If not, why? If it is, what co-operative understanding has been established with local agencies?

8. Are the local doctors and clergymen (if a small community) awake to the problem? What attitude do they take in regard to young unmarried mothers keeping their babies?

The mother herself

9. What was her health as a child? At what age did she mature? Has she any physical peculiarity or deformity? Is there any evidence that she is mentally deficient or abnormal?

10. Did her parents say that she was troublesome as a child? If so, how? Did she disobey her parents, fail to heed their advice, was she disrespectful to them? Did she frequent candy, ice cream, or fruit stores for diversion? What sort of associates did she have while she was growing up? How have they turned out? Can her parents throw light on the reasons for her behavior, if loose? Of what sort are her present girl or women friends?

11. When her parents learned she was pregnant, what, if any, plans did they make for her?

12. What grade in school did she reach? What do the teachers who knew her best think of her? In what studies did she excel? What vocational training, if any, did she receive?

13. What do her employers say of her work? How long has she held her positions? If she was employed in a factory, how much judgment did her work call for? Was it mechanical? If as a domestic, what are the things that she does well, what ill? For instance, can she make good bread. season vegetables? Is she neat and clean about her person and her work? Can she wash and iron? Does she wait on table smoothly and quietly? Has she done ordering for her mistress? How much did she know when her mistress took her? Does she improve—rapidly or slowly? Does she remember directions, or do they have to be repeated? What does she do best, heavy work or light? Is she good with children? Is she capable enough to hold a place with her child?

415

SOCIAL DIAGNOSIS

14. What do her employers say of her character? Is she honest, of a good disposition, industrious? If a domestic, has she been discreet with tradesmen who
come to the house? Has she had men callers, one or many? Have they been
accustomed to go at a proper hour? Has she been given to staying out very
late? Does she dress conspicuously?

15. When did girl's or woman's sexual experience begin? Under what circumstances—was it with a relative, an employer, an older man, a school boy? Has
she accepted money from any man or men for unchastity, or has she received
only a good time—theaters, dinners, etc.—or board? Has she lived for any
period as the wife of any man or men? Has she supplemented her income through
men, or has she made her whole livelihood in this way? If so, for how long and
when? Has she been a common prostitute, has she had a succession of "friends,"
or has she been intimate with but the one man? Has she a court record?* From
what she, her relatives, friends, and employers say, does she seem to seek wrongdoing, or does she merely yield when evil approaches her?

16. Has she had another child or other children by a different man or men? When
were the children born and where? How long did she nurse them? If they did
not live, at what age and of what disease did they die? If they are alive, where
are they—with her, with her family, with the man's family, boarded out, or
adopted? If the latter, through whom was the adoption brought about? What
does she know of the character and circumstances of the adoptive parents of her
child or children? Has she any child in charge of a society or institution? Was
it placed out in a family? How often has its mother seen it? Is it under supervision? If she separated from her child, what has seemed to be the effect upon
her character? If she kept it with her, what?

17. Has she ever been under treatment for syphilis or gonorrhea? When and by
whom?

II The Father[1]

His family

18. What is or was the standing of the man's parents in the community? Did the
father instruct his sons in sex hygiene? Did his influence in this direction tend
towards high-mindedness, towards cautiousness in pleasure, or towards un-
abashed laxity in morals? Did the mother and sisters take a double standard
for granted? (See in addition same topic under The Mother for questions that
apply.)

His community

19. What is the character of the community in which the man grew up? (See
same topic under The Mother for questions that apply.)

The man himself

20. Was he troublesome to his parents as a boy? Respectful and obedient, or the
reverse? What sort of associates did he have while he was growing up? How
have they turned out morally? Have any of them got girls into trouble? If so,

[1] To be used only in cases where the mother is sure who is the father of her child.

416

THE UNMARRIED MOTHER

do they boast of it, or have they the average moral scruples? Where do they draw the line as to the things "a fellow can't do"?

21. Did he spend any part of his childhood in an institution? If so, how long was he there, at what age, and why? What was his record while there?

22. What grade in school did he reach? Why did he leave, and at what age? What have his teachers to say of his character and ability? In what studies did he excel? Has he attended a trade school or a night school?

23. Is he single or married? Is he still living at home? If not, at what age and for what reason did he leave? How has he lived since? What type of associates has he chosen?

24. At what age did he first go to work? With what employer and at what occupation has he worked longest? Where is he now working and how long has he held this place? What do his employers say of the quality of his work? How much judgment does it call for?

25. Does he drink to the point of intemperance? Use drugs? Gamble? Is there any evidence that he has been dishonest?

26. What is his record as to sexual morality? Has he been known as a loose liver? Involved in scandals? Or has he, on the other hand, borne a good reputation, and is this the first affair with a woman in which he has been involved?

27. Has he ever been arrested? At what age and for what offense? If imprisoned, for how long? What was his record at reform school or prison?*

28. Is he of the same social status as the mother of his child?

III The Situation, Past and Present

Man and woman

29. What is the girl's or woman's explanation of her going wrong? Was she engaged to the man? Was she in love with him? If not, was it loneliness, drink, ignorance, force, that led to her shame? Where and when did she meet the man? Was she living at home at the time? With relatives, friends, in a lodging house, or at service? Had she known the man steadily or was he a passing acquaintance? Did she live with him for any time as his wife? Did he promise marriage? Do her family or friends know of his seeing her often at about the time of conception? Had they been expecting that he would marry her? Has she letters from him that go to show his probable paternity? Has the man known her family, called at her home? Does she know his family?

30. Does the man acknowledge paternity? Does he acknowledge having had relations with her? Does he claim that others had also? If so, who? Did she live in a lodging house, or were there men lodgers in the same house or tenement? Is there any evidence that she was intimate with any other man at about the time of conception? Any evidence (such as that of the physician who confined her, regarding earlier abortions, miscarriages, or births) to prove her previous unchastity?

27   417

SOCIAL DIAGNOSIS

31. What is the man's opinion of the girl's character? What suggestions, if any, has he made to her regarding her plans? Did he suggest her consulting any illegal practitioner? Did she follow his advice? Name of the practitioner?

32. Do the man and the girl wish to marry? If so, why have they not done it before? Are they both such human material as to make marriage advisable? What are the man's health and habits? Has he had a medical examination? By whom? Was it clinical only or with laboratory tests? Does marriage in the mother's home state legitimize a child, or must its parents adopt it?

33. Have the couple lived together for several years and had more than one child? (Consult, as circumstances of the case demand, the questionnaires regarding Any Family, a Deserted Family, or a Neglected Child, pp. 378, 395, and 405.)

34. If the man is married, does his wife know of his relations with the girl or woman? Has he legitimate children to support? If unmarried, has he relatives whom he must help?

35. Has the man property? Has he a steady place? What is his income? Would his employers bring pressure on him to help his baby, or would they abet him in eluding his responsibility? Is he a man who would readily leave for another state if prosecuted? (See Deserted Family Questionnaire, p. 395.) How much should he pay?

36. Is there evidence beyond a reasonable doubt as to man's paternity? Has he a lawyer? If so, who? Will the man settle out of court? Is it desirable that he do so? Why? Can he get bonds? If not, is he likely to keep up weekly payments, or is he so unreliable that a lump sum is wiser? Would his family do anything for the baby? Has his father property?

37. Has the mother a lawyer? If so, who? Has she taken out a warrant, started or completed proceedings? If the latter, what was the settlement?* Has the man paid her anything towards the expenses of confinement, etc.? Did she sign a release paper? Is it legally valid? If she has taken no steps against the man, does she wish to prosecute? If not, is this a case in which it is advisable for an outside party to bring suit, supposing state law permits?

38. Is it better that the man pay the money to the girl, or to a trustee who would hold it for the child? In your opinion, is the purpose of payment in this case to punish the man, to help the girl, or to provide for the baby's future?

Mother and child

39. If this is the girl's or woman's first child, does she appreciate the seriousness of her act and of its consequences? Did she leave her home to hide her shame? To give her baby to strangers so that her misconduct might remain unsuspected at home? Does she love her baby? Does she want to keep it?

40. What preparations did she make for the child? How long before confinement did she stop work? What sort of work was she doing during the previous months? What was her physical condition at this time? Did she have instruction in prenatal care and did she follow it?

418

THE UNMARRIED MOTHER

41. Was she confined in a hospital? How long did she stay? Did she receive after-care? If not confined in a hospital, where? Was she attended by a physician or by a midwife? (Name and address of either.) How soon after confinement did she go to work?

42. Is the child's birth correctly recorded?* Has the child been baptized?

43. Have the mother and her baby been examined by a physician? What is his name and address? How soon after confinement did the examination take place? Was it clinical only or was it accompanied by laboratory tests? Is the mother or her child under treatment? What is the physician's report of her health and of the child's, and what is his advice?

44. Does she nurse the baby? If not, is it by a doctor's advice? Can she get pure milk? Does she understand the preparation of food? Has she had instruction in the general care of an infant? Is she capable of profiting by such instruction? Can she easily get a nurse's visits, or take the baby to a clinic?

45. Do her parents know of her situation? Are they so circumstanced that they can help her by taking her home with the baby, by tending the baby while she goes to work, by adopting the child, or by showing their sense of responsibility in any other way? Do they feel that their younger children should be kept in ignorance of her story?

46. What are the unmarried mother's plans for herself and child?

419

Appendix C

Correspondence from Victoria Leach to Betty Graham

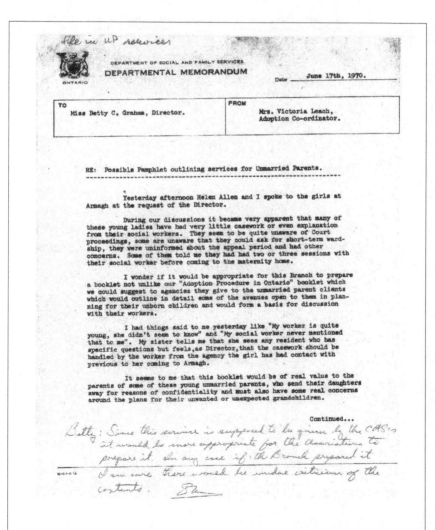

file in UP services

DEPARTMENT OF SOCIAL AND FAMILY SERVICES

DEPARTMENTAL MEMORANDUM

ONTARIO

Date ___June 17th, 1970.___

TO	FROM
Miss Betty C. Graham, Director.	Mrs. Victoria Leach, Adoption Co-ordinator.

RE: Possible Pamphlet outlining services for Unmarried Parents.

Yesterday afternoon Helen Allen and I spoke to the girls at Armagh at the request of the Director.

During our discussions it became very apparent that many of these young ladies have had very little casework or even explanation from their social workers. They seem to be quite unaware of Court proceedings, some are unaware that they could ask for short-term wardship, they were uninformed about the appeal period and had other concerns. Some of them told me they had had two or three sessions with their social worker before coming to the maternity home.

I wonder if it would be appropriate for this Branch to prepare a booklet not unlike our "Adoption Procedure in Ontario" booklet which we could suggest to agencies they give to the unmarried parent clients which would outline in detail some of the avenues open to them in planning for their unborn children and would form a basis for discussion with their workers.

I had things said to me yesterday like "My worker is quite young, she didn't seem to know" and "My social worker never mentioned that to me". My sister tells me that she sees any resident who has specific questions but feels, as Director, that the casework should be handled by the worker from the agency the girl has had contact with previous to her coming to Armagh.

It seems to me that this booklet would be of real value to the parents of some of these young unmarried parents, who send their daughters away for reasons of confidentiality and must also have some real concerns around the plans for their unwanted or unexpected grandchildren.

Continued...

Betty: Since this service is supposed to be given by the CAS's it would be more appropriate for the associations to prepare it. In any case if the Branch prepared it I am sure there would be undue criticism of the contents. BG

TO: Miss Betty C. Graham   - 2 -   June 17, 1970.

For your information, I have also visited other maternity homes and found an equal lack of understanding. I don't want to suggest that I am blaming the case workers. I think it is sometimes due to the fact that the girl is too disturbed to absorb all that is told to her, but might appreciate a reference book she can refer to in a more relaxed atmosphere.

The Ontario Association of Children's Aid Societies has a little booklet called "Where do I turn?" but as you know, it only skims the surface and simply refers the girl to her local Children's Aid Society.

I mentioned this to Mr. Magder who agrees that such a booklet might be useful.

(Mrs) Victoria Leach,
Adoption Co-ordinator.

VL:dj

c.c. to Mr. Magder

Appendix D

Maternity Homes in Canada: List and Images

Salvation Army

NEWFOUNDLAND

The Anchorage
26 Cook St.
St. John's, Newfoundland

Glenbrook Girls Home
Torbay Road, St. John
St. John's Newfoundland

NOVA SCOTIA

Grace Haven/called Parkdale House after 1975
47 Byng Avenue
Sydney, Nova Scotia

Salvation Army Home for Girls, later named Bethany Home
From 1955 at Seymour Street, then in 1960 at 980 Tower Road, former location of Halifax Infant's Home
Halifax, Nova Scotia

Grace Haven
72 Seymour St.
Halifax, Nova Scotia circa 1955

NEW BRUNSWICK

Evangeline Home
36 St. James St. (Est. 1898)
moved to 260 Princess St.

(Rathbone House circa.1916)
Saint John, N.B.

QUEBEC

Grace Haven
6690 Monkland Ave.
Montreal, PQ

ONTARIO

Grace Haven
245 James St. South
—after 1973 moved to
138 Herkimer St.
Hamilton, Ontario

Bethany Home
Until 1958 located at 518 Jarvis St, then to:
450 Pape Avenue
Toronto, Ontario

Bethany Home/House
1140 Wellington St.
Ottawa, Ontario

Bethesda Home & Hospital
54 Riverview Avenue
London, Ontario

Faith Haven
461 Crawford St.
Windsor, Ontario

Grace Haven/Lakehead
Florence Booth Home
497 N. Lillie St.
Thunder Bay, Ontario

Florence Booth Home
Fort William, Ontario

MANITOBA
Grace Haven
Box 2907
Steinbach, Manitoba

Bethany Home
205 Arlington St. 1956-1974
Winnipeg, Manitoba
Changed to Lindenview Place
1974-1993
205 Booth Drive, Winnipeg,
Manitoba

SASKATCHEWAN
Grace Haven
2929 26th Avenue
Regina, Saskatchewan
alternate addresses also found:
2301-15th Avenue, Regina
3302 Dewdney Avenue

Bethany Home & Hospital
802 Queen St.
Saskatoon, Saskatchewan

ALBERTA
Hill Haven/Parkwood House
1402 8th Avenue N.W.
Calgary, Alberta

BRITISH COLUMBIA
Salvation Army Home
Home for unmarried mothers
(1920)

Maywood Home
In Kitsilano from 1909
(address unknown)
then to 7250 Oak St.
(New premises May, 1959)
Vancouver, B.C.

Fig. 1: Evangeline Home, St. John, NB

Fig. 2: Grace Haven, Sydney, NS

Fig. 3: Halifax Infant's Home, later Bethany Home, Halifax, NS

Fig. 4: Bethany Home, Toronto, ON

Fig. 5: Bethany House, Ottawa, ON

Fig. 6: Bethesda Centre, London, ON

Fig. 7: Florence Booth Home, Thunder Bay, ON

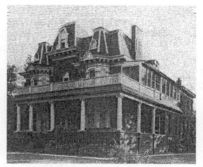

Fig. 8: Faith Haven, Windsor, ON

Fig. 9: Grace Haven, Hamilton, ON

Fig. 10: Bethany Home, Saskatoon, SASK

Fig. 11: Grace Haven, Regina, ON

Fig. 12: Park Wood House, Calgary, AB

Fig. 13: Maywood Home, Vancouver, BC

Roman Catholic Church

PRINCE EDWARD ISLAND

St. Gerard's Home for Unwed Mothers/ Catholic Family Services/
69 Pownal Street
Charlottetown, P.E.I.
(Catholic Family Services offices on first floor -unmarried mothers were housed on top floor)

NOVA SCOTIA

Home of the Guardian Angel
6109 Quinpool Road
also 395 Brunswick St.
Halifax, Nova Scotia

QUEBEC

St.Janvier House
(Sisters of Miséricordia)
1675 Boulevard Gouin East
Montreal, Quebec

Villa St. Michel (Sisters of Miséricordia) 1957-1971
7400 Boulevard Saint-Michel
Montreal, PQ

Foyer Joly (Sisters of Miséricordia) 1958-1970
105 Rue Joly
Trois Riverieres West, PQ
Known as Villa Joly 1970-1976

Foyer Sainte-Dorothee
(Sister of Miséricordia) 1957-1968
Laval, PQ

Carrefour Bethesda
(Sisters of Miséricordia) 1980-1985
355 rue Laviolette
Gatineau, PQ

Villa Marie-Claire
(Sisters of Miséricordia) 1967-1974
225, rue Belvedere nord
Sherbrooke, PQ

Pavillon Jette: Foyer Marie-Lucie et Foyer Marguerite
(Sisters of Miséricordia) 1948-1971
850 Boulevard Dorchester
Montreal, PQ

L'Hopital de la Miséricorde
(Sisters of Miséricordia)
St. Hubert & Rene Levesque Blvd/
address also found at 897 Lagauchetiere est,
Montreal, PQ

Creche St.Vincent de Paul
(Sisters of the Good Shepherd)
1210 Chemin
Ste-Foy, PQ

Creche D'Youville
(The Grey Nuns of Montreal/ Soeurs Grises de Montreal)
5705 Cote de Liesse
Montreal, PQ

ONTARIO

St. Mary's Infants Home
(Sisters of Miséricordia) 1920-1956
550 Jarvis St., Toronto (closed and moved to Scarborough Rosalie Hall)

Rosalie Hall (Sisters of Miséricorde) 1956-Present
3020 Lawrence Avenue East
Scarborough, Ontario
Now operating as Centre for Pregnant and Parenting Teens

Sundale Manor 1960-1976/
Mercy Shelter 1953-1960
(Miséricordia)
140 Park Avenue East
Chatham, Ontario

St. Mary's Home
(Sisters of Providence)
Daly Avenue 1933-1972
Ottawa, Ontario then moved to:
1081 Cadboro Road in Gloucester
1972-1987 then moved to:
659 Church St., Ottawa, Ontario
and taken over by Les Filles de
La Sagesse d'Ontario

Rideau Terrace (in Rockcliffe)
Ottawa, Ontario
St. Martin`s Manor
Catholic Home for Girls
Mohawk Rd. West
Hamilton, Ontario

Miséricordia Hospital Home
(Sisters of Misércordia) 1959-1971
Georgina Avenue, Haileybury
(urgencies only)

St. Monica House
231 Herbert St.
Kitchener/Waterloo, Ontario

Centre Maria
Hawkesbury, Ontario

MANITOBA

Villa Rosa (Sisters of Miséricorde)
1965-1993
784 Wolseley Avenue/
also 99 Cornish Winnipeg,
Manitoba (formerly Rosalie Hall
on Sherbrooke) (There are archival
records going back to 1898, and
upon written request searches can

be conducted, subject to privacy
legislation)

SASKATCHEWAN

Martha House/Mercy Hospital
est 1936 (Sisters of St. Martha/
Sisters of St. Joseph)
1855 2nd Avenue North
Regina Saskatchewan S4R 1Y1
(now home for retired priests)
(It was founded by the Sisters of
St. Martha in the old Mercy
Hospital at the corner of Victoria
Ave and Smith St. at 2416 Victoria
Avenue. The home was relocated
several times; Sisters of St. Joseph
carried on the services from 1984
until June 1994.)

ALBERTA

Providence Creche (Sisters of
Charity of Providence)
5232 – 4th St. S.W
Calgary, Alberta

**The Pineview Home for
Unmarried Mothers**
(Sisters of Miséricordia) 1963-1969
9830, 165th Street/address also
found at 8770, 165th
Jasper Place, West Edmonton,
Alberta

BRITISH COLUMBIA

Our Lady of Mercy
(Catholic Charities)
1050 West 54th
Vancouver, B.C.

Fig. 14: Home of the Guardian
Angel, Halifax, NS

Fig. 15: L'Hopital de la
Miséricorde, Montreal PQ

Fig. 16: Creche St.Vincent de Paul,
Ste-Foy PQ

Fig. 17: St. Gerard's/Catholic Family
Services, Charlottetown, PEI

Fig. 18: St. Martin's Manor,
Hamilton, ON

Fig. 19: Sundale Manor, Chatham,
ON

Fig. 20: St. Mary's Infants Home, Toronto, ON

Fig. 21: Rosalie Hall, Scarborough, ON

Fig. 22: Rosalie Hall, Winnipeg, MAN, Moved to modern Villa Rosa 1965

Fig. 23: Villa Rosa, Winnipeg, MAN

Fig. 24: St. Monica House, Kitchener/Waterloo, ON

Fig. 25: Martha House/Mercy Hospital, Regina, SASK

Fig. 26: Creche D'Youville, 1945

Fig: 27: Providence Creche, Calgary

Fig. 28: St.-Janvier House, Montreal, PQ

United Church of Canada

ONTARIO
Victor Home for Women
1900-1989 – **Massey Centre**
1989-Present[183]
Also Known as **Door of Hope**
1901/Methodist Church/
295 Jarvis St., Toronto
Victor Home for Women 1904
341 Jarvis St.
Toronto, Ontario

Moved in 1948 to:
1102 Broadview Avenue
Toronto, Ontario
Re-named **Massey Centre**[184]
**Cedarvale Home for Unwed
Mothers** (Previously Ontario
Home for Girls) Georgetown,
Ontario

QUEBEC
Elizabeth House, Montreal,
(co-sponsored with Anglican
Church as above) 1968-1973
1973 transferred from church
community to Ministry of
Social Affairs
2131 Marlowe Avenue
Montreal, PQ

Bethany House 1912-1942
Montreal, Quebec

MANITOBA
Church Home for Girls,
Winnipeg (Kildonan) 1911-1974
(co-sponsored with Anglican
Church as above)
2594 Henderson Highway
Winnipeg, Manitoba
new home constructed in
1962 – also associated with:
McMillan House Project
(1972-1976)
824 McMillan Avenue
Winnipeg, Manitoba

BRITISH COLUMBIA
**United Church Home for
Girls** (1913-1973) (co-sponsored,
Presbyterian, Anglican, Baptist)
1750 Sussex Avenue (1923-1967)
7401 Sussex Avenue (1967-1973)
also known as: **Burnaby Home
for Girls** South Burnaby, British
Columbia

184 Many mothers from this home delivered at Burnside Hospital or Mayfair Hospital. These records have not survived. Massey Centre still holds records of Victor Home residents from 1904 onwards.

185 Victor Home was renamed Massey Centre in 1989. It is still operating at 1102 Broadview assisting parenting teens.

Fig. 29: Early Victor Home,
Toronto, ON

Fig. 30: Victor Home, Toronto, ON

Fig. 31: United Church Home for
Girls, Burnaby, BC

Anglican Church of Canada

ONTARIO
Humewood House 1912
40 Humewood Drive
Toronto, Ontario
(As of 2016 operating as
Centre for Parenting Teens at
40 Humewood)

St. Monica House (Huron
Diocese) (Opened May 1968)
30 Sycamore Place
Kitchener, Ontario

QUEBEC
Elizabeth House (Co-sponsored
with Presbyterian & United
Church) 1968-Present
1973 transferred from church
community to Ministry of
Social Affairs
2131 Marlowe Avenue
Montreal, PQ

MANITOBA
Church Home For Girls
(Co-sponsored with United
Church)
2594 Henderson Hwy
Winnipeg, Manitoba

**Bishops Messengers of
St. Faith's** At least in 1969
The Messengers—Anglican Parish
run by lay Anglican women
The Pas, Manitoba—also home
for unwed mothers
Serving Pasandena and Little
Indian Birch Reserves

ALBERTA
St. John's House Anglican
Diocese of Edmonton
11714 – 92nd St. Sisterhood
of St. John The Divine
Edmonton, Alberta

B.C.
Marion Hilliard House
Serle Road, RR#1 1967-2002
Kamloops, B.C.

PRESBYTERIAN
Door of Hope
Sydney, Nova Scotia (circa 1910s)

Presbyterian Home for Girls
123 Yorkville Avenue, Toronto,
1910-1955

Armagh
927 Meadow Wood Road
(replaced Yorkville home)
Clarkson, Ontario

Elizabeth House (co-sponsored
with Anglican Church)
Montreal, Quebec

Fig. 32 Humewood House,
Toronto, ON

Fig. 33 Armagh, Clarkson, ON

Fig. 34 Marion Hilliard Home,
Kamloops, BC

Evangelical

Bethel Home (sponsored by the Pentecostal Benevolent Assoc of Ontario)
115 Bonis Avenue/3762 Sheppard Ave East/Kennedy Road, Scarborough
Agincourt, Ontario
Built in 1926,
new facility late 1950's

Friendly Home – Associated with, but not a facility of the United Church
5867 Cote St. Antoine Rd.
Montreal, PQ

Beulah Home/Woodside Home
13340 101st St.
Edmonton, Alberta
Est 1909 to aid newly arrived women – later unwed mothers

Spruce Cliff Home,
Calgary (1968-)

Jewels for Jesus Mission
2110 Argentia Road
Mississauga, Ontario

YWCA
The Haven (at least 1878 to at least 1913)
Toronto, Ontario

ECUMENICAL

Northern Ecumenical Maternity Homes
P.O. Box 955
Sudbury, Ontario

PRIVATE

Molly Breens Boarding House
18 Wood St.
St. John's, Newfoundland

Ideal Maternity Home
East Chester, Nova Scotia

The Strathcona
32 Gothic Avenue
Toronto, Ontario

(Note: It is not possible to identify all the private homes that may have housed unmarried mothers during the twentieth century.)

Fig. 35: Ideal Maternity Home, East Chester, NS

Fig. 36: Friendly Home, Montreal, PQ

246

Fig. 1   Braydon, Kâté. Photograph, Evangeline Home. In Cunningham, April. "A Daughter's Search Reaches Into a Darker Past." *The Telegraph Journal*, 3 February 2014: C1.

Fig. 2   Google Maps. 47 Byng Avenue, Sydney, Nova Scotia.

Fig. 3   Retrieved from: http://halifaxbloggers.ca/builthalifax/2013/09/halifax-infants-home/

Fig. 4   Kim, Peter. Photograph. 450 Pape Avenue, Toronto. In Kim, Peter "Filming of Stephen King's Horror Classic 'It' Becoming a Nightmare for some Residents." 22 August 2016. Global News. Retrieved from: http://globalnews.ca/news/2896739/filming-of-stephen- kings-horror-classic-it-becoming-nightmare-for-some-residents/

Fig. 5   Schlumberger, Bruno. Photograph. Bethany House. Ottawa. In Reevely, David. "Bethany House Heritage Decision Delayed." *The Ottawa Citizen*, 8 May 2012.

Fig. 6   Glover, Craig/QMI Agency. Photograph. Bethesda Home. In Martin, Chip. "Bethesda Land on Selling Block." *London Free Press*, 11 October 2012.

Fig. 7   Florence Booth Home Thunder Bay, Pamphlet, SAA.

Fig. 8   "Faith Haven Outgrows Itself." *The War Cry*, 15 October 1938: 13.

Fig. 9   "Sally Ann Will Grace New Home." SAA.

Fig. 10 Schnarr, Nancy. Curatorial Research Assistant. *Nowhere Else to Go – Homes for Unwed Mothers in Canada during the 20th Century*. Canadian Clay & Glass Gallery, Art Exhibition. Retrieved from: http://www.theclayandglass.ca/wp-content/uploads/2011/08/Unwed-Mothers-research-Nancy-Final.pdf-FOR-WEBSITE-PROVIDE-PDF-PG2.pdf. Accessed 25 Oct. 2018.

Fig. 11 Salvation Army. Grace Haven Regina. Pamphlet. SAA.

Fig. 12 Salvation Army. Park Wood House Calgary. Pamphlet. SAA.

Fig. 13 "Women's Auxiliary Raises Funds for Vancouver Home." *The War Cry* 19 June 1965: 14.

Fig. 14 Retrieved from: http://freepages.genealogy.rootsweb.ancestry.com/~patwatson/stjoes.htm

Fig. 15 Retrieved from: Google Maps, Musée Bon Pasteur.

Fig. 16 Retrieved from: http://wikimapia.org/19515732/fr/Centre-hospitalier-Jacques-Viger#/photo/1627184

Fig. 17 Provided to the writer via Facebook by a mother who resided in the home.

Fig. 18 Unknown.

Fig. 19 Chatham-Kent Municipal Museums Collection: Frank H. Brown Historic Photo Collection. Book 5, No. 98.

Fig. 20   The Miséricordia Sisters. *Choosing the Life Within: 75 Years of Caring for Single Mothers and their Babies, An Informal History of St. Mary's Infants' Home (1914-1956) and Rosalie Hall (1956-1989).* Archives of the Roman Catholic Archdiocese of Toronto, Pamphlet.

Fig. 21   The Miséricordia Sisters. Choosing the Life Within: 75 Years of Caring for Single Mothers and their Babies, An Informal History of St. Mary's Infants' Home (1914-1956) and Rosalie Hall (1956-1989). Archives of the Roman Catholic Archdiocese of Toronto, Pamphlet.

Fig. 22   Villa Rosa. Email to the author. 13 December 2016.

Fig. 23   Villa Rosa. Email to the author. 13 December 2016.

Fig. 24   Retrieved from: https://www.google.com/maps/contrib/100768358994821790926/photos/@43.460509,-80.515221,17z/data=!3m1!4b1!4m3!8m2!3m1!1e1. Accessed 25 Oct. 2018.

Fig. 25   Courtesy of Rick Williams. City of Regina Archives. Image posted in Facebook Group *Vintage Regina.* Retrieved from: https://www.facebook.com/photo.php?fbid=10151405805955519&set=o.32878811388 7256&type+3&theater. Accessed 25 Oct. 2018.

Fig. 26   Creche D'Youville, 1945. Retrieved from: https://sgm.qc.ca/en/uncategorized/the-youville-creche-nursery/

Fig. 27   Unknown.

Fig. 28   Library and Archives Canada, Home for Unwed Mothers, 1959. Mikan 4170305.

Fig. 29   United Church of Canada. *Twenty-one Years of Mission Work in Toronto, 1886-1907. The Story of the Fred Victor Mission.* Brochure. p. 20. Retrieved from: http://uccdeaconesshistory.ca/wp-content/uploads/biopics/Twenty-One-Years-of-Mission-Work-in-Toronto-Fred-Victor-Mission-1907.pdf. Accessed 25 Oct. 2018.

Fig. 30   United Church Archives. Victor Home, Photograph.

Fig. 31   United Church Archives. *A Concern for People: Directory of Homes and Institutions of the United Church of Canada under the Supervision of the Board of Evangelism and Social Services.* Pamphlet. 1960. Toronto. PAM HV 530 U5B8.

Fig. 32   Retrieved from: https://www.flickr.com/photos/15205252@N00/4911234122. Accessed 25 Oct. 2018.

Fig. 33   Presbyterian Church in Canada. Armagh. Photograph. PA.

Fig. 34   Anglican Church of Canada. "Marion Hilliard House to Close its Doors." Photograph. *The Central Interior Link,* September 2002:8. Territory of the People Diocese. General   Synod Archives.

Fig. 35   Schnarr, Nancy. Curatorial Research Assistant. *Nowhere Else to Go – Homes for Unwed Mothers in Canada during the 20th Century.* Canadian Clay & Glass Gallery. Art Exhibition. Retrieved from: http://www.theclayandglass.ca/wp-content/uploads/2011/08/Unwed-Mothers-research-Nancy-Final.pdf-FOR-WEBSITE-PROVIDE-PDF-PG2.pdf. Accessed 25 Oct. 2018.

Fig. 36   Retrieved from: www.originscanada.org